THE FAITH OF THE ATHEIST

THE FAITH
OF THE
ATHEIST

Arthur Gibson

HARPER & ROW, PUBLISHERS

NEW YORK, EVANSTON, AND LONDON

1817

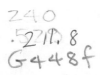

Grateful acknowledgment is made to the following for permission to reprint copyrighted material:

Dover Publications, Incorporated, for excerpts from *Space, Time and Deity* by Samuel Alexander, copyright © 1966 by the Macmillan Company, Ltd., and Dover Publications, Incorporated.

Grove Press, for excerpts from *Nexus* by Henry Miller, copyright © 1965 by Grove Press, Incorporated; *Plexus* by Henry Miller, copyright © 1965 by Grove Press, Incorporated; *Sexus* by Henry Miller, copyright © 1965 by Grove Press, Incorporated.

New Directions Publishing Corporation, for excerpts from *Remember to Remember* by Henry Miller, copyright 1947 by New Directions Publishing Corporation.

Penguin Books, Ltd., for excerpts from *Thus Spoke Zarathustra* by Friedrich Nietzsche.

Alfred A. Knopf, Incorporated, for excerpts from *The Myth of Sisyphus* by Albert Camus, trans. by Justin O'Brien, copyright © 1955 by Alfred A. Knopf, Incorporated; *The Rebel* by Albert Camus, trans. by Anthony Bower, copyright © 1956 by Alfred A. Knopf, Incorporated; *Resistance, Rebellion and Death* by Albert Camus, trans. by Justin O'Brien, copyright © 1960 by Alfred A. Knopf, Incorporated.

Routledge & Kegan Paul Ltd. for excerpts from *Dialectical Materialism* by Gustav Wetter.

Frederick Ungar Publishing Co., Inc., for excerpt from the Introduction by Kurt F. Reinhardt to *The Joyful Wisdom* by Friedrich Nietzsche, copyright © 1960 by Frederick Ungar Publishing Company.

Washington Square Press for excerpts from *Being and Nothingness* by Jean-Paul Sartre, copyright 1946 by Philosophical Library, Incorporated.

FIRST EDITION

LIBRARY OF CONGRESS CATALOG CARD NUMBER: 68-29563

H-S

CONTENTS

TO LILLIAN SNIDER

who early taught me the beauty of words
and the importance of human communication,
as well as English Literature and Composition

1

FAITH AND THE ATHEIST:

MYSTERIES AND IMPONDERABLES

In his manifesto of cosmic optimism, *Building the Earth,* Pierre Teilhard de Chardin sounds an urgent call and makes a drastic analysis:

> To unify the vital human forces, so lamentably disunited at this moment, the direct and effective way would simply be to sound the alarm and to form a block of all those who either on the right or the left, believe that the great affair for modern mankind is to break its way out by forcing some threshold of greater consciousness. Whether Christians or not, the men who are animated by this conviction form a homogeneous category. Although in the march of mankind they take their stations on opposing wings, they can advance hand in hand, because their attitudes, far from being exclusive, virtually prolong each other, and ask only to be completed.[1]

The call here sounded for a common front of all who share at least the conviction that mankind is today in crisis and yet has a real hope of surmounting that crisis—this is the motivating principle of the drive for dialogue between believer and nonbeliever, between theist and atheist. The contention that their attitudes "far from being exclusive, virtually prolong each other, and ask only to be completed" —this is the basic analytical contention which serves as justification for the hope that such a dialogue can be fruitful.

This latter point has been well explored in its philosophico-theological dimension by Leslie Dewart in his recent work, *The Future of Belief.* He is dealing with one specific instance of theist-atheist relations, namely, the "intimate sado-masochistic embrace" that binds Christian theism and Marxist atheism. He concentrates on an odd bipolar phenomenon of our day: ". . . the Christian rejection of the atheism which is genuinely but *unfaithfully* believed in by Marxists" and ". . . The Marxist . . . rejection of the God who is truly that of the Christian faith, but who in fact is *unfaithfully* believed in by us."[2] Dewart's interest here is not the comparatively superficial (though urgently necessary) overcoming of the scandal of mutual disedification occasioned by Marxist practical tyrannies and Christian incompetence in the face of despotism or even connivance with it in Christian lands. He asks, rather, "What are the implications of the unfaithfulness of both Marxists and Christians to their own faiths? I mean, what are the implications of this for an *understanding* of our own Christian or Marxist faith?"[3] And he indicates that it may help us better to understand "the constant, never ending active effort which faith requires under pain of decline, that is, the need for perpetual renewal and growth which corresponds to the faith's always falling short of itself. . . . For faith is always coming-into-being, it is never quite fully faithful, it is always on the way, hence never perfect and achieved."[4] Dewart notes that the problem of mutual appreciation is wide-ranging: "The range is vast indeed, and I cannot explore its full extent."[5]

This book aims at an exploration of one dimension of this problem of appreciation. It is an attempt to detect those valid insights into reality which have historically been offered by atheists and to consider whether such insights are not somehow peculiar to the atheistic approach. If they are, then the theist can sincerely say that he has something to learn from the atheist and the common front will not be simply a makeshift practical accommodation, uneasily papering over irreducible antagonisms.

Every human being must be motivated by some sort of faith. This statement is not intended to prejudge the case. It does not mean that the atheist is really a believer, *in the traditionally accepted sense of that word.* If it meant that, it would inevitably involve an accusation either of hypocrisy or of stupidity against the atheist, neither charge calculated to foster genuine and friendly dialogue: Either the atheist would be being represented as believing in the traditional sense but refusing for tactical reasons or out of Satanic pride to admit this fact; or he would be being accused of not himself being aware of the reality of his own deepest convictions. The former articulation of the charge would degrade him to the status of a deceiver of others; the latter articulation would demote him to the level of a deluded crypto-theist.

The real difficulty inherent in our statement above stems from the fact that Western culture has evolved (and language with it) in a predominantly theistic context. Thus faith has taken on predominantly and often exclusively religious overtones. Webster's second definition clearly shows this: "unquestioning belief in God, religion, etc." Webster's comparative treatment of "belief" and "faith" is illuminating, even if one cannot entirely escape the impression of a somewhat rationalistic bias in the lexicographer responsible: *"belief*, the term of broadest application in this comparison, implies mental acceptance of something as true, whether based on reasoning, prejudice, or the authority of the source; *faith* implies complete, blind acceptance of something, especially of something not supported by reason." Despite its bias, this interpretation puts us on the right track: it is an empirically observable phenomenon that human beings, without exception, find themselves in our world today (or in any age) confronted with a sum total of reality which does not yield without remainder to exhaustive comprehension. There are mysteries and imponderables. The first word, again, has unfortunate religious overtones; the second might seem inappropriate to a Marxist atheist whose ultimate reality, matter-in-motion, would seem to be eminently "ponderable"! Let me try to strip both words of any undesirable connotation. By mystery, here, is meant quite simply a fact, an element or a total situation, not entirely understood by the knowing being to whom it appears as a mystery; by imponderable is meant equally simply some fact, element, or situation that cannot be precisely and exhaustively resolved into ultimate components, each of which will be understandable without remainder. I hope that this will eliminate any skittishness concerning the use of the words throughout this book.

Modern man stands surrounded by mysteries and imponderables, thus understood. The religious-minded man tends to refer all mysteries to the supreme mystery, the personal God who stands behind and outside of the bewildering complex that is creation. The atheist usually bridles even at the word "mystery" but, unless he is a doctrinaire rationalist, he is perfectly willing to admit that there are enigmas. And the doctrinaire rationalist is a gull or a cheat!

The only preliminary concession required for honest theist-atheist dialogue is the readiness *on both sides* to entertain *hypothetically* the theoretical possibility of the statements, especially the basic statements, being made by the other. I do not even mean here a willingness to tolerate the theoretical possibility that the other might be right; merely the willingness to agree that *what* he is saying makes sense, that his statements are not in the order of *nonsense* ("There are bingwals in the boorfunk") or of demonstrable falsehood ("There are no Negroes in the United States of America; there are 550,000,000 persons in the Dominion of Canada today, July 1, 1968"). The atheist partner in the dialogue must agree that the statement "There is a God" conveys a piece of meaningful information, which in his reading of the situation is false information but not devoid of meaning. The theist partner in the dialogue must agree that the statement "There is no God" conveys a piece of meaningful information, which in his reading of the situation is false information but not devoid of meaning.

The theist must not invoke the discredited argumentation of the pseudo-ontological proof of the existence of God to brand the atheist statement "There is no God" as equally meaningless and self-contradictory with the statement "God is dead." For there is a real difference between the form of the two statements. The latter, unless it be interpreted in some variant of a metaphorical meaning, posits God as a reality simply by making Him the subject of an affirmative indicative statement. The predicate ascribed ("dead") is entirely irreconcilable with the fully constituted reality of the subject ("God"). But the atheist's statement "There is no God" in no way constitutes the "God" in question as an admitted reality. Those atheist friends of mine who are lawyers will readily agree that one of the stiffest assignments is to prove a negative. I hope they will accept my sincere sympathy on this point and take note of my impatience with theists who constantly harp (most unadvisedly, as I shall soon show) on the fact that the atheist had not entirely and exhaustively made his case against the existence of God. In practice, the only way to "prove" a negative is to adduce the lack of proof of the contrary positive ("My client was not on the scene of the crime: the prosecution has not produced one witness who saw him there") or to prove another positive that excludes the contrary positive ("My client could not have been there; he was with five witnesses at the football game") or to adduce the inherent improbability of the contrary positive, this last being always the weakest approach, most redolent of total desperation ("Character witnesses will testify that my client would never be seen in that sort of establishment"). Atheists throughout history have, of course, adopted many variants of these three basic approaches, but their strongest arguments have come down to the lack of convincing positive evidence and the inconveniences or indeed insoluble contradictions which, they allege, follow from the assumption (the problem of evil, the problem of Providence and free will, etc.). Of these two, the former kind of argument, the argument from the lack of convincing positive proof, has always seemed to me the strongest. I wish atheists would stick to it more and fall less into the error of introducing totally extraneous material concerning the alleged viciousness of believers. For such an approach exasperates men of good will among believers, and the atheist should know perfectly well that such arguments are really either irrelevant entirely or extremely naïve.

The atheist must not have recourse to the nonsense-argument either, on pain of exposing himself not only to a charge of unfairness and lack of objectivity but also to some very dangerous surprises in our twentieth century. This sort of argument as occasionally used by the atheist comes down to some variant of the trenchant demand of the Bruce Marshall character: "Show me a picture of the Holy Ghost, that's what I always say, show me a picture of the Holy Ghost and I'll believe." To insist, in however refined terms, that every meaningful reality must be susceptible of sensory verification, must be precisely ponderable, is to take a view of reality which science is increasingly outmoding and even outlawing. We shall see that even Lenin in his day warned against any exaggeratedly common-sense empiricism.

The atheist seems to me entirely within his rights in demanding of the theist some kind of intelligible evidence of the existence of God. But in days when scientists are firmly asserting the existence of a neutrino simply on the basis of pictures which show that a neutrino had passed that way, it seems highly imprudent to demand photographic evidence not simply of the path of God or the prints of God but of the very face of God.

The theist must never fall into the tempting error of declaring that the atheist's statement is a demonstrable falsehood. For this would imply that the evidence for the existence of God is immediately cogent in the empirical order (like the presence of Negroes in the United States); it is precisely in terms of the demonstrable falsehood of *that* statement that Fabro establishes his contention that there can be a sincere atheist.[6]

Nor must the atheist rush into the indefensible assertion that the theist's statement is demonstrable falsehood. He would be a brave man indeed today who would positively assert the nonexistence of any object. He would also be a stupid and a dangerous man. In this critical period of our history we must speedily overcome not simply racial and social barriers separating us from one another but above all else our *Terran imperialism,* our supercilious conviction that Earth alone in the universe has produced intelligent life. Man in his own world has had a disastrous history of fearing, hating, and if possible killing the different. Such an attitude in our first encounter with intelligent beings from other worlds could prove absolutely catastrophic for all concerned. And it is a direct contribution to such Terran imperialism to rule out haughtily the reality of anything not conforming to our Terran pattern.

In the matter of existents and existence, I am persuaded the only really satisfactory method of procedure is via direct evidence, never via deductive logical manipulation. The whole tragedy of this latter approach on the part of many theists lies precisely in the fact that the end of the whole business has been not the reality of the living God but the dim opaqueness of a "concept-of-God," a kind of Heideggerian Being with strength only for logical operations and for these only in the hands of a living man! I agree that the burden of proof, in this sense of adducing of evidence, rests here with the theist since he is making the assertion and the positive claim. The problem, of course, is that the evidence simply cannot be restricted by the atheist to evidence of the senses or of human measuring devices. That it cannot be restricted to empirical evidence in any sense is a claim of many theists. I do not agree, if by empirical be understood that kind of human experience (the term "human experience" here being taken in all its richness) which is open to any human being with healthy use of his faculties, without any necessity of a direct supervenient intervention from outside that experience entirely. No man needs God's direct supernatural help in order to discover the existence of God; we need that help only to discover the nature of God. *That* He is we can, I contend, see evidence in natural experience, provided only that the terms of reference and the frame of this experience be not artificially shriveled; *what* He is He must reveal to us. *That* there is a conscious Creator of the universe I contend we ought to be able to (and *are* able to) show from natural experience; *what* precisely that conscious Creator is (personal, Triune, etc.) He must reveal to us.

But the evidence of God in the universe is not of the sort that is immediately cogent, wrenching consent from the intellect like a lamppost collided with on a dark St. Patrick's night! If the theist insists on claiming it is and the atheist insists on accepting no other evidence, of course a stalemate is reached. Too frequently in the past the course of theist-atheist polemic has borne a distressing resemblance either to a political debate or to the sort of adolescent squabble portrayed in Ingmar Bergman's *Wild Strawberries* ("There *is* a God!" "There is *not!*" "There is *too!*"). Because each is determined (often for excellent motives) to *convince* the other, neither very often listens to *what the other is really saying*. This book shall be an effort to listen to what atheists are really saying.

The basic contention of this book is that atheists are faced with exactly the same mysteries and imponderables as are theists in our world today. But, whereas the theist tends to take refuge almost always in, and make reference most often to, the one single transcendent mystery, God, and to "explain" all submysteries in and through Him (which often simply amounts to a more or less pious exclamation that these mysteries are very mysterious indeed, though of course not beyond the understanding of God who achieves it in a fascinating habitat called eternity or a *totum simul*): the atheist, on the other hand, not only grapples much more intensely with these submysteries but frequently ends by putting his faith in one of them. Therefore the atheist has a great deal of important insight for the theist on all matters pertinent to the great submysteries of the universe.

It is now imperative to explicitate exactly what I mean by saying that every human being must live by some faith, that the atheist likewise therefore has his faith by which he lives. I mean basically two things, neither especially arcane but both extremely important: first, the human mind demands that some consistency be discovered in the universe, that some sort of end term be set to its questing, before it will permit the human will to initiate action; second, the most obvious centers for such centripetal searching tendencies, in the absence of the living God, are the great mysteries and imponderables of the universe.

The consistency demanded by the human mind has nothing whatever to do, essentially, with rationality. It is perfectly reconcilable with a strong sense for the absurd. And when Sartre, for instance, speaks so insistently about the absurd in the universe, the absurdity that is the universe, I am persuaded that he means something quite other than total and radical inconsistency and meaninglessness: for it is a vastly different thing to speak of a brute massive primordial "thereness" of meaning (as of existence) and to speak of total and radical meaninglessness. The Sartrean insistence that there is no reason either for the existence of the *en-soi* or of the *pour-soi,* that they are stark facts, is a drastic articulation of atheism but it is not a statement of meaninglessness. It has in fact always seemed to me that the traditional argument against the assertion of one's own nonexistence (to say "I am not," the "I" has to admit its existence and use it) is still more ultimately cogent in the matter of meaning: for the assertion of ultimate meaninglessness (not simply a lack of design, of providential planning, of triumph of the good or the desired, but total lack of all meaning) is a flagrant and arrant self-contradiction, one of the symptoms of drastic dysfunction of the brain, prelude to psychosis, ultimate terminator of all discourse. One may conceivably still be able to play at the game of metaphysical musical chairs in abstraction from existence, but when meaning is categorically denied all possibility of communication ceases. Thus, when the human mind is persuaded (as appears to happen in extreme psychoses) that it has absolutely no security whatever, that every inanimate object may turn into a deadly conscious enemy and every conscious fellow suddenly change into a pumpkin or a hydrogen atom, that the most elementary rules that held today may be utterly abrogated tomorrow, that what worked ten seconds ago may produce exactly the opposite effect now, that water may quench thirst on Mondays and Wednesdays and exactly the same chemical compound may poison and kill on Tuesdays and Fridays, and further that its alternate beneficent and noxious effects can equally well the following week be interchanged so that it vivifies on Tuesdays and Fridays, poisons and kills on Mondays and Wednesdays—in such a state of affairs the human agent would become utterly paralyzed and disoriented. Even the acceptance of a simple series of brute facts without any further possible explanation is already acceptable to the human mind; but the human mind *must* have some firm ground palpably present before it can function or permit the will to execute choices.

It can be further empirically historically demonstrated that the human inquirer most frequently pursues his persistent questing well beyond the absolute minimum of consistency he must have for any human action. Indeed I believe that the initial problematic of this whole questing is traceable to the basic scrabbling, the desperate instinctive thrust for meaningfulness. The human being seems uneasy about the absolute dependability of this meaningfulness until he has traced it back to some kind of ultimate. Indeed the whole tragicomedy of philosophers could be described as this initial conquest of chaos followed by the uneasy effort to widen the beachhead, the terra firma of certainty. And the empirical reason for this tragicomedy is that although the palpable universe around us does indeed yield to the healthily functioning and perceiving human organism a kind of earnest and pledge of minimum consistency, it most definitely does *not*

yield up a pattern of exhaustive clarity. Every facet of the universe
that can be known with that sort of clarity invariably points beyond
itself. And when the atheist Augustine finally comes to rest it must
needs be, ironically enough, in mystery. Incidentally no theist Christian ought to crow over this: St. Catherine of Siena exclaimed, too:
"I am content, for I see that all things are mystery!" It is yet ironic
that the very desire for ultimate clarity and consistency and reliability
drives the human seeker to some ultimate that is full of mystery. Such
are the seven elements of the human universe that I have chosen
here to allow those atheists to speak about, who have chosen them as
their own ultimates. I make no claim that I have here exhausted the
atheistic ultimates; nor do I assert categorically that in every case the
atheist in question has consciously identified this ultimate as his ultimate. But I do say that these are the most immediately important
atheistic ultimates, important for theists so that they may increase
their understanding and the depth of their penetration into some of
the great created mysteries, important to all men of good will for a
better grasp of certain elements of our situation which both atheists
and theists agree to be of cardinal importance in human life.

I have neither desire nor intention of refuting the atheists' statement I shall now adduce. I may from time to time suggest amend-
ments; I shall certainly attempt to interpret and explain. It is high
time, indeed, that both sides stopped this nervous preoccupation with
convincing the other. I am attempting here something midway between a strictly philosophical and critico-creative exposition of men
who sometimes wrote like meticulous reasoners and sometimes like
dithyrambic poets.

The created mystery of which man is most intimately aware, from
which he tries often but always unsuccessfully to escape, is his own
freedom. This freedom has been a genuinely and terrifyingly concreative power ever since man's first appearance on the scene of
evolutionary universal history. Often this freedom has been bagatellized, bowdlerized, and trivialized by overcautious theists. It has been
bagatellized into little more than a new dimension of law, as implacable as that mistakenly assumed to rule the prehuman cosmos with a
rod of iron, reducing events to mechanically predetermined patterns.
It has been bowdlerized into a spineless pother, either mildly abdicat-

ing its own executive position or impotently striving to kick against the good of an omnipotent God. It has been trivialized into a reflex reaction to the magic flummery of a trickster Creator.

Freedom in fact entails, from the moment of its appearance, a constant opening onto chaos or glory. In modern times, Jean-Paul Sartre is its atheist champion and prophet. He forces modern man to face the implications of his own uniqueness defined in function of his freedom.

But freedom pure and simple, freedom sheer and unspecified, at once points beyond itself toward its own implication and concretization. Its key implication is the lonely uniqueness, not only of the human species but of every human individual. Its concretization is the molding executive power exercised by man upon the surrounding nonmental cosmos and upon his fellow human beings.

But again, at the climax of his retreat into the noble lonely hermitage of his individual freedom, man feels the opposing thrust and pull toward the other, a thrust epitomized in the generic phenomenon of human sexuality. Henry Miller has selected as his own creative and redemptive-transformative ultimate precisely this mysterious dimension and act of union between those questing lonelinesses that are human individuals.

Sex can and does ensure a kind of continuing immortality of the race. And it may often thrill the individual with an intuition of that union that conquers loneliness. But death comes as the end, to each successive individual in each successive generation. Albert Camus has himself accepted death as the mysterious brute fact which simultaneously overshadows man's strivings and liberates him from the tyranny of the transcendental.

Balked, then, by this implacable ultimate that seems to sign him with an inescapable terminal limitation, modern man has turned his gaze outside himself entirely to the vast sweep of circling matter, in which the Marxist atheists have seen the face of the truly immortal. We shall see how in fact Lenin ascribes to this ultimate of his choice, matter-in-motion, capacities and properties so extravagant as to justify Wetter's contention that Lenin in fact deified matter.[7]

Such an equivalent deification of matter triggers in the mind and will of the colossus of consistent modern atheism, Friedrich

Nietzsche, a violent opposition. Nietzsche cries out equally against the Infinitely Present Will of God and the infinite scope of deified matter as equally fatally trammeling man's free finite spirit.

Nietzsche is entirely prepared to pay the price of finitude. That price is the cyclic repetition of Eternal Recurrence. Yet one final human irruption occurs against this cramping finitism. The search for ultimate parameters of existence outside of man pursues a triadic dialectical course: first, with the Marxist materialists, a potentially infinite matter-in-motion is chosen; then this infinite is finitized into Nietzsche's cyclic Recurrence; finally, modern man delves beneath matter itself into time as a truly infinite creative source.

Samuel Alexander was the first thinker to take Time really seriously in the context of Einsteinian Space-Time and relativity theories. But he was by no means the only thinker to assign at least implicitly a crucial role to Time. J. A. Gunn has two arresting sentences at the beginning of his 1930 work *The Problem of Time:* "In the Greek mythology Chronos was conceived as a being who begat children and himself devoured them. Thus the early Greeks pictured, in their vivid imagery, the constant becoming and transcience of time, which has impressed the mind of primitive and modern man alike."[8] In effect, finitude as conceived by Nietzsche can scarcely of itself constitute the ultimate; rather, it functions as the limiting factor upon the true ultimate, which for Nietzsche is infinite time. In Nietzsche the marriage of infinite time and finite energy is always both an uneasy and a bleak affair. Camus describes it vividly: "The primordial sea indefatigably repeats the same words and casts up the same astonished beings on the same seashore."[9] But in Alexander's thought the accent has shifted from the finitude of energy to the creative power of Time itself. No man has more eloquently sung the praises of time, and his great epic *Space, Time and Deity*[10] is an undeservedly neglected plaidoyer for Time and taking Time seriously.

All seven of these elements or dimensions of the human environment are suitable candidates for ultimates for the thinker who has rejected God. But for the theist they are equally mysterious elements of created reality which he has too cavalierly dismissed from consideration.

Freedom is an elusive reality, difficult in the extreme of definition, when one considers how facilely it is bandied about by preachers and politicians. As bowdlerized by many who mouth it, freedom amounts to very little more than a capacity to perform. We owe it to Jean-Paul Sartre that there has been restored something of the terror of freedom, that freedom has been again exalted into what it must really be, a direct and horrifying opening onto chaos. Nor can the theist escape this terror by appeals to an omnipotent Big Daddy who will keep firm strings on all freedoms. In effect, causality as operative everywhere else must be held to falter and break down in the face of and in any instance of freedom. The reason the free man acts thus is *because he does!* The free act is in a sense truly recreative and reconstitutive of the entire cosmos. And if one may differ with Sartre on the operational dimension and retroactive consequences of freedom, one can yet accept with gratitude and enthusiasm the amazing insights of a man who is enthralled by freedom! Dostoevski's insistence on the terrors of freedom should persuade the theist to take a long second look at his theory of freedom and see if it be genuine or only sham freedom that is being admitted. The Grand Inquisitor of the institutional Christian Church is represented as precisely reproaching Christ with a lack of love for man because Christ insists on coming to bring them this terrible freedom. Has the theist always understood the implications of freedom? Can he not learn much about the challenge of freedom from an atheist who faces that challenge as an ultimate of the universe, not muffled in the invoked omnipotence of a transcendent God?

One of the most consistently maltreated ultimates of human experience is sex. Too long reduced to a merely functional operation if not directly ostracized as somehow destructive of or degrading to human progress and improvement, sex has found in modern times two great exponents, Lawrence and Miller, the latter the more consistent, monolithic, and revealing prophet of this troubling and uniquely challenging dimension of human existence. Even the most rigorous traditionalist will readily admit that sex, like every other human activity, cannot, on pain of distortion, be reductively demoted to the merely animal dimension. The unfortunate result, however, in very much traditional thinking has been a kind of angelization of sex or a brusque canalization and technicalization of this drive, which misses the entire problematic. It is much too easy to dismiss Miller as a mere scrawler of obscenities. A closer and less nervous inspection of his writings reveals a kind of natural prophetic vision of potentials he himself may not entirely or perfectly have realized. Furthermore, what seems most urgently indicated as a demand of our age is a realistic posture in this whole dimension, neither giving way to the facile romanticism of genuinely pornographic writers (for all pornographers are incurable and even psychotic romantics), nor yet taking refuge behind barricades of pseudo-rationalistic devotion to a sterile chastity which is here but a synonym for cowardice and obtuseness. The sex-prophets again have unerringly spotted still another dimension of the human phenomenon that has been neglected by each of the authors we have hitherto considered. All but one of these authors have located their ultimate, their object of total faith, outside the concrete individual; and Sartre has located that ultimate within individual concrete man, to be sure, but precisely *not* at that crucial nexus of his relation to his fellow human beings. The sex-prophets courageously examine the implications of a positioning of the ultimate human constitutive element at that dramatic meeting place of existent human beings, the rendezvous wherein the lonely individual is most totally and irrevocably exposed to another human self.

That professed modern atheist who is most congenial to theistic trains of thought, yet surely the most consequential of atheists, has devoted the vast majority of his writings to solemn warnings against the tyranny of ultimates other than God, the despotism of atheistic ultimates. Albert Camus stresses the supreme beneficence of the only real and genuine human ultimate, death, the most universally feared and hated of ultimates, the most likely to seduce individual man into the murky swamps of faith in pseudo-redemptive saviors, human or divine. In death, Camus sees the perfect relativizer, the single pledge of human moderation and realism; and he bids us become friends with death, which we have feared and sought vainly to overcome, either by faith in a God and a divinely sustained hereafter, or by devotion to the Moloch of the species or the human future and posterity, that devouring idol that consumes the children of each generation in the name of a succeeding generation that never arrives, that is basically as illusory as any transcendent divinely guaranteed immortality. Man carries death within him; but for Camus this seed of death, far from being the supreme enemy that must alienate man from himself and make him miserable, represents man's final salvation from the whole pantheon of greedy and impotent idols.

The three external parameters of reality chosen as ultimates by other atheists have been just as indefensibly neglected or trivialized by theists. Matter has often been dismissed in a way that is both cowardly and on occasion grotesquely evil, spawning Manicheanism, the most pernicious of all heresies on both the theoretical and the practical levels. And even when accepted at least as a reality and as not basically perverse, matter has often been treated much too gingerly and neglectfully by Christian commentators and by theists generally. This palpably opaque, vibrantly alive, and mysteriously ultimate passive and even laggard reality has many a secret which its devotees can uncover for all men, at least a little.

Finitude is often dismissed as little more than a dimension separating, or distinguishing creature from Creator: Nietzsche first squarely asks the terrible question: What does it feel like to know that specifically finitude is the ultimate and that it is in some strange way a good ultimate? The theist can benefit substantially from Nietzsche's statements because, for the theist's reckoning too, there is finitude and in its own order, *which is our order,* it is ultimate. Too often the theist effects a facile leap beyond finitude, forgetting that so to do avoids both his real cross and his most precious possession: for the finitude of man is indeed a burden for those with an appetite for infinity; but it is man's guarantee of continuing personhood, and to suppress or overleap it thrusts man into the deadly danger of reabsorption into the infinite eternal One.

Time has often been relegated by theists to the entirely contemptible level of a home remedy and unpaid private eye ("Time is the great healer and the great revealer"). Theists have seldom indeed asked themselves just in what sense time, or more accurately temporality, can be called a specially substantial and drastic and radical dimension of creaturehood and what is its significance for us men today.

At the end of this book, I shall attempt to confront the atheist with *the faith,* with faith in God. I believe the honest atheist must tolerate this faith as a legitimate countervision to the atheist's insights with which the theist has been being confronted throughout the book. I also believe that this terminal presentation of a theistic point of view will prove to have taken serious account of those insights which the atheists have provided.

The common task of all men of good will is to build the future and on that future no preconceived limits ought to be set. For that reason, I hope that the terminal presentation of theism will prove to have taken account precisely of these insights of modern atheists, so that the end product will be a common vision. It has been frequently said in recent times that the only theism which has real hope for survival and relevance is that theism which includes and makes a place for atheism:[11] and Roger Garaudy in both his recent books, *From Anathema to Dialogue* and *Le Marxisme du 20ᵉ Siecle* stresses that Marxist atheists must take meaningful account of the phenomenon of religion and religious belief. One of the oldest arguments in favor of religious belief is the tale of the king's councillor who comments on the little bird that has just flown through the flickering light of the royal encampment: "Sire, if this religion can tell us anything about the two great darknesses, that out of which the bird came in and that into which it flew out, let us hear it!" The theist might be reminded that, if the atheist can furnish precious clues about the dimension of the flickering firelight so often swallowed up in theist thought by the two darknesses, we ought likewise to listen to the atheist.

The most imperative need of our world is not for more and more speaking, subtler and subtler enunciations. It is for more, much more, *listening*. I am persuaded that listening is indicative of a much greater personal serenity of conviction than stormy and discourteous refusal to allow a divergent opinion to be expressed. As I extend the courtesy of such listening to the atheists throughout, so I hope at the end they will extend it to me, not so that I may slyly prove my case and confound them but so that we may both see a little more clearly. Perhaps if we can together for a while look away from the dead center of our disagreement we may find common areas of insight gradually converging to a living center of agreement. That center may not be God but it may well be fuller, richer, and more deeply comprehended man. And that will already have been very much indeed.

2

FAITH IN FREEDOM

The subtitle of Jean-Paul Sartre's *Being and Nothingness* defines its scope as "An Essay on Phenomenological Ontology" with overtones in the original French of an "attempt" to sketch such an ontology. The reader accustomed to seek the basic bias in the substantives of a title will therefore assume that the venture is ontological, metaphysical. It is conceivable that Sartre likewise considered his essay to be metaphysics. But I find this hard to believe: if he does consider this lengthy outline a thorough ontology, even extensively, he shows a positively staggering nonchalance and even blindness vis-à-vis the whole of chronologically premental reality. The mind boggles at the notion being seriously advanced that man by a nihilating act constitutes being as such for the first time. But there is nothing mind-staggering (though there is much exciting) in the notion of man constituting by a negating act his specific kind of being, that which sets him off from the rest of beings. The statement early in the book —"Nothingness lies coiled in the heart of being—like a worm"[1]—is either poetic or senseless if taken strictly ontologically; but it is profound and potent if taken ethically. An intelligent and consistent ontology can grant to nothingness no more substantial status than a formal-logical one in the dimension of the human imagination. But a perfectly intelligent and consistent ethic can certainly grant to nothingness a very substantial status indeed; or more accurately can grant to the act of negation of the practical intellect, the will, a power to alter reality very substantially.

I believe Sartre himself felt it unnecessary to explain in detail that the adjective "phenomenological" in his subtitle effectively transformed "ontology" into "ethics"; that a truly phenomenological ontology, taking as starting point man's immediately evident special status and distinctive act, *must* issue in an ethic. For man cannot *con-*

naturally penetrate beyond the bounds of that precarious but reflectively patent freedom that separates him from the rest of the world. And I believe that Sartre's true greatness can only be appreciated if his questioning be understood in categorically ethical terms; not as asking any such musty pseudo-question as whether nothingness is somehow central to or co-constitutive of being; but, rather, as asking the spine-chilling question in the moral, ethical order and dimension, as to whether an act of will must be negative in order to be genuinely constitutive, whether an emergent moral entity must indeed "secrete a nothingness which isolates it."[2]

Even those who take *Being and Nothingness* seriously as an ontology agree that Sartre's faith is squarely placed in freedom. We shall here endeavor to contribute a new dimension to the interpretation and evaluation of Sartre by taking this major work as an unequivocal ethic, one might indeed say ontological ethic or ethical ontology if this be understood to mean not that Sartre claims to be describing exhaustively the whole of reality but that he is delimiting himself, in the context of a vague materialistic background, to the dimension of being which he considers to be the only meaningful one, the dimension of freedom. We shall consider what new light can be shed on *Being and Nothingness* when it is regarded as an ethic.

Our inspection will proceed in five stages: (1) the relations between the *in-itself* and the *for-itself;* (2) the relations between freedom and nihilation; (3) the relations between nihilating free agents; (4) the despair of apotheosis or theology; (5) the horror of the slimy. We would specify once again that we here understand ethic to mean not the normative science of free human actions but the descriptive science of free human agents. The watershed Sartre places at the center of his evolving and emergent picture of cosmic progress is the generic act whereby moral action emerges from premoral being. From the scientific descriptive point of view, Sartre's treatment of premoral being is utterly inadequate to the multiplicity and complexity of physical objects and relations (to say nothing of chemical ones); his entire "ontology" is balanced upon the act that to him is truly and meaningfully creative, the act whereby moral being emerges from a solid mass which *from the moral point of view,* i.e., with retrospective hindsight and described *in terms of* already emerged moral freedom, can reasonably adequately be described as Sartre in fact describes the in-itself. But we stress again that *only* an ethicization of ontology can justify such a description of prehuman cosmological evolution.

1. The Implacable War

Macquarrie gives us the first valuable clue to Sartre's drastic contradistinction between

the two incompatible modes of being which Sartre's philosophy recognizes—the en-soi or in-itself and the pour-soi or for-itself. The en-soi consists of material things, and is characterized by being—massive, uncreated, opaque being, almost nauseating in its senseless plenitude. The pour-soi is consciousness, which constitutes itself by an act of negation whereby it separates itself from the en-soi. The pour-soi is freedom and transcendence—a freedom to order a world and to create values. But freedom is precisely a lack of being.[3]

Collins specifies the clash as between "the fullness and solidity of material being" and "the openness and agility of consciousness,"[4] between "inert, opaque being and active, translucent consciousness" which "are at constant war with each other."[5]

Thus, in this initial presentation of the challenge and enigma of free man, Sartre is quite clearly setting up two domains of being, preconscious and conscious. In direct opposition to the Teilhardian version of modified panpsychism, Sartre is radically and utterly contradistinguishing these realities and realms. The opaque monolithic self-identity of material being has been historically shattered by the emergence of consciousness as a nihilation of that monolithic character.

It may be readily admitted that Sartre's stress on the drastic and novelty-creating character of the emergence of consciousness is a healthy corrective to a possible exaggeration of gradualism that could be derived from the Teilhardian formulation. But to our present purpose it is supremely relevant to detach the precise reason Sartre adduces for the implacable war between conscious freedom and preconscious being. It will be most useful to juxtapose his three main distinctions:

Being-in-Itself	*Being-for-Itself*
1. It is in-itself.	1. It is not in-itself.
2. It is what it is.	2. It is not what it is.
3. It is.	3. It is not.

We may not adduce the key Sartrean texts pertinent to each pair of assertions. Thus:

A. Of being-in-itself, he writes that it

> has no *within* which is opposed to a *without* and which is analogous to a judgment, a law, a consciousness of itself. The in-itself has nothing secret; it is a solid [massif]. In a sense we can designate it as a synthesis. But it is the most indissoluble of all, the synthesis of itself with itself.[6]

He further specifies in a highly important parenthetical remark:

> In the in-itself there is not a particle of being which is not wholly within itself without distance.[7]

Of being-for-itself, Sartre writes, on the contrary,

> The law of being of the *for-itself,* as the ontological foundation of consciousness, is to be itself in the form of presence to itself. . . . Actually *presence to* always implies duality, at least a virtual separation. The presence of being to itself implies a detachment on the part of being in relation to itself. . . . Presence to self . . . supposes that an impalpable fissure has slipped into being.[8]

The constitutive parameter of preconscious being, then, is continuity and radical homogeniety. The constitutive parameter of free being is discontinuity and radical heterogeneity. Now this is surely palpably absurd, at least in its first part, if that be taken as a factual description of the preconscious world. And equally obviously, Sartre does not intend to introduce spatio-temporal dimensions into his notion of duality in the conscious, at least not in the crude material sense. In fact his two descriptions come into proper focus and become highly revealing precisely when they are taken as generic descriptions of the two dimensions, sheer (material) being and freedom. The preconscious is indeed spatio-temporal in the extreme; and since it possesses no time-transcending consciousness, its only conceivable principle of identity is utterly continuous togetherness. And for Sartre's purpose it is quite irrelevant that a conscious being can look at the preconscious world and distinguish granite and manganese and further distinguish discontinuous individual clumps of either. His point is that if two clumps of granite and two of manganese were set side by side in the order: granite, manganese, manganese, granite, neither granite nor manganese would have any inkling of where its own dimensions end and the next clump begins, whether that clump be homogeneous or heterogenous. It is significant that he describes the *within,* lacking in the in-itself and obviously a constitutive parameter of conscious freedom, as being "analogous to a judgment, a law, a consciousness of itself." What Sartre is here seeing and pointing up brilliantly is the sobering and even chilling fact that, with the emergence of the dimension of freedom, there occurs an "impalpable fissure," large enough to separate subject and predicate in a judgment, large enough to admit that emergence of the distinction between general principles and particular instances which is a mandatory requirement of a law, large enough to permit of awareness. Now patently this is not a spatio-temporal fissure in the usually understood sense of that term; but it is no less ominous for all that. It indicates that a radical new parameter has been added, has emerged with the inception of freedom, and that this parameter has to do with a kind of otherness, alienation, negation, nihilation, unknown to that homogeneous behemoth, the preconscious.

B. The nature and significance of the new parameter emerge more clearly when we confront the Sartrean text on the degree of identity in the in-itself and the for-itself. Of the in-self, he writes:

It is full positivity. It knows no otherness; it never posits itself as *other-than-another-being.* It can support no connection with the other. It is itself indefinitely and it exhausts itself in being.[9]

Of the for-itself, on the other hand, Sartre says:

The being of consciousness does not coincide with itself in a full equivalence.[10]

And again he specifies:

The distinguishing characteristic of consciousness . . . is that it is a decompression of being. Indeed it is impossible to define it as coincidence with itself.[11]

We are here far less concerned with Sartre's own mental and lin-

guistic gymnastics and those of his critics concerning the nature of
this decompression and the "pre-reflective *cogito*" than we are with a
set of crucial observations linking these degrees of identity and differ-
ence-from-self in the in-itself and the for-itself with the quality of
temporality. For Sartre writes of the in-itself:

> It is not subject to temporality: . . .[12] an in-itself, whose present is
> what it is, can not "have" a past.[13]

Of the for-itself, on the contrary, he writes:

> . . . the For-itself can not be except in temporal form. The For-itself
> rising into being as the nihilation of the in-itself constitutes itself simul-
> taneously in all possible dimensions of nihilation. . . . temporality can
> only indicate the mode of being of a being which is itself outside itself.
> . . . Temporality is the being of the For-itself in so far as the For-itself has
> to be its being ecstatically. Temporality is not, but the For-itself tem-
> poralizes itself by existing.[14]

This represents a most drastic definition of temporality in terms of
conscious freedom. It is for Sartre precisely because a certain new
mode of being emerges, the mode that can be "itself outside itself,"
that temporality comes into the picture. "Prior to" conscious being,
time would have no meaning; and temporality is simply the mode of
existence of that being which can be itself outside itself. "Prior to"
this conscious mode of being, there simply prevailed being-in-itself in
its radically atemporal opaqueness. There had not yet emerged or
been introduced into the cosmos that disturbing capacity for standing-
at-gaze-over-against-itself which is the constitutive parameter of consciousness and which Sartre considers in the "spatial" sense as
productive of theoretical judgments and in the "temporal" sense as
productive of temporality itself and moral decisions.

We said above that the preconscious is for Sartre spatio-temporal
in the extreme; we implied that the conscious has a time-transcending
power. How is this to be reconciled with his contention that the
conscious can exist only temporally and that the in-itself is not subject to temporality? The first reconciliation is effected by recognizing
that the emergence of conscious freedom is for Sartre an absolute
starting point. He does not, of course, assert that "nothing happened"
before that emergence; but he clearly indicates himself not to be
interested in it nor yet to feel it meaningful. The crucial watershed for

Sartre is the point at which a fissure was able to be introduced into opaque, solid being-in-itself. This being-in-itself was spatio-temporal in the extreme in the sense that, in its dispensation, space, time, and all other distinctions were paralyzingly simply one. It was with the dramatic breakthrough of nihilation that differentiation set in. When therefore we speak, above, of a time-transcending power as accruing to the in-itself, we mean radically that ultimate and irreducible explosive power that can differentiate and therefore start time going or itself existing as temporal. Unless we are willing to reduce Sartre to a level of extremely crude and simplist materialism (and I am not, in view of the extremely subtle and penetrating psychological insights he displays), I hold we are compelled to admit that he is speaking, at this crucial anterior node of his system, not ontology at all but descriptive ontological ethics, i.e., not of the origin of being but of the origin of *Bewusstsein* (conscious being or being-conscious).

Sartre's *en-soi* (in-itself) is almost indistinguishable from the Marxist ultimate, *almost but not quite;* the distinction is crucial and can be properly appreciated only if we maintain a sane outlook on perspective and angles of vision and refrain from pusillanimous insistence on unidimensionality in terminology. For the Marxist ultimate, as we shall be seeing in detail later, is precisely matter-*in-motion* and the Marxist "dialectical materialists" conceive of this motion as an ontological ultimate, i.e., pertinent to premental reality. Sartre's purely descriptive anterior ultimate may indeed be at least likened to matter, stark and simple; *but it is not in meaningful motion.* The whole complex of conundrums of cosmology simply do not interest Sartre. The *motion* he introduces at his crucial nodal point is already in the dimension of consciousness and freedom; it is a differentiating, nihilating, contradistinguishing motion which at once constitutes and is constituted by the irreducible act of consciousness.

Before we pass to a consideration of the absolutely capital question in Sartre's ontological ethic, the question of what constitutes what, whether freedom nihilation or nihilation freedom, we must cope with his treatment of the third crucial difference and distinction between the in-itself and the for-itself, a distinction that provides the first and major clue to a proper answer to the capital Sartrean question.

Sartre's first distinction may crudely be called a pseudo-spatial distinction, his second distinction may equally crudely be called a pseudo-temporal distinction, in the sense that two terms, space and time, normally used primarily of premental reality, are here not only transposed to constituent parameters of conscious being (*Bewusstsein*) but moreover alleged to have real meaning only in terms of the emerging fact and act of conscious freedom. Thus the preconscious is said to be *"in*-itself" and the conscious to be *"not-in*-itself"; the preconscious is said to be what it is (i.e., innocent of the change produced and measured by time), the conscious is said to be not what it is but rather precisely that decompression which, by conscious acts of judgment and will, creates temporality. Now Sartre proceeds to the most ultimate distinction which appears incomparably more grotesque than the other two, *if we persist in making him speak absolutely ontological language* rather than that of ontological ethics.

C. For he asserts that, ultimately the preconscious is and the conscious is not. His remarks concerning the brute facticity of the preconscious clearly underscore his deliberate decision to shift the fulcrum of meaningfulness from cosmological evolution to the creative emergence of consciousness:

> Being-in-itself is never either possible or impossible. It *is*. This is what consciousness expresses in anthropomorphic terms by saying that being is superfluous [*de trop*]—that is, that consciousness absolutely can not derive being from anything, either from another being, or from a possibility, or from a necessary law. Uncreated, without reason for being, without any connection with another being, being-in-itself is *de trop* for eternity.[15]

To equate this Sartrean statement with vulgar materialism, or a fortiori with dialectical materialism, is to trivialize impermissibly the whole drama Sartre intends to treat. For the vulgar materialist reductively levels consciousness into a mere function of matter and the dialectical materialist endows anterior matter with the inseparable attribute of motion which allows the emergence of consciousness to be explained as a qualitative leap of one type of matter, bunching up quantitatively at a certain point in already flowing time to a crisis-point, at which it explodes into another type of motion. But for Sartre the situation is quite other: brute facticity paralyzed in the toils of absolute identity; and then the explosion of consciousness which institutes and *is* true motion, dynamism, effort—and ultimate tragedy. Of the conscious he writes:

In fact the *self* cannot be apprehended as a real existent; the subject can not *be* self, for coincidence with self, as we have seen, causes the self to disappear. But neither can it *not be* itself since the self is an indication of the subject himself. The *self* therefore represents an ideal distance within the immanence of the subject in relation of himself, a way of *not being his own coincidence,* of escaping identity while positing it as unity —in short, of being in a perpetually unstable equilibrium between identity as absolute cohesion without a trace of diversity and unity as a synthesis of multiplicity.[16]

The caveat we would here suggest relates to Sartre's confusion between the rational explanation of a knowing being and the actual factual construction of such a being. Sartre seems not to have grasped the full force of material being nor yet its full potential for consciousness, or else to have opted against any such tenets. Consequently, he sees consciousness as a wildly new emergent on the bland indeterminate opaque face of this material mass. And he is by no means entirely wrong; and to the extent he is right, he is chilling for theists and salutary for theist and atheist alike. But we submit that his angle of vision is not adequate. Certainly from *his* angle of vision, the human conscious knower *is* wildly unique and must indeed be described in all the Sartrean terms. But *the constitutive reality of a human being is not simply the conscious epistemological act but the total act of being comprising also his own body* (which Sartre treats simply as a mode of presence to others, a compromising thing indeed, because it partakes of the monolithic unconscious unity of the sheerly material).[17]

But proceeding on Sartre's terms and toward the goal of that ultimate freedom in which he puts his faith, we must say that the point-event of the emergence of consciousness precisely initiates real history by introducing real becoming, real meaningful motion, real temporality. And Sartre gives us the clue we have been seeking to the hierarchy of his two candidates for ultimate, when he writes:

Presence to self . . . supposes that an impalpable fissure has slipped into being. If being is present to itself, it is because it is not wholly itself. Presence is an immediate deterioration of coincidence, for it supposes separation. But if we ask ourselves at this point *what it is* which separates the subject from himself, we are forced to admit that it is nothing.[18]

And this nothingness as here produced by nihilation is a separation that

cannot be grasped or even conceived in isolation. If we seek to reveal it, it vanishes . . . appearing when we do not wish to see it, disappearing as soon as we seek to contemplate it. This fissure then is the pure negative . . . the nothingness which arises in the heart of consciousness *is not.* It *is made-to-be*.[19]

The hierarchy, as between nothingness and nihilation, is thus crystal clear. With all possible force and emphasis, Sartre is shifting the fulcrum from any anterior parameter merely utilized by man to man's act of nihilation itself. This act causes that nothingness which is at once the guarantee of man's autonomous contradistinction from the not-self. Simultaneously, by virtue of its very nothingness, of the fact that it "is not" but *"is made to be,"* of the fact that it is exhausted in the act itself, it can function as the guarantee of man's meaningful operative identity.

Nihilation then is an act that produces nothing and yet, and *therefore,* constitutes the nihilator as an autonomous being while safeguarding his identity. We have effectively removed nothingness itself as an operative ultimate:

Nothingness does not nihilate itself: Nothingness "is nihilated."[20]

The implacable war rages then between two types of being . . . two radically separated regions of being . . . which *in theory* are without communication,[21]

the solid in-itself whose identity is paralyzing and the fluid for-itself whose identity is at once supremely fragile and supremely activizing. And the bridge is the nothingness produced by nihilation. But we must now inspect the relation between nihilation and freedom to establish Sartre's true ultimate.

2. An Original Freedom[22]

Sartre has clearly repudiated any contention that nothingness can have an ontological status as subject. He continues:

> it follows therefore that there must exist a Being (this can not be the In-itself) of which the property is to nihilate Nothingness, to support it in its being, to sustain it perpetually in its very existence, *a being by which nothingness comes to things.*[23]

He then proceeds by a series of nervous precisions to eliminate various possibilities of relationship between this "being by which nothingness comes to things" and that nothingness itself. The nihilating being cannot be subject of his own nihilation in the merely passive sense, cannot receive it; nor can he produce it without change to himself. Finally Sartre arrives at the startling conclusion that the nihilation in question here is not, in the strict sense, an act at all, but "an ontological characteristic of the Being required. It remains, [he adds, somewhat wryly,] to learn in what delicate, exquisite region of Being we shall encounter that Being which is its own Nothingness."[24]

He identifies the being as man and "this possibility which human reality has to secrete a nothingness which isolates it"[25] as *freedom.* He then proceeds to a clear statement of the hierarchy, as between freedom and nihilation: "freedom [he says, is] "the requisite condition for the nihilation of nothingness."[26]

But is this freedom then "a *property* which belongs among others to the essence of the human being?"[27] In other words, is man after all a more basic ultimate, subject of this freedom but not himself constituted by it? Sartre's answer is categorical and of capital importance:

> What we call freedom is impossible to distinguish from the *being* of "human reality." Man does not exist *first* in order to be free *subsequently;* there is no difference between the being of man and his *being-free.*[28]

Much later in *Being and Nothingness,* when he is ready to attack the *problem* of freedom as such, Sartre remarks on a profound preliminary difficulty:

Ordinarily, to describe something is a process of making explicit by aiming at the structures of a particular essence. Now freedom has no essence. It is not subject to any logical necessity. . . . Freedom makes itself an act. . . . if we wish to reach the constitutive power, we must abandon any hope of finding it an essence.[29]

It must be described, rather, in terms of the existence that is the free being; and

For the for-itself, to be is to nihilate the in-itself which it is. . . . It is through this that the for-itself escapes its being as its essence. . . . I am condemned to exist forever beyond my essence, beyond the causes and motives of my act. I am condemned to be free. This means that no limits to my freedom can be found except freedom itself or, if you prefer, that we are not free to cease being free.[30]

Freedom is thus original to man in two senses: it emerges first *as* man; and it *constitutes* him man.

The stark tragedy and exhilarating challenge of this situation is revealed in Sartre's most pungent passages on his ultimate, which we here telescope into a single consecutive articulation:

If we admit that human reality can be determined to action by a prior state of the world or of itself, this amounts to putting a *given* at the beginning of the series. Then these acts disappear as acts. . . . The existence of the act implies its autonomy.[31]

The freedom of the for-itself is always *engaged;* there is no question here of a freedom which could be undetermined and which would pre-exist its choice. We shall never apprehend ourselves except as a choice in the making. But freedom is simply the fact that this choice is always unconditioned. Such a choice made without base of support and dictating its own causes to itself, can very well appear *absurd,* and in fact it is absurd. This is because freedom is a *choice* of its being but not the *foundation* of its being. . . . Thus freedom is not pure and simple contingency in so far as it turns back toward its being in order to illuminate its being in the light of its end. It is the perpetual escape from contingency; it is the interiorization, the nihilation, and the subjectivizing of contingency, which thus modified passes wholly into the gratuity of the choice.[32]

Freedom can exist only as *restricted* since freedom is choice. Every choice . . . supposes elimination and selection; every choice is a choice of finitude. Thus freedom can be truly free only by constituting facticity as its own restriction. . . . Without facticity freedom would not exist—as a power of nihilation and of choice—and without freedom facticity would not be discovered and would have no meaning.[33]

Sartre has here articulated, in a context of total immanentism, the very mystery that is the creative act of the Truly Free Eternal Infinitely Present God, degrading that act to the level where, as *self-constitutive* act of temporalized *finite* man, it becomes a constant danger and absurd challenge. The God of whom we have just spoken does not emerge by a desperate cast or upsurge out of a preconscious mass endowed with and constituted by paralyzing unity. His parameter of action in creating is not a continuous mobilization of his sheer potential geared to attain to a self-perfecting that is not yet; it is, rather, an absolutely primordial pleromization and dimensionalization of his transcendent act of simple being, so that there may begin to exist a manifold initially possessing not static unity but the exact reverse, *utterly uncentered centrifugal plurality,* which then gradually centers into those admittedly fragile foci of conscious action that are conscious free being. Nor is this God limited anteriorly by *finitude,* as is Sartre's human self-constituting chooser. Finitude is the parameter not of God's choice for self-perfection but of his creative making of the pleroma with its inherent finite tensions and drive to a species of infinity, in the sense of unboundedness, realized at last in truly tormented man, tormented however not by a terminal finitude imposed on his strivings but rather by an *initial finitude* deriving from his solidarity in the order of creation, existence, with the finitized pleroma, and clashing with that emergent thirst and thrust for unboundedness which constitutes him a man.

Yet Sartre is not only right but the most inward and consistent and adequate of all atheists, *if man is indeed God-bereft and Godless.* Viewed in abstraction from God, man's plight is quite as tragic, quite as desperate, as Sartre describes it in a curious passage in which he sets man upon the vacant awful throne of the nonexistent God:

. . . man being condemned to be free carries the weight of the whole world on his shoulders; he is responsible for the world and for himself as a way of being. . . . the responsibility of the for-itself is overwhelming since he is the one by whom it happens that *there is* a world; since he is also the one who makes himself be, then whatever may be the situation in which he finds himself, the for-itself must wholly assume this situation with its peculiar coefficient of adversity, even though it be insupportable. He must assume the situation with the proud consciousness of being the author of it.[34]

It is our firm contention that at least the substance of what Sartre here says about free man must be accepted entirely and unreservedly by the theist. The trivialization of human freedom on the part of predestination-besotted and security-minded theists is put to shame by this courageous outburst of a professed atheist who takes freedom seriously. What the theist can and ought to do about this disgusting state of affairs—this we shall treat in the final chapter. For the moment, suffice it to note that the appeal to omnipotence and merciful love is no escape for free man; and that the urgency of a proper reckoning with freedom is mounting sharply in our own day. A crusading contemporary novelist prefaces his most challenging and unsettling novel with the words of Albert Einstein:

We can only sound the alarm, again and again; we must never relax our efforts to rouse in the peoples of the world, and especially in their governments, an awareness of the unprecedented disaster which they are absolutely certain to bring upon themselves unless there is a fundamental change in their attitude toward one another as well as in their concept of the future.

Our world is threatened by a crisis whose extent seems to escape those within whose power it is to make major decisions for good or evil. The unleashed power of the atom has changed everything except our ways of thinking. Thus we are drifting toward a catastrophe beyond comparison. We shall require a substantially new manner of thinking if mankind is to survive.

To meet this threat has become one of the most urgent tasks of our times.[35]

And the same novelist eloquently expresses this whole dilemma in this brief dialogue:

"You say, 'God cannot allow it—God ought not to allow it.' God ought, God must! The same sort of hypocrisy—blackmail, as it were—that has prevailed for thousands of years. As the final test He has permitted mankind to split the atom—the unsplittable atom. He has placed the sun's heart in the hands of mortals—to use for light and warmth or to burn themselves up with."

"God is merciful—isn't that so?"

"He is endless and eternal. A world that goes up in flames is like a speck of dust on his mantle. To God the history of mankind is like a single breath. It is enough to know that God is!"[36]

The magnificence of Sartre's exposé of theistic Platonism is well articulated by his translator, Hazel Barnes, in her description of his notion of "bad faith": "It is to pretend that one is born with a determined self instead of recognizing that one spends one's life pursuing and making oneself."[37]

She also pinpoints what we believe to be the chief and central of many reasons for Sartre's rejection of God: "If the creature is still inwardly dependent on God, then he is not separate, not free, not an independent existent. But if in his inner being he is not dependent on God, then he no longer can receive from God any justification for his existence or any absoluteness. He does not 'need' a Creator. Either man is free and does not derive his meaning from God, or he is dependent on God and not free."[38]

Freedom is therefore original to man in a mysterious third sense: not only does it originate with him and originate him; it posits him as supreme originator: "Consciousness is its own foundation but it remains contingent *in order that there may be* a consciousness rather than an infinity of pure and simple in-itself. The absolute event or for-itself is contingent in its very being."[39] And this freedom is ultimately a supremely individual existence: "I could not describe a freedom which would be common to both the Other and myself. . . . actually the question is of *my* freedom."[40] Having thus arrived, by his own unique path, at *the free individual existent* as the ultimate fulcrum and originator of meaningful reality, Sartre is compelled, by his own honesty, to face the question of that self-constituting chooser-actor's relation to other nihilating free agents; and to explain, on his own terms, the phenomenon of the God-problematic, which Collins incisively notes Sartre to reduce to "that of the idea of God" which is but "the product of man's creative consciousness" and yet "an inevitable one for the human mind to bring forth, since it expresses a necessary tendency of our nature, albeit in a deceptive way."[41]

3. Hell Is Other People[42]

The ultimate fulcrum of the world is therefore the individual as free. Precisely because of the constitutive function of the individual's own free act, precisely because the self is in constant process of coming into being, there can *be* no self as such (the for-itself is that precisely whose being is its nothingness). Small wonder then that one commentator should remark: ". . . it does seem that his ontology, in the strictest sense, does not leave much room for an ethics of interpersonal relationships."[43]

But there is much worse to come and the same commentator sums it up neatly thus:

> The other's gaze, as such, just because it is directed toward the part of the world in which I am, constitutes me as *object-in-the-world* and alienates me from myself. That look breaks up my own universe and regroups objects, including my body, around it. Thus simply by appearing, the other has stolen my world. He has undermined the centralization that I was effecting for myself. The opposite is equally true. By perceiving the other, I congeal him into an object, as a thing among things. . . . He and I are two liberties affronting each other and trying to paralyze each other by our look. . . . the other's look solidifies me in the world and endangers my being-subject and my liberty.[44]

Cumming, in his Introduction to *The Philosophy of Jean-Paul Sartre,* succinctly describes the sequel:

> . . . the dialectic of my relation with him does not remain a duel at a visible distance, but culminates in tactile forms of self-aggrandizement and humiliation, in which my body changes sides in the dialectic, and my consciousness of myself as something embodied participates in my alienation by the caress, which embodies the other's tactile consciousness of me.[45]

Sartre presents the whole complex of sexuality as a somber and bitter business. His observations form an ideal background of contrast to the attitude of Henry Miller, whose faith in sex we shall be presently treating. Sartre sees sex as a doubly frustrating passion, exceeded in pathos and pointlessness only by the hopeless passion of man to be God. Sex (the over-all complex of psycho-physical events articulating interpersonal commitment, love) is frustrating because it is a parallel effort on both sides to possess the other; and because moreover it is an effort by a radically nonexistent to possess an equally nonexistent. In his strange ethical ontology, Sartre sees the only hope of possession as lying in a quasi or attempted reduction of the other nihilating free willing agent in some sense to the inert stability of the *in-itself via the flesh:*

Desire is an attempt to strip the body of its movements as of its clothing and to make it exist as pure flesh; it is an attempt to *incarnate* the Other's body. It is in this sense that the caress is an appropriation of the Other's body. . . . the caress is designed to uncover the web of inertia.[46]

But the seeker, not after mere gratification nor even affection but after the self-reassuring knowledge that he has triumphed over and appropriated the other, finds to his horror that he can do this only at nameless expense to himself:

I destroy my possibilities in order to destroy those of the world and to constitute the world as a "world of desire"; that is, as a destructured world which has lost its meaning, a world in which things jut out like fragments of pure matter, like brute qualities. . . . As soon as I throw myself toward the Other's facticity, as soon as I wish to push aside his acts and his functions, so as to touch him in his flesh, I incarnate myself, for I can neither wish nor even conceive of the incarnation of the Other except in and by means of my own incarnation.[47]

It is somberly typical of this ethical ontology of identity-destroying freedom that sadism should strike Sartre as a specially adept way of seeking what is sought in sex:

. . . as the sadist neither can nor will realize the Other's incarnation by means of his own incarnation . . . he seeks to utilize the Other's body as a tool to make the Other realize an incarnated existence. . . . The body of the torturing For-itself is no longer anything more than an instrument for giving pain. Thus from the start the For-itself can give itself the illusion of getting hold of the Other's freedom instrumentally; that is, of plunging this freedom into flesh without ceasing to be the one who *provokes,* who grabs hold, who seizes. . . .[48]

But in the context of a stunning and brutal quotation from Faulkner, Sartre pricks the balloon of the sadist's dream:

The sadist discovers his error when his victim *looks at* him; that is, when the sadist experiences the absolute alienation of his being in the Other's freedom. . . . He discovers then that he can not act on the Other's freedom even by forcing the Other to humiliate himself and to beg for mercy, for it is precisely in and through the Other's absolute freedom that there exists a world in which there are sadism and instruments of torture and a hundred pretexts for being humiliated and for forswearing oneself. . . . this explosion of the Other's look in the world of the sadist causes the meaning and goal of sadism to collapse. The sadist discovers that it was *that freedom* which he wished to enslave, and at the same time he realizes the futility of his efforts.[49]

The significance of such an approach in the context of a situation involving the most urgent necessity of using sexuality in the widest sense as an instrument of centering and centripetal unification of a new mankind will be treated in part in the chapter on Miller and in part in the final chapter. For the moment it is essential to note that this hell that is being-for-others derives ultimately from the fact that men are free.

It should be specially stressed that the emphasis in Sartre's treatment of interpersonal relationships is definitely not on grasping aggressive egotism; rather, he poignantly evokes the desperate defensive stance of every for-itself in any relation to its fellow nihilators. He speaks of "my desperate effort to *be*" and immediately notes ominously:

there is a freedom beyond my freedom, a situation beyond my situation and one for which what I live as a situation is given as an objective form in the midst of the world.[50]

Consequently,

we are always . . . in a state of instability in relation to the Other. We pursue the impossible ideal of the simultaneous apprehension of his freedom and of his objectivity. . . . But . . . we shall never place ourselves concretely on a plane of equality; that is, on the plane where the recognition of the Other's freedom would involve the Other's recognition of our freedom. The Other is on principle inapprehensible; he flees me when I seek him and possesses me when I flee him.[51]

And Sartre proceeds to articulate the most trenchant and drastic consequences of this ineluctable tragedy of freedom, as totally destructive of viable interpersonal relationships:

To train the child by persuasion and gentleness is no less to compel him. Thus respect for the Other's freedom is an empty word; even if we could assume the project of respecting this freedom, each attitude which we adopted with respect to the Other would be a violation of that freedom which we claimed to respect. The extreme attitude which would be given as a total indifference toward the Other is not a solution either. We are already thrown in the world in the face of the Other; our upsurge is a free limitation of his freedom and nothing—not even suicide—can change this original situation. Whatever our acts may be, in fact, we must accomplish them in a world where there are already others and where I am *de trop* in relation to others.[52]

In his intriguing recent book, Jolivet speaks hopefully of a **Sartre** who "healed and clairvoyant as he was when (after having struggled with his lobsters and his crabs for a long time) he declared magnificently one day, 'I'm tired of being crazy,' still has before him a handsome career."[53] And he cites equally hopefully from Sartre's 1964 work *Les Mots,* to back his optimism. At the end of this work, Sartre declares:

I see clearly, I've lost my illusions, I know what my real jobs are, I surely deserve a prize for good citizenship. For the last ten years or so I've been a man who's been waking up, cured of a long, bittersweet madness and who can't get over the fact, a man who can't think of his old ways without laughing and who doesn't know what to do with himself.[54]

We may soberly reply that the dynamic evolution of a thinker is of less interest to us here than the *scripta* which *manent;* and that a possibly enlightened Sartre may indeed rejoice the angels but will, we hope, repudiate nothing of the true observations he wrote, out of his "bittersweet madness," when his angle of vision, distorted out of true, as we readily agree, yet caused him to see deep truths which the enlightened too easily pass lightly over.

For, though we are persuaded that Sartre's bitter vision of the unviability of interpersonal relationships is ultimately untrue, yet we are equally convinced that his insight into the ultimate loneliness of every created free being, the unstable compromise that is a relationship between created free nihilators, the radical incapacity of the lonelinesses that are free creatures ever really resolving their mutual problematic *in terms of their own dimension,* is a permanent truth, whose applicability need only be modified accidentally in function of the further progress in communication that those free creatures will undoubtedly effect. Man may indeed, in Sartrean terms, be "incapable of motivating his conduct metaphysically or morally" (which, on our analysis, would amount to the same thing, i.e., man's radical incapacity to assume the burden of a creator of the world and of meaning) and he may indeed be unable to "stand this conflict much longer without becoming a tortured neurotic."[55] But we cannot agree with Jolivet that this "could be just another *mal de siècle* analogous to the one that fed the disgust and nausea of the Romantics."[56] To agree to this would be to abrogate our initial assumption, that modern atheists, *precisely as atheists,* can contribute vital insights to the human community.

Sartre's conclusion that "I am *de trop* in relation to others" articulates a profound insight often diluted and washed away into sentimental and bowdlerized pseudo-humanism by the great wave of an incautious and childishly unquestioning faith. The Sartrean man is *de trop* to all his fellow nihilators *because he is making himself* in opposition to them. But the free created agent is *de trop* to all his peers in a way the theist must acknowledge, on pain of fatal distortion. He is *de trop* because each proportionate participation in the Infinite Act of Being is separated from all other such participations by the great gulf of the unalterable distinctness of the vertical line, which binds individual man to his Creator and which supersedes (in the dictionary sense of causing "to be set aside or dropped from use as inferior or obsolete and replaced by something else"[57]) all horizontal lines joining man the individual to his fellow men. Hell is, indeed, other people when each person is a God in process of self-construction. But when each human person on our planet is a proportionate participation of the fullness of Being of an anterior Personal Creator, then the relation is neither hell, as Sartre's grim atheism would have it, nor yet heaven-on-earth, as incautious theoretical (and practical!) Christian humanists would all too often have it but, rather, that exciting and unstable nexus of the communion of saints, i.e., of creatures in process of being saved; it is the comradeship of wayfarers building the Mystical Body of Christ.

The witness of Sartre in *Being and Nothingness* would reject this whole vision as inconsistent and unacceptable. We must now examine this rejection.

4. Man Is a Useless Passion[58]

These are the well-known last words of *Being and Nothingness*. They are preceded by and sum up a profound and nervous analysis of human theologizing: "Human reality is the pure effort to become God without there being any given substratum for that effort."[59]

The free being, by whose nihilating act of freedom the world as meaningful antithesis to that self-constituting free being has come into existence and that being himself is constantly being built in desperate battle, finds himself patently cheated of any harmony, even unstable and provisional, with other nihilating self-constructors. He sees himself cheated here by virtue of the fact that satisfying communion can be bought only at the price of the destruction of even the embattled and emergent selfhood of both himself and the other. They can meet and embrace only at the level of a mutual and mutually triggered relapse into the opaque paralysis of the *in-itself*. But, untaught by or impervious to this sobering rebuff, he extrapolates to infinity the unsuccessful merger, and aspires in narcissistic yearning to achieve an ultimate stable merger *with himself!* The for-itself wishes (by another "useless" act of will in freedom) to become the in-itself-for-itself:

> That is, the ideal of a consciousness which would be the foundation of its own being-in-itself by the pure consciousness which it would have of itself. It is this ideal which can be called God.[60]

The creator-man who creates by nihilating, i.e. constitutes himself in and as his perilous freedom by using that freedom to hide from the mass of uncreated (or precreated or at least pre-existing) being all around him, now wishes to possess the stability of that precreated being and so makes the useless thrust to Godhood. It is useless basically because the two kinds of being can never be united: they are perpetually at war. See how precisely Sartre describes this:

> The act of causation by which God is *causa sui* is a nihilating act like every recovery of the self by the self, to the same degree that the original relation of necessity is a return to *self,* a reflexivity. . . . Being has its possibility outside of itself in the pure regard which gauges its chances of

being; possibility can indeed be given *to us* before being; but it is *to us* that it is given and it is in no way the possibility *of* this being. . . . But possibility can also appear to us as an ontological structure of the real. Then it belongs to certain beings as *their* possibility; it is the possibility which they are, which they have to be. In this case being sustains its own possibilities in being; it is their foundation, and the necessity of being can not then be derived from its possibility. In a word, God, if he exists, is contingent.[61]

This analysis is unanswerably correct if you start from the epistemologico-moral act of man as ultimately constituent of being, thus reducing being to consciousness or moral action. But in God, or better still *as* God, being is sheer power, sheer act; and quite simply not governed by the limitations of consciousness as ultimate ground. Sartre's "God" has been imprisoned in the epistemologico-moral dimension and his nihilating Intellect has been made his basic constitutive ground. But it is not, for this basic constitutive ground is God as Being, as *him*self not *it*self. Thus, to Sartre's Being-in-itself must be added Being-as-himself where the genderized pronoun is intended to express simply fully constituted personality grounded in fullness of being as act. Thus the entire Sartrean gymnastic should firmly persuade the theologian that God must necessarily be conceived and articulated as a personal Being. Only inasmuch as He is such a fully powerful anterior personal Creator can man's personality possess, given by Him, anything more than the lonely freedom of nihilation articulated by Sartre.

The dangerous ambiguity of Sartre is rooted in two errors:

A. The human being, this man, is not constituted as radically and exclusively human by virtue of the fact that he wills (nihilates). The reality is more complex by far. When the species differentiates itself from the genus or the genus from the class or kingdom, it does not thereby nihilate the generic reality. Therefore man as man is constituted and held in contradistinguished being not simply and exclusively by his act of freedom but by the complex interplay of that act of freedom and the generic inertia of prehuman reality out of whose womb he has sprung.

B. The apparent contradictions of the God-idea stem from the fact that this idea is an effort by creatures to represent to themselves a transcendent Creator. I bypass deliberately the whole question of the legitimacy of Sartre's failure even to touch, in over seven hundred pages of treatise, on the phenomenological fact of revelation. I concentrate on his alleged problems of the God-idea:

Every human reality is a passion in that it projects itself so as to found being and by the same stroke to constitute the In-itself which escapes contingency by being its own foundation, the *ens causa sui,* which religions call God.[62]

Barnes, in her Introduction, echoes this anthropocentrism: "This is an obviously self-contradictory ideal, for the essence of the For-itself is the power to secrete a Nothingness, to be always in the process of becoming, to be-about-to-be."[63] Nothing more clearly reveals Sartrean radical anthropocentric, indeed epistemologico-ethico-centric atheism than these words. In a much more radical sense than Heidegger, Sartre is in effect making man into the Creator and alleging that the creation of such a fragile Creator must necessarily be absurd, brute contingency.

The Sartre we know and love (in defiance of his own contention that this latter is impossible) for his trenchant exposure of human foibles, of second-best solutions, is a resolute battler with words, a shrewd and supremely competent (psycho) analyst because also a poet, i.e., a man who sees intuitively as well as discursively beneath the shimmering seductive surfaces. He repeatedly delights in exposing the inner existential core of apparently edifying sentiments. Therefore we presume to hope that he will not cavil at our own interpretative articulation of that section of *Being and Nothingness* which seems to us to betray (not in the sense of the treachery of the weary mind and heart exploited by the snide commentator, but in the sense of the unconscious self-revelation precisified by the admiring friend) Sartre's own deepest motivation in terms of his faith in freedom.[64]

5. The Slimy Offers a Horrible Image

We have said that it is in the name of total human freedom that Sartre is protesting so violently against any God-reality. His section on the slimy is richly revelatory not only of how Sartre subconsciously conceives God but also of how he conceives fellow human beings. There is, we again stress with all possible force, one kernel of truth in his furious protest, a kernel every theist of squamously and mystagogically sociological pretentions must take seriously: the lonely individual human existent does indeed retain his individuality and does have the inescapable assignment of making being, the being of his own ultimate free choices. But it is because Sartre has set up the free human being too exclusively in terms of consciousness as an active transformer of nonmental reality rather than as in any sense also a passive receiver of that nonmental reality, that Sartre shows this pathological horror of slime. Before we cite the nub of Sartre's disquisition on slime, we would articulate our conviction that the theist must take serious cognizance of that disquisition not only, indeed not primarily, in the dimension of ontology where Sartre can, we believe, relatively easily be overthrown, but predominantly in the dimension of ethics (or ethical ontology, the ontological survey of man, the lonely maker), where his waspish voice is pre-eminently topical.

Of the slimy, Sartre says:

> . . . it represents in itself a dawning triumph of the solid over the liquid—that is, a tendency of the indifferent in-itself, which is represented by the pure solid, to fix the liquidity, to absorb the for-itself which ought to dissolve it. Slime is the agony of water. It presents itself as a phenomenon in process of becoming; it does not have the permanence within change that water has but on the contrary represents an accomplished break in a change of state. This fixed instability in the slimy discourages possession. Water is more fleeting but it can be possessed in its very flight as something fleeing. The slimy flees with a heavy flight which has the same relation to water as the unwieldy earthbound flight of the chicken has to that of the hawk. Even this flight can not be possessed because it denies itself as flight. It is already almost a solid permanence.[65]
>
> The slimy is *docile*. Only at the very moment when I believe that I possess it, behold by a curious reversal, *it* possesses me. . . . it sticks to me, it draws me, it sucks at me. . . . It is a soft, yielding action, a moist and feminine sucking, it lives obscurely under my fingers. . . . it draws me to it as the bottom of a precipice might draw me. There is something like a tactile fascination in the slimy. I am no longer the master in *arresting* the process of appropriation. It continues. In one sense it is like the

supreme docility of the possessed, the fidelity of a dog who *gives himself* even when one does not want him any longer, and in another sense there is underneath this docility a surreptitious appropriation of the possessor by the possessed. . . . there is a possibility that the In-itself might absorb the For-itself. . . . it is a fluidity which holds me and which compromises me.[66]

The slime is like a liquid seen in a nightmare, where all its properties are animated by a sort of life and turn back against me. Slime is the revenge of the In-itself. A sickly-sweet, feminine revenge which will be symbolized on another level by the quality "sugary." . . . A sugary sliminess is the ideal of the slimy; it symbolizes the sugary death of the For-itself (like that of the wasp which sinks into the jam and drowns in it). But at the same time the slimy is myself, by the very fact that I outline an appropriation of the slimy substance.[67]

. . . the being of the slimy is a soft clinging, there is a sly solidarity and complicity of all its leech-like parts, a vague, soft effort made by each to individualize itself, followed by a falling back and flattening out that is emptied of the individual, sucked in on all sides by the substance. . . . It is an ideal being which I reject with all my strength and which haunts me as *value* haunts my being, an ideal being in which the foundationless In-itself has priority over the For-itself. We shall call it an Antivalue.[68]

An analysis of the self-revelation here articulated must proceed from the humblest to the most exalted, passing by that very cross-roads creature, man, whom Sartre resolutely insists on lifting entirely out of the dimension of matter. And the end will be seen in the beginning, for everywhere the clue is passivity, a quality totally present in the preconscious reality of which Sartre speaks as related to man, present in complex function of this material parameter complicated by the spiritualized emergence of freedom in man the crossroads creature, and utterly absent (but potent in its absence, which becomes a retroactive relational presence in the creature, pre-eminently the free creature) in God. For slime is precisely the meeting point of the fluid and the solid.

"Slime is the revenge of the In-itself." It is indeed the revenge of a matter-parameter of spatio-temporal creaturehood, against a consciousness falsely set up over against it in the first place. What Sartre hates about the slimy, matter, is that it cannot be known. Not being able to absorb it into his ruthless male dominance-bent consciousness, he judges it by himself and fears it will try to absorb him. Sartre comes close to identifying matter with God and then hating both as restraining man, human luminous consciousness, from the eternal quest for more being. Matter of course is not God. But it comes from God and has a vital message for us as revelation of an arc of the immanent God, an arc that is in us too, in its radical passivity and strange amorphous state between solidity and fluidity. It instructs our senses as to what creaturehood means.

But slime is also, as we have said, in us nihilating free beings as well. Not by accident does Genesis speak of man as being fashioned of "the slime of the earth."[69] Human beings have slime in them, or rather are spiritualized slime, because they are not sports of an atheistic cosmos but evolved creatures of the materialized pleroma. The parameter of their most fruitful interpersonal relationships is precisely this slime that is the parameter of their creatureliness. When they encounter one another on this level, they can most surely communicate because precisely this is the dimension, still present in them, at which they are least contradistinguished from each other and closest to their pleromizing Creator. That will be the great, though perversely and short-circuitedly articulated, insight of Henry Miller. They do indeed transform the materialized pleroma prior to any contact between them. That is why Miller's sex mysticism cannot stand as he himself articulates it. But they do contact each other in a genuinely creative fashion at this level; and this is the Miller rectification of Sartre's unnecessary loneliness which the searcher would do well to mark.

Sartre's words "a sickly-sweet feminine revenge" articulate in subverted and inverted fashion the great insight that before the Creator every creature is feminine, i.e., radically ontologically passive. The "revenge" of the slimy which he articulates at this level ("the sugary death of the For-itself like that of the wasp which sinks into the jam and drowns in it") is not a revenge at all but that taking-possession by the ontologically active, God, of the ontologically passive, the creature, which is the essence of mystical experience. When the ontologically passive sets itself up as ontologically active at the deepest level, then it may well see itself drowning in this taking-possession. But the reality is otherwise: the creature must effect only one rectification of perspective and then the taking-possession ceases to be a violation or a drowning. For in the instant in which the creature knows (and admits) that as created emergent he is fundamentally passive in relation to an active *in another dimension,* then the taking-possession is neither a rape nor (let theists beware!) even a shift of responsibility. It is merely a supreme ontological powering for the thrust that must be accomplished by the creature.

Sartre's final conclusion can be enthusiastically approved by the aware and responsible theist. The God known by the questing creature can very easily emerge as a "new danger, a threatening mode of being which must be avoided," for He can emerge, to the flagging and pusillanimous heart and mind of the tired creature, as the God who *takes over* the creature, rather than as the God who *inspires* or *powers* the creature. The creature cannot, even if he would, surrender his freedom absolutely to this God, much less to any creature and still less to any human institution. And this, not because he is perpetually making himself in the absence of any transcendent God and against any fellow nihilator but, rather, because to him has been entrusted the lonely dignity of real created freedom, which can be redeemed only by the power of the Creator, operating along the parameters of materiality, finitude, and temporality, and coalescing, in an ultimately unanalyzable encounter, with that created freedom itself, doughtily operative. This created freedom, encapsuled in the lonely individual, can be socialized only by the power of sex, the free conscious creature's most intimate analogue to divine creativity. But that is the subject of a subsequent chapter.

We shall not be impermissibly anticipating if we say that sex is (and should more and more be recognized by the theist as being) a multidimensional phenomenon; but its *analogatum primum* is the procreative function, the biological drive to make new human beings. Now precisely the slimy is the milieu of biological generation. The aqueous fluidity of water must be weighed down and metamorphose under the action of the solid germ-cells and in turn dampen these solid cells so that generation may proceed. Slime may well be called the agony of water, a phenomenon in the process of becoming, from this biological point of view. It is the very native habitat of that reality which cannot but change, and change radically, if it is not to perish, namely the embryo.

In generation, the sire especially is indeed no longer the master in arresting the process of appropriation. Even the seed of grain must fall into the ground and die that it may bring forth fruit a hundredfold (a kind of pale analogue of pleromization itself). But the higher the level of distinctively sexual generation, the more grievous the demand made upon the generating parents and especially the father to surrender a vital part of themselves so that the new may emerge. This is the generosity demanded of concreators. And the whole affair is a slimy business; no amount of romantic and sentimental embellishment should ever be allowed to obscure that fact. The point is, however, that this sliminess is intolerable or disaffecting only to the psyche that clutches its spiritual identity to it overpassionately and sees that identity namelessly threatened by any materialization. Embryology is not the supreme branch of aesthetics, nor are we setting up the fetus as the goal of human beauty. But the generative process has something invaluable to tell man, and it is connected with slime. In this process the individual emergent human being recapitulates the phylogenetic path of ancestors, from the proximate to the most distant, right back to that link between the animate and lifeless matter. "Where there's life, there's hope" expresses the teleological forward-driving thrust of the crossroad creature, man. "Where there's life, there's slime" expresses the anterior terminal milieu of living material being, a milieu that never entirely forsakes that being until he is finally resolved, so far as his material element is concerned, into the dry dust that is perhaps aesthetically more tasteful but biologically dead.

Slime is not specially correctively pertinent to the system of the human thinker who leans heavily on matter anyway, nor yet of the thinker who puts his faith in either of the ultimates that are not and cannot be of themselves antimaterialistic, finitude or time. But slime is supremely relevant to the system of a thinker who puts his faith in freedom. For it is a palpable demonstration of how that created freedom must function if it is not to become the brittle lifeless nihilation of sheer pseudo-spiritual negation. Again and again that freedom must go down into the sliminess of matter, a sliminess perceptible only (or at least so dramatically and terrifyingly palpable only) to the existent who is spiritual and yet immatered. Into slime must be resolved the life-giving cells of human procreators; out of slime must gradually emerge the new human being.

And this biological parameter of sex is the only sound and sane one for any discussion of the many other dimensions of this complex relational phenomenon. At the level of total person-to-person relationships, the picture is necessarily complicated by a whole host of problems, stemming from the emergence of fear and hate and all centrifugal aspirations. But always a certain amorphousness must prevail at the heart of the relation or else it is little more than utilitarian collaboration. The human being who would truly love must entirely and integrally expose himself; and so must the partner. Love among human beings is not entire possession by either partner but, rather, a mutual ingress into a new dimension wherein each in some sense dies in order to come to life again in a wider and deeper unity. The operation of love from human being to human being is something only beginning to be properly and seriously attempted. The survival of our world may depend on its outcome. And the outcome will certainly depend on the seriousness and courage with which it is attempted. Theism has here an unenviable record of pusillanimity. It seems to have been terrified by precisely the danger, a very real danger and a danger to which Miller, we feel, falls victim, that the surrendering existent may so far surrender as to nihilate or compromise his own identity and dignity. This is precisely the mystery that makes the nonbiological act of love so delicate and dangerous: there must indeed be a total surrender but the goal is not the production of a new human being; rather, it is the deepening and ratification of the identity of each partner and ultimately the production of a new species, one might almost say, the new unified and unitary mankind. To a consideration of this entire problematic we shall proceed in the chapter on Henry Miller.

3

FAITH IN SEX

It is grotesque to call Henry Miller a pornographer in the legal sense: his description of sexual activity is patently narrative and subsidiary; not intended to titillate but to move, a little, to pity; moreover such passages become less and less frequent as his writing career progresses, especially through the trilogy *The Rosy Crucifixion*. Not a single one of Henry Miller's really memorable passages would have the slightest difficulty with the censor. Yet Miller can, we fear, be called quite simply a bad writer, or at least a less than successful writer, in his passages dealing with the neuro-muscular dimension of sex. He has not succeeded in creating a poetry of this dimension. His descriptions have a numbing banality; and such dialogue as there is reduces to series of staccato imperatives of a mind-staggering ordinariness. It may be that, as he himself alleges, he has "endeavored to withhold no part of himself in his written work."[1] It may be that this creative genius in whom the neuro-sexual and the artistic creative were so intimately conjoined, was indeed under compulsion to write in detail of what he says he had to experience in detail as preliminary to his genuine creative insights: "Before I could make a proper start I had to go through my 'little death.' The false start, which lasted ten years, enabled me to die to the world.[2] Undoubtedly he is reporting an honest evaluation when he writes:

And there was sex. But what *was* sex: Like the deity, it was omnipresent. It pervaded everything. Perhaps the whole universe of the past, to give an image for it, was none other than a mythological monster from which the world, my world, had been whelped, but which failed to disappear with the act of creation, remaining below, supporting the world (and its own self) upon its back.[3]

46

However all this may be, the fact remains that Miller's probings into the mechanics of sex are much less revealing than his probings into the mental-volitional motivations. Even in his specifically sexual passages, his really arresting descriptions deal with the spiritual-personal aspect and almost always with some form of the selfish fear and pride and greed that has to be overcome precisely in order properly to realize such an encounter:

> An expression of utter selfish pleasure filled the full, roving orbs. . . .[4]
> There was something almost anthropophagous about his tenderness; he demanded not the promptings and stirrings of the heart but the heart itself, and with it, if possible, the gizzard, the liver, the pancreas and other tender, edible portions of the human organism. In his exalted moments he seemed not only eager to devour the object of his tenderness but to invite the other to devour him also. His mouth would wreath itself in a veritable mandibular ecstasy; he would work himself up until the very soul of him came forth in a spongy ectoplasmic substance. It was a horrible state of affection, terrifying because it knew no bounds. It was a depersonalized glut or slop, a hangover from some archaic condition of ecstasy—the residual memory of crabs and snakes, of their prolonged copulations in the protoplasmic slime of ages long forgotten. . . .[5]
> As I look at her, as I get to her morsel by morsel, I find that the totality of her escapes me. My love adds up like a sum, but she, the one I am seeking with desperate, hungry love, escapes like an elixir. She is completely mine, almost slavishly so, but I do not possess her. It is I who am possessed. I am possessed by a love such as was never offered me before —an engulfing love, a total love, a love of my very toenails and the dirt beneath them—and yet my hands are forever fluttering, forever grasping and clutching, seizing nothing.[6]

If we would appreciate Miller's crucial contribution to the dynamic of modern thought, we must be aware from the outset that he uses and thinks of sex in the widest possible meaning of that word, as the dimension of intense and ultimately merging contact between lonely individuals. If the steaming jungles of specifically copulative contact taught him anything, they taught him that not by mere mechanics could the merger he deems mandatory be effected; and they simultaneously taught him that this contact is nonetheless a kind of supreme analogue, a paradigm of a terrifying, in some sense mortal, crucifixion which the lonely individual must undergo so taxingly to the end that the merger may be effected. He has some sections which might have been written by Teilhard, as we shall see. We can usefully survey the sprawling genius of his thought and insight systematically under seven headings, before addressing ourselves to his specifically sex-metaphysic work, *The World of Sex.* Thus, we shall consider: (1) Miller's conviction of man's need for a transformative liberation; (2) his articulation of the main fakery that stands in the way of this liberation; (3) his confidence in an act that can only be described, in the deepest sense, as sexual, to effect that transformative liberation; (4) the intensely and distinctively atheistic framework of this endeavor, at least at the practical level; (5) his elevation of sex to the status of a metaphysical ultimate; (6) his convergent conjunction of physical sex and creative art; (7) his vision of the reconciled future.

1. Need for Liberation

The dynamic of this recognition can most usefully be traced through the great trilogy, garnering additional evidence from several other works.

At the outset of *Sexus,* Miller articulates this need as a tremulous and uncertain vision warring against apparently overwhelming odds:

> I'm love-sick. Sick to death. A touch of dandruff and I'd succumb like a poisoned rat. . . . I *believe.* I *believe,* because not to believe is to become as lead, to lie prone and rigid, forever inert, to waste away. . . . Looking out on the contemporary landscape. Where are the beasts of the field, the crops, the manure, the roses that flower in the midst of corruption? I see railroad tracks, gas stations, cement blocks, iron girders, tall chimneys, automobile cemeteries, factories, warehouses, sweat shops, vacant lots. Not even a goat in sight. I see it all clearly and distinctly: it spells desolation, death, death everlasting. For thirty years now I have worn the iron cross of ignominious servitude, serving but not believing, working but taking no wages, resting but knowing no peace. Why should I believe that everything will suddenly change, just having her, just loving and being loved?[7]

A little later the same truth is borne in on Miller the creative writer as he reads a really fine piece of his own work:

> I was so moved that the tears came to my eyes. It wasn't something to show an editor: it was something to put away in a drawer, to keep as a

reminder of natural processes, as a promise of fulfillment. . . . It was revealed to me that I could say what I wanted to say—if I thought of nothing else, if I concentrated upon that exclusively—and if I were willing to bear the consequences which a pure act always involves. . . .[8]

The third revelation is already on the social level:

We are accustomed to think of ourselves as a great democratic body, linked by common ties of blood and language, united indissolubly by all the modes of communication which the ingenuity of man can possibly devise; we wear the same clothes, eat the same diet, read the same newspapers, alike in everything but name, weight and number; we are the most collectivized people in the world, barring certain primitive peoples whom we consider backward in their development. And yet—yet despite all the outward evidences of being close-knit, inter-related, neighborly, good-humored, helpful, sympathetic, almost brotherly, we are a lonely people, a morbid, crazed herd thrashing about in zealous frenzy, trying to forget that we are not what we think we are, not really united, not really devoted to one another, not really listening, not really anything, just digits shuffled about by some unseen hand in a calculation which doesn't concern us. Suddenly now and then someone comes awake, comes undone, as it were, from the meaningless glue in which we are stuck—the rigmarole which we call the everyday life and which is not life but a trance-like suspension above the great stream of life—and this person who, because he no longer subscribes to the general pattern seems to us quite mad, finds himself invested with strange and almost terrifying powers, finds that he can wean countless thousands from the fold, cut them loose from their moorings, stand them on their heads, fill them with joy, or madness, make them forsake their own kith and kin, renounce their calling, change their character, their physiognomy, their very soul. And what is the nature of this overpowering seduction, this madness, this "temporary derangement" as we love to call it? What else if not the hope of finding joy and peace?[9]

Yet Miller clearly accepts as starting point a lonely individualism.

In *The World of Sex,* this is expressed with succinct poignancy: "To be in love. To be utterly alone. . . . Thus it begins . . . the sweetest and bitterest sorrow that one can know. The hunger, the loneliness that precedes initiation."[10]

Nonetheless, toward the end of *Sexus,* the imperious call to communalization sounds out in accents that would cause a Randian objectivist's blood to run cold! This brief passage is among the most tightly packed of Miller's paragraphs:

Prisons and even lunatic asylums are emptied of their inmates when a more vital danger menaces the community. When the enemy approaches, the political exile is recalled to share in the defense of his country. At the last ditch it gets dinned into our thick skulls that we are all part and parcel of the same flesh. When our very lives are threatened we begin to live. Even the psychic invalid throws away his crutches, in such moments. For him the greatest joy is to realize that there is something more important than himself. All his life he has turned on the spit of his own roasted ego. He made the fire with his own hands. He drips in his own juices. He makes himself a tender morsel for the demons he liberated with his own hands. This is the picture of human life on this planet called the Earth. Everybody is a neurotic, down to the last man and woman. . . . To be cured we must rise from our graves and throw off the cerements of the dead. Nobody can do it for another—it is a private affair which is best done collectively. We must die as egos and be born again in the swarm, not separate and self-hypnotized, but individual and related.[11]

There is here a simultaneous gentle and genuine acknowledgment of the lonely individual, the imperious call for his communalization, the insistence that it can ultimately be achieved *viably* only from within, and the hint that there is yet a collective element or dimension involved. This is precisely the dimension of sex.

It is no surprise to find the theme recurring initially in *Plexus*, predominantly concerned with the endeavor of the creative artist, in the dimension of creative art:

I sat down at the machine immediately after breakfast. By noon I had finished my article on Coney Island. It had come without effort. Why? Because instead of forcing it I had gone to sleep—after due surrender of the ego, *certes*. It was a lesson in the futility of struggle. Do your utmost and let Providence do the rest! A petty victory, perhaps, but illuminating.[12]

The next major revelation of the transformation drive highlights the communalization of solitudes:

A landscape truly Tibetan beckons me onward. I know not whether it is a creation of the inner eye or some cataclysmic disturbance of the outer reality attuning itself to the profound reorientation I have just made. I know only that I am more solitary than ever. Everything that occurs now will have the quality of shock and discovery. I am not alone. *I am in the midst of other solitaries.* And each and every one of us speaks his own unique language! It is like the coming together of distant gods, each one wrapped in the aura of his own incomprehensible world.[13]

Miller subsequently expands this vision to truly cosmic proportions, writing in a vein that unwary theists might too hastily applaud but that comes really, as we shall show, from the very radically atheistic framework in which he begins. The isle at this point is truly full of voices and we must listen most discriminatingly in order to sift the true from the misleading:

A phrase like *"la fin des temps"*—what *does* it mean? Can there really be an end to time? And if so, could it possibly mean that time's end is really *our* beginning? . . . When the *end* comes, we will take our world with us. . . . But to approach this end business from another angle. All it can possibly mean . . . is the emergence of a new and fecund chaos. Were we living in Orphic times we would speak of it as the coming of a new order of gods, meaning, if you like, the investiture of a new and greater consciousness, something even beyond *cosmic consciousness.* . . . The phrase so widely used today—the common man—strikes me as an utterly meaningless one. There is no such animal. . . . Perhaps we will have to begin all over again from where the Cro-Magnon man left off. One thing seems highly evident to me, and that is that the note of doom and destruction, which figures so heavily in all prophecies, springs from the certain knowledge that the historical or world element in man's life is but transitory. . . . Man's descent into the illusory realm of matter must continue until there is nothing left to do but swim up to the surface of reality—and live in the light of everlasting truth. The men of spirit constantly exhort us to hasten the end and commence anew. Perhaps that is why they are called paracletes, or divine advocates. Comforters, if you like. They never exult in the coming of catastrophe, as mere prophets sometimes do. They indicate, and usually illustrate by their lives, how we may convert seeming catastrophe to divine ends. That is to say, they show us, those of us who are ready and aware, how to adapt and attune ourselves to a reality which is permanent and indestructible.[14]

Man, we agree most enthusiastically, will take his own world with him; but this is precisely the world of time and matter! Of the ultimate transformation, the ultimate mysterious leap of time into eternity, we shall be speaking in later chapters. But here it must be noted that Miller is mixing two dimensions or visions: the cosmic consciousness, of which we thoroughly approve, and a kind of quasi-Nirvana notion which is further developed even more blatantly later[15] and which is a mistaken erasing of the parameters of creatureliness. The tension between the authentic and the Nirvana notion of ultimate man's state remains in Miller throughout. But the final relevant *Plexus* section can certainly bear an interpretation with which again we can enthusiastically agree:

> That gulf between the dawn man, who participated mystically, and contemporary man, who is unable to communicate except through sterile intellect, can only be bridged by a new type of man, the man with a cosmic consciousness.[16]

Nexus brings to a climax this felt need for transformation and already introduces dominant notes of the reality that will effect and characterize it:

> "In pure love (which no doubt does not exist at all except in our imagination)," says one I admire, "the giver is not aware that he gives nor of what he gives, nor to whom he gives, still less of whether it is appreciated by the recipient or not." With all my heart I say "D'accord!" But I have never met a being capable of expressing such love. Perhaps only those who no longer have need of love may aspire to such a role. To be free of the bondage of love, to burn down like a candle, to melt in love, melt *with* love—what bliss! Is it possible for creatures like us who are weak, proud, vain, possessive, envious, jealous, unyielding, unforgiving: Obviously not. For us the rat race—in the vacuum of the mind. For us doom, unending doom. Believing that we need love, we cease to give love, cease to be loved. But even we, despicably weak though we be, experience something of this true, unselfish love occasionally. Which of us has not said to himself in his blind adoration of the one beyond his reach—"What matter if she be never mine! All that matters is that she be, that I may worship and adore her forever!" And even though it be untenable, such an exalted view, the lover who reasons thus is on firm ground. He has known a moment of pure love. No other love, no matter how serene, how enduring, can compare with it.[17]

The goal is noble but here, more clearly than in any portion we have thus far cited, the atheistic background emerges: Miller is right to a degree he cannot suspect in this terrifying business of loving, too often bowdlerized by the antisex thinkers as much as by the atheistic evolutionists even blander than Miller himself. Creatures cannot aspire to give totally unrequited love; to do that, one must be a Creator: *quia bonus est, sumus.* But neither is that sort of heroism demanded of creatures. They are indeed commanded by the thrust of the immanent God who is the fulcrum and lever of evolution to go into a dark and terrible crucifixion. But they are not commanded to surrender their very egoistic need for love, because this they can surrender only on one of two presuppositions, both unthinkable: that they should become themselves Creator; or that they should lapse into total nothingness. So long as they exist, in whatever modality, creatures will demand and need love.

The same drastic vision of a doom-filled apocalypse that can and must be a redemptive transformation comes out very strongly in the last words of Miller's preface to *Remember to Remember:*

> Somewhere in the black folds which now enshroud us I am certain that another being is gestating, that he is but waiting for the zero hour to announce himself. Hope never dies, passion can never be utterly extinguished. The deadlock will be broken. Now we are sound asleep in the cocoon; it took centuries and centuries to spin the seeming web of death. It takes but a few moments to burst it asunder. Now we are out on a limb, suspended over the void. Should the tree give way, all creation vaults to its doom. But what is it that tells us to hasten the hour of birth? What is it that, at precisely the right moment, gives us the knowledge and the power to take wing, when heretofore we knew only how to crawl ignominiously on our bellies? If the caterpillar through sleep can metamorphose into a butterfly, surely man during his long night of travail must discover the knowledge and the power to redeem himself.[18]

This is the first of those Miller passages we mentioned above which might have been written by Teilhard: cosmic optimism, persuasion of crisis, hope of transformation and all, right down to the self-redemption, albeit otherwise understood than Miller will understand and articulate it.

The same theme, with special reference to the place of the creative artist, is sounded in *Big Sur,* in a passage of which we cite here only the initial portion, immediately relevant to this point of transformation-longing:

The theme of separation and isolation—"atomization" it's now called—has as many facets to it as there are unique individuals. And we are all unique. The longing to be reunited, with a common purpose and an all-embracing significance, is now universal.[19]

In the essay "The Wisdom of the Heart," Miller stresses the need for transformation and its ineluctably communal dimension:

> We are chained to one another by invisible links, and it is the weakest in whom our strength is revealed, or registered. "Poetry must be made by all," said Lautréamont, and so too must all real progress. We must grow wise together, else all is vain and illusory.[20]

In prophetic vein again, Miller writes in his "Open Letter to Surrealists":

> The Minotaur is we ourselves standing on the threshold of a new era. We must be devoured whilst devouring. . . . The miracle is MAN, man full blown and travelling with his mother the earth in a new field of constellations. Now he is busy weighing the stars and measuring the distance between them; *then* he will be of the stars and there will be no need to record, neither with instruments, nor with paper and ink, nor with signs and symbols.[21]

Finally at the international level, on the touchy subject of war, Miller writes with exceptional and perceptive serenity during World War II, writes words that are even more realistically topical today and all the more compelling because they indict no one—and everyone:

> Nations reflect the cowardice and selfishness of the peoples which constitute them. It may have been possible once to serve God and country simultaneously. That is no longer true. The peoples of the earth have a great and compelling urge to unite. The boundaries established by nationalism are no longer valid. People are now murdering one another in a confused effort to break down these boundaries. Those who realize the true nature of the issue are at peace, even though they wield the sword. . . . The warrior of the future will murder freely, without orders from above. He will murder whatever is murderous in human nature. He will not be an avenger but a liberator. He will not fight to destroy an "ism" but to destroy the destroyers, *whoever* they be and *wherever* they be. He will go on fighting after peace is declared. He will make war until war becomes the lifeless thing which at heart it is.[22]

Miller sees then the need for a transformation and liberation of man the individual, man the citizen, man the Terran; he sees all these liberations as modalities of a single deep liberation that will allow presently fragmented and earthbound (even, as he erroneously believes, deleteriously matter-bound) man to pass over through the narrows of the rosy crucifixion into the next stage of evolution. He sees this liberation as involving absolute uniquenesses somehow meeting in mutually fertilizing embrace; and he sees with devastating clarity the obstacles that stand in the way of that liberation.

2. Obstacles to Liberation

The chief barriers Miller pinpoints as standing in the way of this desired and mandatory liberation are: rationalism, false passivity, fearful egotism, pride, fluid inertia, mistaken pity, and an ultimate stark fear of the unknown that lies ahead.

The dangers of rationalism are hinted at continuously, also in some of the sections already cited above, but nowhere more succinctly than in the passage at the beginning of the "Open Letter to the Surrealists":

Below the belt all men are brothers. Man has never known solitude except in the upper regions where one is either a poet or a madman—or a criminal.[23]

Nor will Miller concede that the transformation can be achieved simply by mechanical surrender of responsibility. There is a false passivity which inhibits it irretrievably:

For, since the beginning of time the picture which the world has presented to the naked human eye can hardly seem anything but a hideous battle ground of lost causes. It has been so and will be so until man ceases to regard himself as the mere seat of conflict. Until he takes up the task of becoming the "I of his I."[24]

With nimble dialectic, Miller almost immediately proceeds to demolish the hope, especially in the dimension of transformation via sex, of any retention of the ego as inviolable:

She didn't want the in between realm, the surrender, the fusion, the exchange. She wanted to keep that little tight core of self which was hidden away in her breast and only allow herself the legitimate pleasure of surrendering the body. That body and soul could not be separated, especially in the sex act, was a source of the most profound irritation.[25]

In his attempted psychoanalysis of Kronski, Miller uncovers still another barrier to transformation and ensuing cure of the psychic ills, the psyche-ill, of individuals:

It was taking a big gamble, however, to presume that I could break down his pride. There were layers of pride in him, just as there were layers of fat around his girdle. He was one vast defense system, and his energies were constantly being consumed in repairing the leaks which sprang up everywhere.[26]

With persistent penetration, Miller probes through the more obvious egotistical defenses to arrive at the most drastic barrier to transformation, the fluid inertia of squamous souls:

There is a texture and substance even to the psychic fortifications, as you discover when you begin to penetrate the forbidden precincts of the ego. The most difficult ones are not necessarily those who hide behind a plate of armor, be it of iron, steel, tin or zinc. Neither are they so difficult, though they offer greater resistance, who encase themselves in rubber and who, *mirabile dictu,* appear to have acquired the art of vulcanizing the perforated barriers of the soul. The most difficult ones are what I would call the "Piscean malingerers." These are the fluid, solvent egos who lie still as a foetus in the uterine marshes of their stagnant self. When you puncture the sac, when you think Ah! I've got you at last! you find nothing but clots of mucus in your hand.[27]

To this elusive fluidity, symptom of a supreme regressive desire to escape the forward-looking transfiguration by a womb-regression fantasy, is often conjoined a mistaken pity, fake and calculated to evade, by a surreptitious abortion of their true selves into mere empathizing collaborators, the terrible agony of real crucifixion:

They bleed with every bleeding soul in the universe—but they never fall apart. At the crucifixion they hold your hand and slake your thirst, weep like drunken cows. They are the professional mourners from time immemorial: they were so even in the Golden Age, when there was nothing to weep about. Misery and suffering is their habitat, and at the equinox they bring the whole kaleidoscopic pattern of life to a glaucous glue.[28]

Finally Miller unerringly pinpoints the most ultimate and deepest-lying cause of man's paralysis within the shell of his unviable ego:

We live on the edge of the miraculous every minute of our lives. The miracle is in us, and it blossoms forth the moment we lay ourselves open to it. The miracle of miracles is the stubbornness with which men refuse to open themselves up. Our whole life seems to be nothing but a frantic effort to evade that which is constantly within our grasp. This which is the very reverse of the miraculous is nothing else but FEAR. Man has no other real enemy than this which he carries within him.[29]

I might have told my friend who was so debilitated by the unremitting copulation in Miller's novels simply to read on past the two *Tropics* and *Sexus:* he would have found a startling decline in such technical scenes as the pitiable characters begin wrestling with the spiritual dimensions of human relationships, as more and more poignant and somber deviations are introduced into the picture until the reader almost nostalgically longs for another of those unidimensional scenes of horizontal play. In his essays, especially the later ones, Miller often reads like a Buddhist monk and often like a militant but somewhat pessimistic cosmopolitan. One might say he has grown up. I regret this. I would express it differently: he has transmuted his own ultimate, sex, conceived erroneously from the outset in an atheistic framework, into the only redemptive ultimate it could ever become in a consequential thinker of his sort: the ultimate of some kind of reabsorption. Sex *is* an ultimate created parameter of man, both in the strictly biological sense and in the wider and deeper sense in which it stands for the tremulous ultimate contact between created free rational beings. As we shall soon be pointing out, this ultimate, legitimate in its relative status, has more than any other been truly bowdlerized and devastated by religion. But sex can function as a salvific relative ultimate only if activated within the context of a Creator God.

Nevertheless, for all his adult deviation and betrayal of the true sinews of his chosen ultimate, Miller remains to this day a superb poet; and therefore even his distorted vision (and much more drastically his earlier and less clouded vision) retains a tang of this healthy ultimate. For throughout he is stressing, often unconsciously, that the act that effects the transformative liberation of man is a sexual act.

3. Sex as Liberation: Liberation as Sex

Miller characterizes the liberating act as one of ultimate and existential acceptance; of technical and metaphysical surrender; of supreme confidence in others; of movement through death to life; of that mysterious energy called Love with its poignant charm and its bitter hardness; of ultimate reconciliation between the male and female principles, a reconciliation which Miller articulates perfectly in one essay even as he swerves it into an uneasy triumph of the female principle in two other essays, one articulating a legitimate relative supremacy (and this one we shall have occasion to cite at some length) and the other more dubiously enunciating the much more questionable Molly Bloom syndrome, precursor to Buddhistic Nirvana (and this we shall have occasion to identify in a note).

Our process of proof here will be quite simply a process of identification. The tenor of the Miller passages cited in support of each characteristic of his liberating act mentioned above will adequately support the contention that the act of liberation is a sexual act of which the physical sexual act is a pale analogue.

The liberating act is an act of ultimate existential acceptance:

> He divines that the great secret will never be apprehended but incorporated in his very substance. He has to make himself a part of the mystery, live *in* it as well as with it. Acceptance is the solution; it is an art, not an egotistical performance on the part of the intellect.[30]

The liberating act involves technical surrender; and in his description here Miller quite openly refers to the physical act and dimension of sex:

> The man who admits to himself that he is a coward has made a step towards conquering his fear; but the man who frankly admits it to everyone, who asks that you recognize it in him and make allowance for it in dealing with him, is on the way to becoming a hero. . . . To be able to give oneself wholly and completely is the greatest luxury that life affords. Real love only begins at the point of dissolution. The personal life is altogether based on dependence, mutual dependence. . . . To become the

great lover, the magnetiser and catalyzer, the blinding focus and inspiration of the world, one has to first experience the profound wisdom of being an utter fool. . . .[31]

But there is a deeper metaphysical surrender involved too. At a critical juncture in his own development, Miller sees the appalling truth of this fact in his own case:

> At this strange moment, dead but not dead, the doors of memory swung open and down through the corridors of time I beheld that which no man should be permitted to see until he is ready to give up the ghost: I saw in every phase and moment of his pitiful weakness the utter wretch I had been, the blackguard, nothing less, who had striven so vainly and ignominiously to protect his miserable little heart. I saw that it never had been broken, as I imagined, but that, paralyzed by fear, it had shrunk almost to nothingness. I saw that the grievous wounds which had brought me low had all been received in a senseless effort to prevent this shriveled heart from breaking. The heart itself had never been touched; it had dwindled from disuse. It was gone now, this heart, taken from me, no doubt, by the Angel of Mercy. I had been healed and restored so that I might live on in death as I had never lived in life.[32]

The liberating act requires a supreme confidence in others. In his diagnosis of Kronski, Miller tells him: "You realize, I suppose, that one of the things you've come to me for is to acquire confidence and trust in others. Your failure to recognize this is part of your illness."[33]

The liberating act is a progress through death to life. This most mysterious of all dimensions of the redemptive action in which the human individual must participate actively and passively at once is epitomized in the haunting conclusion of Miller's essay on Anais Nin:

> In this extraordinary unicellular language of the female we have a blinding, gem-like consciousness which disperses the ego like star-dust. The great female corpus rises up from its sleepy marine depths in a naked push towards the sun. . . . The voices of the earth mingle in an eternal resonance which issues from the delta of the fecundating river of death. It is the voice of creation which is constantly being drowned in the daylight frenzy of a man-made world. . . . Nothing lost, nothing used up, nothing relinquished. The great mystery of conservation in which creation and destruction are but the antipodal symbols of a single constant energy which is inscrutable. . . . Adopting the universal language, the human

being in her speaks straight out from under the skin to Hindu, Chinaman, Jap, Abysinnian, Malay, Turk, Arab, Tibetan, Eskimo, Pawnee, Hottentot, Bushman, Kaffir, Persian, Assyrian. The fixed polar language known to all races: . . . The language of bells without clappers, heard incessantly throughout the nine months in which every one is identical and yet mysteriously different. In this first tinkling melody of immortality lapping against the snug and cosy walls of the womb we have the music of the still-born sons of men opening their lovely dead eyes one upon another.[34]

In *Plexus,* moving out to the cosmic dimension, yet retaining all the warm mystery of the physical sex act, Miller articulates the very name of this liberating act. It is essential to retain all the previously mentioned characteristics of that act; otherwise we shall read in this section nothing more than a pious Victorian platitude. No, it is sexual love, with its challenge, its terror, its mystery, and its great resurrection promised after death to self, that Miller is here articulating:

Imagine, if you can, a total, drastic silence, all ears cocked to catch the fatal words! *Would it even be necessary to utter the words?* Can you not imagine that everyone, in the silence of his heart, would supply the answer himself? There is only one response that humanity longs to give— and it can be voiced in one little monosyllable: *Love.* That little word, that mighty thought, that perpetual act, positive, unambiguous, eternally effective—if that should sink in, take possession of all mankind, would it not transform the world instantly? Who could resist, if love became the order of the day? Who would want power or knowledge—if he were bathed in the perpetual glory of love?[35]

The deepest dimension of this liberating act of love is a reconciliation of the male and female principles. In *Remember to Remember,* Miller articulates this reconciliation in entirely acceptable terms and with poetic insight. In his essay "The Universe of Death," however, the equilibrium is shattered and the passively creative female takes the upper hand, spinning out of the womb of her amorphous creaturehood a kind of perpetuity which is less than individual survival. The genuine articulation is pivoted on Miller's reaction to the women of France:

The women of France were the palpable symbol of that flowering spirit; they were not merely idolized, eulogized, worshipped in verse, stone and music, they were enthroned in the flesh. These vast musical cages, immune to everything but treachery, vibrated with feminine ardor, feminine resistance, feminine devotion. They were courts of love and scenes of valor; all the dualities modulated through their ribs and vaults. The flowers, the animals, the birds, the arts, the mysteries, all were permeated by the marriage of the male and female principles. It is not strange that the country which is so gloriously feminine, *la belle France,* is at the same time the one in which the spirit, which is masculine, has flowered most. If proof were needed, France is the living proof that to exalt the spirit both halves of the psyche must be harmoniously developed. The rational aspect of the French *esprit* (always magnified by the foreigner) is a secondary attribute and a much distorted one. France is essentially mobile, plastic, fluid and intuitive. These are neither feminine nor masculine qualities exclusively; they are the attributes of maturity, reflecting poise and integration.[36]

This immense thrust toward integration of male and female principles, this drive to rebirth of the individual in a larger community, this liberation of the ego from its repressive bounds, this cosmic sex act of surrender and of active-passive crucifixion is framed against an essentially atheistic background.

4. Atheism of the Sex Thrust in Miller

All the dubious elements in his multidimensional description of the liberation of man via sex stem from Miller's anterior atheism of perspective. Not having grasped the essential femininity of rational creatures over against an utterly active, anteriorly constituted Creator, a God who is Pure Act, Miller inevitably attempts the impossible, assigning to man along this ultimate parameter of sex, a self-deification.

Miller's atheism begins with an exaggerated immanentism, close to the truth of the Immanent God but tainted already with immanent-*ism:*

Incorporated in it. Suddenly it becomes clear to you, that when God made the world, He did not abandon it to sit in contemplation—somewhere in limbo. God made the world and He entered into it; that is the meaning of creation.[37]

The weasel word here is *incorporated.* Such a Creator instantly becomes an anterior myth and a consequent Cosmic Force at best, powerless to do more than cosuffer with the universe in its own hermaphroditic thrust to reality, actuality and perfection. Hence Miller's alleged reconciliation of male and female principles is really an uneasy collaboration in which the male gradually succumbs to the female and man eventually knows the joy of perfect passivity, but passivity not in the hands of a Creator entirely active; rather, in the womb of a cosmic whole impotently bringing at last to birth the great quiet of the unborn sons of man!

Man's role is therefore transformed into that of redemptive creator: not absolute creator as in Sartre, but *redemptive* creator. The male in the creature must voluntarily crucify itself so that the great liberation may occur. And at last Miller's relatively true absolute reveals its impotence and horror against which every Western creature rebels furiously. This is the crucially exorbitant price that must be paid by those who would have faith in a mystery torn from its proper context, absolutized, split off from the only support that can give it meaning in its very mystery, the Transcendent Creator.

When we take leave of one another we shall return to the world of chaos, to the realm of space which no amount of activity can exhaust. We are not of this world, nor are we yet of the world to come, except in thought and spirit. Our place is on the threshold of eternity; our function is that of prime movers. It is our *privilege* to be crucified in the name of freedom. We shall water our graves with our own blood. No task can be too great for us to assume. We are the true revolutionaries since we do not baptize with the blood of others but with our own blood, freely shed. We shall create no new covenants, impose no new laws, establish no new government. We shall permit the dead to bury the dead. The quick and the dead shall soon be separated. Life eternal is rushing back to fill the empty cup of sorrow. Man will rise from his bed of ignorance and suffering with a song on his lips. He will stand forth in all the radiance of his godhead.[38]

Still more clearly is this deification motif articulated in another passage of the same book: "We should cease worshiping and inspire worship. Above all, we should cease postponing the act of becoming what in fact and essence we are."[39] And most unequivocally of all does Miller enunciate his own commitment to deification of man via the rosy crucifixion of sex surrender to chaos, fecund and fecundating chaos and the great unknown that is the next stage of cosmic evolution, in the concluding words of that great testimony wrenched out of him by his pilgrimage through Greece: "I refuse categorically to become anything less than the citizen of the world which I silently declared myself to be when I stood in Agamemnon's tomb. From that day forth my life was dedicated to the recovery of the divinity of men."[40] This deification is to be reached via that ultimate in which Miller puts his faith, sex as expressive of man's ultimate thrust into nonpersonhood:

5. Sex, the Metaphysical Absolute

This absolutizing of sex is of course best articulated in *The World of Sex,* to which we shall presently turn. But we may note two poignant statements of it from the great trilogy:

My heart, cleansed of its iniquities, had lost all fear; it ached now to offer itself to the first comer. Indeed I had the impression that I was all heart, a heart which could never be broken, nor even wounded, since it was forever inseparable from that which had given it birth.[41]

The dynamic of this new parameter of endeavor, of redemption, of redemptive crucifixion, is brilliantly exposed in *Sexus:*

But, you quibble, how can I sing when the world is crumbling, when all about me is bathed in blood and tears? Do you realize that the martyrs sang when they were being burned at the stake? They saw nothing crumbling, they heard no shrieks of pain. They sang because they were full of faith. . . . Between the planes and spheres of existence, terrestrial and superterrestrial, there are ladders and lattices. The one who mounts sings. He is made drunk and exalted by unfolding vistas. He ascends surefootedly, thinking not of what lies below, should he slip and lose his grasp, but of what lies ahead. *Everything lies ahead.* The way is endless, and the farther one reaches the more the road opens up.[42]

To this persistent thrust forward via self-crucifixion is conjoined the creative artist's task of communication, which is also sexual, implying a total frankness of surrender in communication.

6. Creative Artistic Copulation

Precisely thus does Miller describe the only kind of creative artistic endeavor with any chance of success, with any hope of making a redemptive contribution to struggling humanity:

> The writer who wants to communicate with his fellow-man, and thereby establish communion with him, has only to speak with sincerity and directness. He has not to think about literary standards—he will make them as he goes along—he has not to think about trends, vogues, markets, acceptable ideas or unacceptable ideas: he has only to deliver himself, naked and vulnerable.[43]

In an apparently joyous outburst of advice to creative artists, Miller reveals the ultimate atheistic or pantheistic ground of all his hope of communication, redemption, and articulation. For he says in effect that the artist must surrender to the sheer explosive sexual act of giving of talent, realizing that nature herself is the dam of any offspring he can hope for in the dimension of art.

> Take this everyday world and embrace it! That is what the spirit urges. What better world can there be than this in which we have full responsibility, each and every one of us? Labor not for the men to come! Cease laboring altogether and create! For creation is play, and play is divine.[44]

7. Vision of the Reconciled Future

It is at this point that our careful inspection of all dimensions of Miller's forward thrust of hope and trust becomes vital to a proper comprehension. For his picture of the world to come, after the great liberation, is a scene from *The Millennium of Hieronymus Bosch* which Miller makes his own. It is the second of the Miller articulations which might have been written by Teilhard. But these very same words as scanned by Miller include two maggots Teilhard would never have permitted to enter into his vision: the material has been spiritualized, for Miller, at this point, to the ultimate limit where it has ceased to exist and consequently ceased to obstruct; and the happy beings, though a single family indeed, are not concentered on One who is not only Omega but Alpha as well and so capable of

retaining in existence in their own beings even what they have voluntarily surrendered along the way.

The Bosch passage Miller cites reads:

. . . These fair-headed people of both sexes are all so alike that they
could scarcely be told apart, and their attitudes are anonymous and
selfless. They are a single family, reminding us of a plant family all the
more in that their expression is confined to a silent dreaminess and mute
gazing. Theirs is a stillness as of vegetation, so that the fine-drawn, grop-
ing hands appear like tendrils seeking neighboring flowers for support.
And they seem to grow up out of the ground as much at random as wild
flowers in a meadow. For the vague uniformity of this naked life is not
subjected to any formal discipline. Yet however arbitrarily the pattern of
the moving bodies may be concentrated and condensed in one place and
may loosen and scatter in another, there is nowhere any overcrowding
and nowhere any random emptiness. However free each may be to follow
his own inclination, there remains an invisible bond holding them all
together. This is the *tenderness* with which all these inhabitants of the
heavenly meadows cling together in brotherly and sisterly intimacy.[45]

The World of Sex draws together in succinct fashion all these many
strands of thought and hope and faith in sex to a dramatic articulation of a sex-metaphysic. In astonishingly brief compass, he sets his
aim, outlines his generic hope, articulates the practical atheism inherent in his view, centers sex in this whole context as liberating force,
warns of the impersonality of his ultimate, integrates sex into the
totality of man's striving, formulates in a slogan his deepest reason
for faith in sex, and paints a brief picture of the end effect of such
faith.

The aim:

. . . the highest goal an author can set himself. The same aim—unification—is implicit in all religious striving. Perhaps, without knowing it, I
have always been a religious person.[46]

The generic hope:

A new world is in the making, a new type of man is in the bud.[47]

The practical atheism:

Like everyman, I am my own worst enemy. Unlike most men, however,
I also know that I am my own saviour.[48]

Sex centered as pivot of liberation:

Real life begins when we are alone, face to face with our unknown self.
. . . The crucial and truly pivotal events which mark our way are the
fruits of silence and of solitude. . . . When I think of sex, I think of it as a
domain only partially explored. . . . I have charted certain islands which
may serve as stepping stones when the great routes are opened up.[49]

Sex as impersonal:

Love is the drama of completion, of unification. Personal and bound-
less, it leads to deliverance from the tyranny of the ego. Sex is impersonal,
and may or may not be identified with love. Sex can strengthen and
deepen love, or work destructively.[50]

Sex integrated into the totality of man's striving:

The sexual drama is a partial aspect of the greater drama perpetually
enacted in the soul of man. As the individual becomes more integrated,
more unified, the sex problem falls into its proper perspective. The geni-
tals are impressed, so to speak, into the service of the whole being. There
is simultaneous procreation in all spheres. What is new, original and
fecund issues only from a complete entity.[51]

The slogan:

Not to go the full length, that is man's fatal error.[52]

The picture of the end effect:

I can imagine a world—because it has always existed!—in which man
and beast choose to live in peace and harmony, a world transformed each
day through the magic of love, a world free of death. It is not a dream.[53]

Religion generally has rather badly mauled the question of the
ultimate personal and corporate relationship between human beings.
Though almost every religion speaks of this relationship under some
terms as vital to human well-being and a component part of religious
living, there has been an exaggerated tendency to misread it, to fear
it, and to mislocate it.

Religion has *misread* the question by a too drastic departmentali-
zation of man into spirit and flesh, however those two terms be
interpreted in the individual religion. Thus often religion has read the
whole question as the problem of causing the "higher" spiritual char-

ity to dominate the "lower" eros which is alleged to be sinful or at best selfish. This has taken the vital strength out of agape by desexing it and has rendered eros too undisciplined. Worst of all it has split man.

Religion has *feared* the very notion of love relationships for two widely differing reasons: because of its misreading of the whole love question as such, religion has tended to consider that human love is somehow opposed to divine charity and all too capable of perversion or distortion or at least exaggerated emotionalism; and because religion has worried about any drive that could lead to a consolidation of humanity, fearing such a consolidation could trammel the direct vertical individual relation of the human being to God.

Religion has totally *mislocated* love. First, in its too rigid division between charity and eros there is already a fracture of man. Second, and more seriously, it has overrated the utilitarian aspect in what it does see as human love, namely the mating drive, and exaggerated out of all proportion the romantic and nuptial love which is merely a nicer name for a perfectly healthy but decidedly limited function of the total human being, namely the prolongation and proper education of the young of the species. Husband and wife have too often been related one to the other by religion as little more than a functioning breeding-and-training team, with undue neglect of the fact that here, in marriage, as nowhere else, the person-to-person relationship is absolutely essential to the proper functioning even of the utilitarian community.

The cumulative result has been a divorce of meaningful (and all too often meaningless!) human loving and the search for human love from the whole religious frame of reference even to the extent of triggering a strange kind of atheism in the practical order, a neglect of or contempt for God as inhibitory of or inimical to proper personal relationships. And the human being, thus torn from his roots in his Creator at this vital point, has then vainly striven to find again that spontaneous reaction of sympathy and attraction for all his fellow human beings which is the key to a truly human loving and the only safe guarantee of a loving human community.

Thus twentieth-century man, the more civilized and modern he is, has the more desperately and despairingly cast about for some way to retrieve the sense of community which only this spontaneous human love could have given him. By ethical and even legal sanctions he has striven to eliminate the barriers of calling, class, and race which have come between human beings, oblivious to the patent fact that you cannot legislate loving: that man must either know instinctively the thrill of sympathy in the mere presence of a fellow human being or else limp badly in his deliberate efforts to be nice to those he instinctively considers as different from him, inferior to him, or inimical to him.

The theist must then accept the sex dimension precisely as the impersonal or apersonal or transpersonal dimension in which and via which love in the deepest and most abiding sense alone can be realized. And Miller is unerringly right in this, his analysis of what that dimension demands: a kind of mysterious surrender, a combination of the supremely active and the supremely passive collaboration of the individual toward the engendering of a new reality. Sex is too terrifying to be taken lightly. It is so terrifying in its biological and in its wider analogical sense because it brings home to the creature the extent of the crossroads nature of man: on the one hand compelled like the amoeba to surrender a portion of self, expelling that portion sooner (in the case of the male) or later (in the case of the female) so that a new being may appear; on the other hand, somehow caught up into the highest creative act of God, bringing into being a living soul, another rational creature destined for the loneliness and total independence of all such creatures (a point parents all too often hastily and protectively forget); and finally questing as person for a total personal union with another created loneliness.

But in the wider analogical sense, sex is a still greater torment and terror for free individualized rational conscious creatures. The sex act is the paradigm of meaningful creative contact between human beings, whether biologically or on the level of interpersonal and dynamic social relationships. And the pith of the act is so rarely achieved and realized even at the biological level, where hasty congress consoles itself later for the total failure by the pseudo-comfort that at least a new human being has been born into the world. Such unbridled vertical utilization of sex without any corresponding horizontal utilization can only compound the confusion of which Miller writes so pessimistically and bitingly, the spirit of the hive, the pathetic milieu of the rabbit warren where the sheer weight of human flesh is multiplied unbearably until the earth bulges, in the lethal absence of any corresponding volatilization of the horizontal thrust. Then truly is every newborn baby merely another mouth to feed, another competitor for the material goods of the earth, for its very air.

We enthusiastically endorse Miller's modest claim to have charted some islands. More important he has been a trail-blazer setting an attitude. We regret his later divagation into unacceptable Nirvana-substitutes, into the phenomenon of Nirvana without the deep Eastern sense of Nirvana which redeems the concept, so dangerous to Western minds, from its lethal effects.

The sex act is the supreme analogue of three vital dimensions of any genuinely meaningful and creative interpersonal contact: absolute honesty, absolute trust, and consequent absolute surrender on both sides into a new dimension. This act is one in which the human individual is supremely exposed. It is an incomparably more poignant and drastic act than any other. It is an essentially fluid act, momentary and therefore supremely demanding. For this very reason, from it and it alone can human beings perhaps individually and generically learn those desperate virtues (strengths) they need for those apparently less demanding acts which are in fact just as demanding but whose levy on the individual is not so concentrated, not so climactic, and therefore more easily evaded.

Absolute honesty is demanded in the sex act by a force greater than either of the participants. Here all deception must end. "Abandon sham, all ye who enter here" might be written over the portals of such communication. *Nemo dat quod non habet* (No one gives what he does not have), applies here more desperately than anywhere else, for here the inadequacy can never be covered up by diplomatic phrases. This holds true from the absolutely minimal biologico-neuro-muscular phenomenon of potency to the subtlest spiritual dimension of worth.

Absolute trust is demanded in the sex act, again by a power greater than either partner. *For there must be trust in a mysterious coming third.* Not trust merely in the partner, for then the act degenerates into a mutual titillation, a narcissistic exhibition, wherein both take refuge in the safety of their own or their reflected ego and neither is properly satisfied and both squander the treasure entrusted to them. No, there must be a trust in the mysterious third, the coming one. Both partners must realize or at least trust that the act being consummated goes beyond themselves, that they are not two lonelinesses probing and entirely uncovering one another (for that they cannot ever do), but that they are two earnest if intoxicated collaborators, intent on a thrust into procreative activity. I am not for a moment saying that every sex act must, in order to be legitimate, be *biologically* procreative. At the minimal level of consideration, this is beyond the power of the collaborators in the most favorable of cases! But I am saying that any sex act, to be meaningful, must extend beyond the boundaries either of each individual partner (for if one restricts it to a divisively personal boundary to be thrown round the other in an act of annexation, it becomes a rape) or of both partners taken collectively as a community. The community of two can be founded in a hundred other ways, homey and subtle. But it can never be founded sanely by the sex act itself. That act points by its very innermost nature beyond both partners.

Consequently there must be absolute surrender on both sides into a new dimension. Here is precisely the point at which Miller's perception falters and fails. He is betrayed by his own too hastily and too little analyzed masculinity. Initially appearing as the truly generous male, ready, in defiance of his male urge to domination, to surrender meaningfully and ultimately to the partner, he terminally appears as the hopeless would-be Creator intent to surrender to the All-Mother, the ultimate Lorelei, the totally passive cosmic consciousness. He is betrayed by his own failure to penetrate at the biologico-psychological level into the innermost working of the genuine female at the procreative level. He sees her all too fleetingly as the actual human mother-to-be and all too quickly as the Ultimate Mother, who merely allows to be. The existential female human being must contribute actively in the extreme to any genuine procreation, and this both in the dimension of collaboration and of surrender. She must collaborate actively in the psychological formation of the life that is to be; she cannot be simply an incubator, for her chromosomes likewise contribute to the very psyche of the child. And she must contribute at the level of surrender, for she must not only welcome a guest for a time, but give that guest genuine freedom after a time. And this again in two stages: first, the purely physical freedom of birth, which benign nature usually takes care of, and much later at the psychic level, where benign nature is powerless against the cannibalistic protective tendency of an egotistical mother.

When we now pass to the analogical level of sex, the most volatile and subtle contact possible between individual human beings, the same holds true. Restrictive communities are always sterile communities. Defensive alliances are unholy alliances. Nor can the ultimate frame of reference be even the entire human race, for that would merely give free rein to Terran imperialism against possible encounters with other intelligent life from other worlds. The ultimate frame of reference of this outward-thrusting encounter can be no less than the perfect creature; and if even here the thrust falters and wishes for the false security of finitude and boundaries, then the thrust is doomed to ultimate sterility. The absolute frame of reference of the sex thrust can be no less than the supremely and totally active Creator himself, who, in the final mysterious encounter, answers to the ultimate outward thrust of total passivity with His supreme activity, reconciling all things to Himself.

The mystery of sex is the mystery of total contact between created existents. This is the mystery that is often lived so badly, in hasty miscalculation or egotistical restrictiveness. The whole world is heavy with sex in this sense, but on the subhuman level it functions basically without deviation. Elements combine in a sexual act to form compounds; plants and animals obey an instinct greater and more potent than their individual selves. But with the free conscious being, a new danger and a new glory is introduced. For out of their creative contact, their only total contact, the new being can arise, on whatever dimension, of biology or of wider analogical reality, only by the most mysterious of all acts: the free surrender of the total person for an end that will leave that total person intact. How close we are to the creative act of God himself! How ignorantly and impiously we often trample this proximity, seeking to glorify and extend ourselves in our progeny (especially our elaborative artistic progeny, states, treaties, and new formations)! Above all, how subtle is the siren's song of the sham-eternal Mother, beckoning each generation to entrust their finest specimens to her, that she may mold a new and greater reality, a reality that will ultimately devour them, for which they are supposed to be ready to surrender themselves entire.

The sexual collaborator dare neither surrender personality thus completely, nor yet regard the issue of his act as a mere projection of himself. Imitating, in trust and faith, the creative act of God, the creature must here be total goodness overflowing. At each new stage of the cosmic development, the lonely individual creature will always remain exactly that. But at the same time a new being will have been brought to birth, with a genuine autonomy.

We have here arrived at the drastic ultimates: on the one hand, the absolute encapsuling drive to self-sufficiency; on the other hand, the forlorn and desperate thrust to total annihilation. The former is a sluggishness of the heart which can only retard, perhaps fatally on our planet, the progress of evolution. But the latter is the more subtly perverted drive, epitomized by Miller's sex ultimate in its terminal manifestation. The thrust to annihilation has beckoned some of the noblest free creatures, and always exercises a strange fascination on truly generous souls. Total annihilation, complete absorption into the Creator at least—this has been a religious and secular motif of amazing seductive power. It stems ultimately from an atheistic approach to life in the widest terms. It pictures the Creator as either finite or passive. The great Pure Act, our Creator-God, is able to and wills to give being and give it more abundantly, without requiring or needing to require any ultimate return. Man must strive to imitate Him here with all the power He freely gives to free creatures. In the awful dimension of sex, man must know the ultimate analogical parameter of creation which is procreation: the giving of being which is genuinely independent though dependent, which does not require the annihilation or transmutation of the giver, nor can demand the ultimate reabsorption of the issue.

Miller frequently refers to the twin pair, sex and death. But the false and security-minded death that Miller would have us die in sex, in order to evade the somber destiny of material temporal free finitude rendered eternal, is the false face of the next ultimate of modern atheists which we must consider: real death, the terminal temporal finitude of free rational creatures.

It is a singular fortune that we have a modern atheist who deals with this ultimate with none of the evasive tactics of other atheists who have bowdlerized it out of existence, like the Marxists, or erroneously attempted to transcend it, like Miller. Albert Camus is preeminently among modern atheists an utterly honest man. This is not a moral or psychological evaluation; rather, an assessment of ontological sinew. For the theist, death is indeed the relativizer, the reconciler of the many, the manifold parameters of man's creatureliness, but not absolute; and supreme only in the context of created reality. For the honest atheist, Camus, death is the final absolute, the supreme relativizer.

4

FAITH IN DEATH

From the dark horizon of my future a sort of slow, persistent breeze had been blowing towards me, all my life long, from the years that were to come. And on its way that breeze had levelled out all the ideas that people tried to foist on me in the equally unreal years I then was living through.[1]

In this way does the young condemned murderer of Albert Camus' *The Outsider* muse on his approaching death. He has been visited by the prison chaplain who has striven mightily to win his soul. But the youth continues to meditate in the same vein:

What difference could they make to me, the death of others, or a mother's love, or his God; or the way one decides to live, the fate one thinks one chooses, since one and the same fate was bound to "choose" not only me, but thousands of millions of privileged people who, like him, called themselves my brothers. Surely, surely he must see that? Every man alive was privileged; there was only one class of men, the privileged class. All alike would be condemned to die one day; his turn, too, would come like the others'. . . . As a condemned man himself, couldn't he grasp what I meant by that dark wind blowing from my future?[2]

Camus alone among atheist existentialists offers a genuinely empirico-practical code of living, consistent and held in its precarious consistency by the supreme relativizing principle, death; not viewed with terror or hate or cynicism, but gently and with a kind of respect. In his great analytical essay *The Rebel*[3] he warns that rebellion against the infinite transcendent God brings with it its own special dangers: chiefly that of the erecting by finite man of new tyrannies, which Camus lumps together under the global designation of Caesarism. The rebellion itself, Camus holds, is vitally necessary to man's very existence; but it must respect its own limits:

74

Man's solidarity is founded upon rebellion, and rebellion, in its turn, can only find its justification in this solidarity. We have, then, the right to say that rebellion which claims the right to deny or destroy this solidarity loses simultaneously its right to be called rebellion and becomes in reality an acquiescence in murder. . . . In order to exist, man must rebel, but rebellion must respect the limit it discovers in itself—a limit where minds meet and in meeting begin to exist.[4]

At the end of this essay, Camus notes the practical consequences of this demand:

The world is not in a condition of pure stability; nor is it only movement. It is both movement and stability. The historical dialectic, for example, is not in continuous pursuit of an unknown value. It revolves around the limit, which is its prime value.[5]

This limit, this prime value, this supreme relativizer, this catalyst of genuine, moderate love of life, is *death,* the ultimate in which Camus places his faith, to an extent not often realized by interpreters who have been, quite understandably and justifiably, dazzled by his courage, his wry wisdom, and the perceptiveness of his analysis.

1. The Praise of Death

Camus has faith in death as an implacable ultimate, revealing to man his own essential evanescence and that of all things; moderating all excesses of striving that devour self and others; imparting to man an intransigent and undivided allegiance to the real *now* which is not the passing moment but the totality of moments circumscribed by one sentient consciousness; infusing into man a genuine and unshakable sympathy with his fellow mortals; steeling man to an all-out living of his finite existence; and unexpectedly delivering him from the grotesquerie of the absurd.

A. Death the Revealer

Death, for Camus, reveals to man his own essential evanescence. The theme is sounded in *Caligula* in the strange litany of Venus which the mad emperor forces the patricians to recite after Caesonia:

Welcome your wandering children home, to the bleak sanctuary of your heartless, thankless love. Give us your passions without object, your griefs devoid of reason, your raptures that lead nowhere. . . . O Queen, so empty yet so ardent, inhuman yet so earthly, make us drunk with the wine of your equivalence, and surfeit us forever in the brackish darkness of your heart.[6]

It is proclaimed as the bitter, inebriating wisdom learned by the Emperor in the wake of his many murders and on the threshold of his last murder, that of Caesonia: "I know now that nothing, *nothing* lasts. Think what that knowledge means! There have been just two or three of us in history who really achieved this freedom, this crazy happiness."[7] Death has wrought a bitter but salutary cure upon Camus' own beloved Algerians:

> This race, wholly cast into its present, lives without myths, without solace. It has put all its possessions on this earth and therefore remains without defense against death. . . . And yet, yes, one can find measure as well as excess in the violent and keen face of this race, in this summer sky with nothing tender in it, before which all truths can be uttered and on which no deceptive divinity has traced the signs of hope or of redemption. Between this sky and these faces turned toward it, nothing on which to hang a mythology, a literature, an ethic, or a religion, but stones, flesh, stars, and those truths the hand can touch.[8]

Death seen as the relativizing end gives Sisyphus a new vigor:

> At that subtle moment when man glances back over his life, Sisyphus returning toward his rock, in that slight pivoting he contemplates that series of unrelated actions which becomes his fate, created by him, combined under his memory's eye and soon sealed by his death. Thus, convinced of the wholly human origin of all that is human, a blind man eager to see who knows that the night has no end, he is still on the go. The rock is still rolling.[9]

The creative thrust of man is delivered from paralysis and restored to a more poignant probing and a more ardent articulation of evanescence once the single fatality of death is unreservedly accepted:

> All that remains is a fate whose outcome alone is fatal. Outside of that single fatality of death, everything, joy or happiness, is liberty. A world remains of which man is the sole master. What bound him was the illusion of another world. The outcome of his thought, ceasing to be renunciatory, flowers in images. It frolics—in myths, to be sure, but myths with no other depth than that of human suffering, and, like it,

inexhaustible. Not the divine fable that amuses and blinds, but the terrestrial face, gesture, and drama in which are summed up a difficult wisdom and an ephemeral passion.[10]

B. Death the Moderator

Death moderates the excessive striving which leads to destructive cruelty. The dangers of such acquiescence in cruelty are vividly sketched in *The Rebel:*

> Historical Christianity postpones to a point beyond the span of history the cure of evil and murder, which are nevertheless experienced within the span of history. Contemporary materialism also believes that it can answer all questions. But, as a slave to history, it increases the domain of historic murder and at the same time leaves it without any justification, except in the future—which again demands faith. In both cases one must wait, and meanwhile the innocent continue to die.[11]

And the root cause of such preposterous cruelty, even nay precisely, in the self-proclaimed atheist is pinpointed as just this effort to deny death as the supreme ultimate, to escape the finality of the tomb by some sort of appeal beyond it: "Nietzsche, at least in his theory of super-humanity, and Marx before him, with his classless society, both replace the Beyond by the Later On."[12] Yet as soon as the relativizing finality of death is accepted, Camus proclaims all reformers harmless:

> All may indeed live again, side by side with the martyrs of 1905, but on condition that it is understood that they correct one another, and that a limit, under the sun, shall curb them all. Each tells the other that he is not God, this is the end of romanticism. At this moment, when each of us must fit an arrow to his bow and enter the lists anew, to reconquer, within history and in spite of it, that which he owns already, the thin yields of his fields, the brief love of this earth, at this moment when at last a man is born, it is time to forsake our age and its adolescent furies.[13]

The crucial misstep of those just delivered from the transcendental Moloch is to attempt to replace that Moloch with some other devouring idol, not so much supratemporal as, rather, transcending the life span of the individual:

> The decisive step that he [Nietzsche] compelled rebellion to take consists in making it jump from the negation of the ideal to the seculari-

zation of the ideal. Since the salvation of man is not achieved in God, it must be achieved on earth. Since the world has no direction, man, from the moment he accepts this, must give it one that will eventually lead to a superior type of humanity. Nietzsche laid claim to the direction of the future of the human race.[14]

But as soon as the terminal finality of death is accepted, the reforming crusader is transformed into the doughty but moderate fighter for a limited happiness:

> We shall choose Ithaca, the faithful land, frugal and audacious thought, lucid action, and the generosity of the man who understands. In the light, the earth remains our first and our last love. Our brothers are breathing under the same sky as we; justice is a living thing. Now is born that strange joy which helps one live and die, and which we shall never again postpone to a later time. On the sorrowing earth it is the unresting thorn, the bitter brew, the harsh wind off the sea, the old and the new dawn.[15]

C. Death the Inspirer

Death accepted as ultimate imparts to man an intransigent and undivided allegiance to his own *now,* the span of his conscious life. Of his fellow Algerians, he says:

> These men have never sinned against life. For if there is a sin against life, it consists perhaps not so much in despairing of life as in hoping for another life and in eluding the implacable grandeur of this life. These men have not cheated. Gods of summer they were at twenty by their enthusiasm for life, and they still are, deprived of all hope. I have seen two of them die. They were full of horror, but silent. It is better thus. From Pandora's box, where all the ills of humanity swarmed, the Greeks drew out hope after all the others, as the most dreadful of all. I know no more stirring symbol; for, contrary to the general belief, hope equals resignation. And to live is not to resign oneself. This, at least, is the bitter lesson of Algerian summers.[16]

The Europeans, on the other hand, he castigates precisely for their lethal devotion to dim futures:

> The men of Europe, abandoned to the shadows, have turned their backs upon the fixed and radiant point of the present. They forget the present for the future, the fate of humanity for the delusion of power, the misery of the slums for the mirage of the eternal city, ordinary justice for

an empty promised land. They despair of personal freedom and dream of a strange freedom of the species; reject solitary death and give the name of immortality to a vast collective agony. They no longer believe in the things that exist in the world and in living man; the secret of Europe is that it no longer loves life.[17]

In a perceptive evaluation of *The Plague,* Camus' greatest novel, it has been well said that "the sentence of death is the central theme of his work. It matters little here whether it is nature, fate, justice, or human cruelty which pronounces the sentence."[18] And the same commentator adds: ". . . for the man who starts to struggle, living is not enough. Man regains control of himself in the revolt against death, and henceforth this recovery itself, the good will to begin anew without illusions as to the outcome of the struggle, becomes for him the primary value. To be a man condemned, with and among other men likewise condemned: therein lies our task. For Camus, this is the province of ethics—of the *we* engaged in a desperate venture, beneath a narrow sky darkened by the plague."[19] It might here seem that death as the plague is a hostile ultimate in which no man can put his faith. And there can be no question of Camus' persuasion that man must struggle: not, however, *against* death (for that would be futile) but precisely within the limits imposed by death, which give pith and verve to man's struggle. There is a tiny phrase at the end of *The Plague* which must be overlooked or rendered unintelligible by anyone wishing to maintain that Camus' faith in death wavers, even in that awful and protesting novel. Speaking of the plague bacillus which man must constantly fight, he says: "perhaps the day would come when, *for the bane and the enlightening of men,* it roused up its rats and sent them forth to die in a happy city.[20] Even in its most apparently inimical form, then, as snuffing out in torment the lives of innocent children, this plague is called an enlightener.

D. Death the Humanizer

Death infuses into men a genuine and unshakable sympathy with his fellow mortals. Such otherwise utterly diverse and even disparate characters as Rieux, Tarrou, Grand, and Paneloux are welded into an effective fellowship by their campaign against the plague; and it is solely in function of that great relativizer that the young Meursault is ready to meet the chaplain and call him brother. Rieux articulates Camus' conviction when he says of himself as chronicler of the plague:

Summoned to give evidence regarding what was a sort of crime, he has exercised the restraint that behooves a conscientious witness. All the same, following the dictates of his heart, he has deliberately taken the victims' side and tried to share with his fellow-citizens the only certitudes they had in common—love, exile and suffering.[21]

And in the emotion-charged encounter between tormented priest and atheist doctor after the Othon boy's death, both stress the unifying force of the fight against death, *of the joint recognition of their common mortality.*

Says the priest: "We're working side by side for something that unites us—beyond blasphemy and prayers. And it's the only thing that matters."[22]

Replies the doctor, who is unwilling to admit any transcendentals into this encounter: "What I hate is death and disease—as you well know. And whether you wish it or not, we're allies, facing them and fighting them together."[23]

E. Death the Strengthener

Death steels man to an all-out living of his finite existence. The youth of Oran, a spot "without soul and without reprieve,"[24] are nonetheless, indeed precisely for this reason, "happy to be alive and to cut a figure, indulging for an hour in the intoxication of perfect existences."[25]

As the other side of this coin, Camus links Europe's war-madness and destruction mania ("Europe . . . philosophizes . . . by shooting a cannon."[26]) directly to a refusal to accept mortality and love it creatively:

Ulysses can choose at Calypso's bidding between immortality and the land of his fathers. He chooses the land, and death with it. Such simple nobility is foreign to us today. Others will say that we lack humility; but, all things considered, this word is ambiguous. Like Dostoevsky's fools who boast of everything, soar to heaven, and end up flaunting their shame in any public place, we merely lack man's pride, which is fidelity to his limits, lucid love of his condition.[27]

In a continuing antiphonal contrast, Camus describes his return to Tipasa, the scene of his

Turbulent childhood, adolescent daydreams in the drone of the bus' motor, mornings, unspoiled girls, beaches, young muscles always at the peak of their effort, evenings slight anxiety in a sixteen-year-old heart, lust for life, fame, and ever the same sky throughout the years, unfailing in strength and light, itself insatiable, consuming one by one over a period of months the victims stretched out in the form of crosses on the beach at the deathlike hour of noon.[28]

Out of this return, he draws an ultimate wisdom:

O light! This is the cry of all the characters of ancient drama brought face to face with their fate. This last resort was ours, too, and I know it now. In the middle of winter I at last discovered that there was in me an invincible summer.[29]

On the eve of the liberation of Paris, Camus wrote in the clandestine *Combat* a concentrated cry of the hope and determination and dedication to life born out of an intimate intense existential encounter with death:

The Paris that is fighting tonight intends to command tomorrow. Not for power, but for justice; not for politics, but for ethics; not for the domination of France, but for her grandeur.

Our conviction is not that this will take place, but that this is taking place today in the suffering and obstinacy of the fight. And this is why, despite men's suffering, despite the blood and wrath, despite the dead who can never be replaced, the unjust wounds, and the wild bullets, we must utter, not words of regret, but words of hope, of the dreadful hope of men isolated with their fate.

This huge Paris, all black and warm in the summer night, with a storm of bombers overhead and a storm of snipers in the streets, seems to us more brightly lighted than the City of Light the whole world used to envy us. It is bursting with all the fires of hope and suffering, it has the flame of lucid courage and all the glow, not only of liberation, but of tomorrow's liberty.[30]

F. Death the Deliverer

Death accepted as ultimate unexpectedly delivers man from the grotesquerie of the absurd, indeed works hand in hand with the recognition of absurdity to bring man's mind back into equilibrium:

> Death, too, has patrician hands, which, while crushing, also liberate. Losing oneself in that bottomless certainty, feeling henceforth sufficiently remote from one's own life to increase it and take a broad view of it—this involves the principle of a liberation. Such new independence has a definite time limit, like any freedom of action. It does not write a check on eternity. But it takes the place of the illusions of *freedom,* which all stopped with death. The divine availability of the condemned man before whom the prison doors open in a certain early dawn, that unbelievable disinterestedness with regard to everything except for the pure flame of life—it is clear that death and the absurd are here the principles of the only reasonable freedom: that which a human heart can experience and live. This is a second consequence. The absurd man thus catches sight of a burning and frigid, transparent and limited universe in which nothing is possible but everything is given, and beyond which all is collapse and nothingness. He can then decide to accept such a universe and draw from it his strength, his refusal to hope, and the unyielding evidence of a life without consolation.[31]

2. The Critique of Death

Death is undoubtedly the relative ultimate, the created mystery that has been most vulgarized by theists. Others, like matter and time, have not been understood; still others, like freedom and productive power, have been trivialized; others again, like finitude and sex, have been distorted. But death has been vulgarized by what amounts to a total denial of its existence, which nonetheless so palpably assails every sentient observer who does not willfully evade it. Either death is inflated into a pseudo-mystery of completion of life; or it is wrenched into an event wherein the mortal subject is alleged to be supremely active, in patent defiance of the solid fact that death, of all human events, is precisely the one in which the mortal is totally passive; or else death is surreptitiously extirpated (one might even say, expatriated) by a faith that insists that redeemed human beings have already put on immortality.

In such a context, the witness of a modern atheist who chooses death as his sacred ultimate is of capital importance. It may well be that "Camus, like Malraux and Sartre, belongs to a generation which history forced to live in a climate of violent death. At no other time, perhaps, has the idea of death been linked so exclusively to that of a paroxysm of arbitrary cruelty."[32] It may likewise be true that this very paralyzing absurdity which has desecrated death has brought about a situation in which "the immense certainty that there is a cure which the Christian associated with death, and his infinite hope that death was the winged sentinel of a fatherland, have slowly been wearing out. Nothing remains but naked death, in a storm of cold violence. Never before had death come to man with the new face now modeled by its millions of slaves. Neither the cult of the dead, nor any belief in glory, nor any faith in eternal life accompany death into this hell."[33]

It is beyond dispute that Camus' revolt is "without hope (for the rebel is always aware of death), but without resignation (for he continues to rebel against death)."[34] But it would be an egregious blunder of blunted perception to lower on this continuing rebellion and process it prematurely into a crypto-Christian phenomenon or a sort of proof that Camus was moving in the direction of the Christian faith. The point we made so strongly concerning the living Sartre, we must repeat even more drastically concerning the dead Camus. Whatever the "might have been" of Camus' tragically shortened life, it is the "was" that interests us here. Thomas Hanna, in his essay "Albert Camus and the Christian Faith," is perceptive in this respect:

Against aspiration for totality, conquest and perfection in human history, Camus places a history in which men have limits, and knowledge has uncertainties, and values have relativity. To attempt to transform men into the image of an absolute value is not to fulfill them but to murder and deform them. For men are not infinitely plastic; they are not things which can be endlessly molded and changed. They have limits, and to go beyond these limits is only to add to the total of suffering in human history. It is this limit which all men find within themselves and which is shared in common by all men that is the only source of value which men possess. It is the only real value in human existence.[35]

Robert Kanters quite unintentionally expresses the real contribution of Camus' death-faith, in a remark calculated to be caustically critical: "His dialectic is a reassuring conversion; he settles down, forsaking desperate thought for the ideas of a good family man. With great and noble words he channels the energy of death to make it irrigate our dear moderate slopes."[36]

The theist is too prone to use the argument or reasoning from human longing. This argument, legitimately stated, holds that the existence of aspirations in the human existent are and must be treated as component elements of reality, cannot be shrugged off as mere figments. But often this argument is used in a short-circuited fashion to allege that aspiration proves the existence of its object; and, in the specific case we are now treating, that the first sign of revolt against death proves the rebel to be a "crypto-immortalist." To argue thus in the case of Camus is to display an alienating obtuseness to the crux of his message. For Camus is proclaiming that man must *first* accept death as an ultimate, as the ultimate relativizing parameter of man, not merely a single event at a specific terminal point-instant but pervading every moment of man's existence, pervading and accompanying man's every moment in the mode and shape of that potentiality for death which is mortality. *Then and only then,* must man revolt, not in a futile effort to defeat death entirely but in a tragic-heroic effort to wrest the maximum of meaning and joy from every death-accompanied moment before the potency of mortality shall have been actualized as the implacable reality of death.

Here again Hanna's critical evaluation of Camus' "humanism" is most perceptive: ". . . a humanism whose final and only goal is the uncertain and mortal lives of men, creatures who are not infinitely pliable and suffering but are limited and infinitely precious and must at all costs be defended against those who would judge their lives and history by that which is foreign to their lives and history."[37] And in that chilling and challenging document, "Letters to a German Friend," Camus makes, flatly and sadly, the very point he would make against theists:

I continue to believe that this world has no ultimate meaning. But I know that something in it has a meaning and that is man, because he is the only creature to insist on having one. This world has at least the truth of man, and our task is to provide its justifications against fate itself. And it has no justification but man; hence he must be saved if we want to save the idea we have of life. With your scornful smile you will ask me; what do you mean by saving man: And with all my being I shout to you that I mean not mutilating him and yet giving a chance to the justice that man alone can conceive."[38]

In the matter of mortality, theists all too often reveal the quintessence of their vulgarizing sacrilege against created mysteries. Incomprehension, misunderstanding, trivialization, and even distortion can be intellectual errors, though they all participate to some extent in the volitional error of vulgarization. But total volitional abolition of a patent fact is an unmixed and unmitigated vulgarization of the most pernicious sort. It represents a sinking, on the part of intelligent thinkers, to the coarse level of wishful superstition.

3. The Seriousness of Mortality

Much has been written and said about Camus' reproach to Christians that they do not take this life seriously enough. That is certainly one of the effects of the vulgarization of death; but this reproach is by no means peculiar to Camus. Much has likewise been said and written about Camus' contention that rejection or neglect of death leads to a distortion and mutilation of man; but this reproach, though more distinctive of Camus, is by no means limited by him to theists. In fact, over half of his essay *The Rebel* presents precisely a charge-sheet against atheists for their mutilation of man in terms of some pseudo-transcendental future. The real crux of Camus' charge in this matter against theists and more particularly against Christians is the reproach that *they do not take man's mortality seriously.* Camus was nurtured in a too bloodstained generation to devote the bulk of his powers to any serene scholarly argument about this-worldliness. He and his generation were concerned with human *survival* rather than, and as a necessary preliminary to, the full flowering of this-worldly human activity.

In a masterpiece of frankness, moderation, clarity, precision, and devastating articulateness, Camus, the unbeliever, told his audience at the Dominican monastery of Latour-Maubourg in 1948 precisely what the unbeliever-rebel, dedicated to death as an ultimate and rejecting all transcendent Molochs, demands of the Christian theist:

> I share with you the same revulsion from evil. But I do not share your hope, and I continue to struggle against this universe in which children suffer and die. . . . For a long time during those frightful years I have waited for a great voice to speak up in Rome. I, an unbeliever? Precisely. For I knew that the spirit would be lost if it did not utter a cry of condemnation when faced with force. It seems that the voice did speak up. But I assure you that millions of men like me did not hear it and that at that time believers and unbelievers alike shared a solitude that continued to spread as the days went by and the executioners multiplied.
>
> It has been explained to me since that the condemnation was indeed voiced. But that it was in the style of the encyclicals, which is not at all clear. The condemnation was voiced and it was not understood! Who could fail to feel where the true condemnation lies in this case and to see that this example by itself gives part of the reply, perhaps the whole reply, that you ask of me. What the world expects of Christians is that Christians should speak out loud and clear, and that they should voice their condemnation in such a way that never a doubt, never the slightest doubt, could rise in the heart of the simplest man. That they should get away from abstraction and confront the bloodstained face history has taken on today.[39]

Theists are often guilty of a regrettable confusion of the orders of nature and grace, amounting to a proclamation that man is naturally immortal, or to a practical activity which presupposes this untenable contention.

Against the priest who tries to persuade him that he is working for man's salvation, Dr. Rieux protests: "Salvation's much too big a word for me. I don't aim so high. I'm concerned with man's health! and for me his health comes first."[40] And it is highly significant that the same Father Paneloux is reported, almost immediately after this conversation, as preaching his famous second sermon on the plague, a sermon in which he swerves notably away from the first sermon in which he had spoken of

> that radiant eternal light which glows, a small still flame, in the dark core of human suffering. And this light, too, illuminates the shadowed paths that lead towards deliverance. It reveals the will of God in action, unfail-

ingly transforming evil into good. And once again today it is leading us through the dark valley of fears and groans towards the holy silence, the well-spring of all life.[41]

The second sermon Paneloux concludes with the terrible peroration:

The love of God is a hard love. It demands total self-surrender, disdain of our human personality. And yet it alone can reconcile us to suffering and the deaths of children, it alone can justify them, since we cannot understand them, and we can only make God's will ours. That is the hard lesson I would share with you today. That is the faith, cruel in men's eyes, and crucial in God's, which we must ever strive to compass. We must aspire beyond ourselves towards that high and fearful vision. And on that lofty plane all will fall into place, all discords be resolved, and truth flash forth from the dark cloud of seeming injustice. Thus in some churches of the south of France plague victims have lain sleeping many a century under the flagstones of the chancel, and priests now speak above their tombs, and the divine message they bring to men rises from the charnel, to which, nevertheless, children have contributed their share.[42]

But it is the gloss of the unbeliever Tarrou which is most crucial to an understanding of the message Camus wished to communicate with this sermon preached by a tormented but still believing priest. For there is genuine dialogue in *The Plague,* not merely the unresolved juxtaposition of irreducible oppositions. It is the dialogue which Camus welcomed and called for in his remarks to the Dominicans:

. . . the world needs real dialogue. . . . falsehood is just as much the opposite of dialogue as is silence, and . . . the only possible dialogue is the kind between people who remain what they are and speak their minds.[43]

The priest has not merely swerved from a more facile, poetic optimism of faith to a more somber dark night of faith. He has grasped precisely the fact which Tarrou articulates:

Paneloux is right. . . . When an innocent youth can have his eyes destroyed, a Christian should either lose his faith or consent to having his eyes destroyed. Paneloux declines to lose his faith, and he will go through with it to the end. That's what he meant to say.[44]

The believing priest has accepted death as a genuine component of human reality, has agreed that in the midst of life we are in death, and has drawn from the acceptance of mortality as a genuine if not ultimately impenetrable curtain the stern lessons of duty incumbent on mortals throughout the vicissitudes of this mortal life, quite especially in times of stress, which periods of testing, however, merely serve to make clearer a demand levied at every moment of mortality.

4. The Threat of Death

The intelligent and humane atheist, not bewitched by counsels of epistemological despair at the meaninglessness of life, seeing one young innocent human being die, by disease, by violence, or by neglect, must feel a crusading sense of revolt. The theist, strong in his conviction that this death is a portal to eternal life, must, by an equal acceptance of the relative ultimacy of death, attain to the same crusading dedication. In our world today, the theoretical dispute about this-worldliness is decidedly an outmoded luxury. The real problem is whether this world, at least as a planet habitable by human beings, shall continue to survive at all. And Albert Camus, seasoned by many desperate nights and days of clandestine underground combat, tortured and enlightened by the spectacle of irreverence for life on the part of misguided crusaders for ideals, and at the examples of heroism in defense of life, has fashioned a challenge for every theist: Learn to love man as mortal. To your supernaturally motivated charity for the salvation of his eternal immortal soul, learn to add a tormented and heroic natural crusading love for the perishable entity, the existent human being in the here and now, the mortal human being. Consider if this second and vital devotion can be triggered by anything less than the clear-eyed and honest acceptance of the sobering pathos manifested in epitome in the inscription so prevalent in Greek pagan cemeteries: *Houtos athanatos* (Nobody is immortal).

We do not feel that Camus himself would have regarded our next remarks as mere puerile impertinence. Surely the theist precisely can say: No*body* is immortal; and this without prejudice to his faith. And from this accepted mortality of the body he can learn a new reverence for a crusading interest in the body, not merely in the sphere of medical research into and attempted conquest of the ills that beset that body and the centrifugal drive that destines it for disintegration at the end; not merely in the dimension of research into the problems of cultivation and distribution connected with the adequate sustenance of that body with earthly food; not only in the dimension of a new reverence for the participation of that body in the intimate communication that is sexuality; but also, but above all, in a new and deeper reverence for the most crucial of all single parameters of man's crossroads being, matter itself, the distinctive parameter of mortality, the atheist ultimate to an investigation of which the next chapter will be devoted.

Death as ultimate centrifugal force broods loweringly over all five converging and maturing influences by which modern man is being driven into a crisis at once grim and exciting.

No single one of the discoveries of the scientific-technological explosion of the last hundred years since Darwin can, taken alone, account for the vague but desperate malaise of modern man; but all converging discoveries have led him to question deeply and unhappily (or in some cases with a forced and brave show of happiness) the traditional picture on which he built his hopes, a picture with everything in its proper place: God in his heaven and all basically right with the world. Rather, man sees a swirling mass of an evolving and *devolving* universe, thrusting upward, to be sure, by the mysterious forces that defy entropy, only to be forced and fated ultimately to run down into total entropy so that heat will be evenly distributed again and nothing left of man's dreams and vital desires but a vast uniform waste, utterly unrecognizable to man as he is and dreams today. Twin magnitudes, the astrophysical and the microcosmic at the antipodes of the starry hosts in the heart of the atom, dizzy man and make him acutely conscious of his own smallness; and the loping shadow of the death of the universe itself disturbs man's pleasant evenings.

Man's ever more terrifying glimpses into the depth of his own self, where dark and savage powers prowl and threaten, reveal yet another kind of death-drive. Such glimpses render even the notion of sin itself curiously irrelevant and legalistic to describe the ultimate horror that man must look upon, namely a vast centrifugal force operative within his very self, a savage and destructive and trampling instinct by no means yet tamed. Even if he thinks still in the old categories, man realizes with piercing clarity that he can never really hurt God with all his sinning, but that the sword of his own rioting unbridled centrifugal powers is turned ineluctably, as often as it is unsheathed, against his own poor self and against that self reflected in his neighbor whom at odd instants he sees as equally defenseless but at the next moment is willing to strike down; and throughout he longs obscurely for a bright day on a sunlit island where he can love without fear.

Man's increasing, furious cry for an unrestricted freedom is by no means a consistently self-assured cry. What he seeks with divided heart he fears with divided mind. For while freedom may seem bracing at first glance, it soon emerges out of the mists of sentiment as a dreadful power, a perpetual opening onto chaos in the absence of an omnipotent benignity.

Finally there is death threatening in the most desperate form of all: the increasingly demanding requirement for man to arrive at a meaningful and consistent interpretation of reality, in the interests of his own self-preservation, at a moment precisely when reality seems to be becoming more and more complex and uncontrollable, more and more fragmented and ultimately indeterminate, more and more inimical to man as a part of it. This urgency once again is connected with the liberation of the heart of the atom, the volatilization of matter.

In the context of modern atheism, the death problem can be articulated thus: From the dimmest beginnings of his history man has been poignantly conscious of the *thrill of life* and has as constantly sought to eternalize it. Indeed burial mounds with their mute testimony to a hope of something beyond have been long considered the distinguishing watershed dividing man from other animals. This tormented higher animal, then, throughout long millennia of endeavor, has grasped at an indefinite extension of that thrill of life he feels pulse within him when he is most alive, in the sex act or in the rapture of artistic creation or apprehension or in contemplation of nature in motion. In great pulsing rhythms he has played out his various moods in this ultimate question. Now he has entered ineluctably the ages of analysis and his former infant faith is sicklied o'er with the pale cast

of thought and the disintegrative dynamic of analysis, that pulls entities apart into simpler elements and thus often begins to lose the very
feel for their totality, their over-all living pattern. In our century for
the first time, whole masses of men are trying to live with the accepted fact of ultimate mortality. That is a distinctive atheistic feature
of our age. And the death problem and the atheism problem form a
kind of vicious circle: man's increasingly scientized approach has led
him to be most wary of the chief historically adduced evidences of
survival and thus to doubt the existence or at least the meaningful
relevance of God; and conditioned increasing doubt of or lack of
sensitivity to an anterior personal Creator has led to a more and more
full acceptance of the grim fate of ultimate mortality.

But Camus requires more of man than simply to accept his fate
passively or in resignation. He demands struggle, to be sure, but he
demands something more subtle and deeper even than struggle. He
requires man to accept death not as a hostile malignant destroyer but
as a friendly benignant relativizer. Then let man struggle against it
with all his heart, the tang of living intensified by the very persuasion
of the evanescence, the *irrevocable evanescence* of the life man lives.

5. The Dynamic of Camus' Death Dedication

This attitude on Camus' part is no innate bent of mind or easily
won victory. In one of his earliest essays, "L'ironie," Camus describes the emotions of a young man (obviously himself) who becomes interested in the strange and pathetic case of an old, dying
woman: "He believed that there was such a thing as truth and at the
same time knew that this woman was going to die; and he did not
worry about resolving this contradiction."[45] A commentator well
remarks: "All Camus' later thought is an effort to draw such meaning
and value as can be drawn from this contradiction between desire and
reality.[46]

In another, slightly later, essay, "Le Vent a Djemila," we encounter a further step along the road of total yet resisting acceptance:

But men die in spite of themselves, in spite of their pious shams.
Someone says to them: "When you are better . . ." and they die. I want
none of that. For if there are days when nature lies, there are days when

she tells the truth. Djemila is telling the truth this evening, and with what sad and compelling beauty does she speak! For my own part, faced with this world, I am unwilling to lie or to be lied to. I want to push my clear-eyed vision to the extreme and look my own death straight in the eye in the full spate of my jealousy and my horror.[47]

The beginning of an antitranscendental theory of salvation, pivoted on an unconditional acceptance of death as ultimate, emerges in another essay of this same period, just before World War II: "The world is beautiful and outside the world there is no salvation. The great truth this landscape was patiently teaching me is that the mind is nothing, no nor even the heart itself."[48]

But the almost antihuman Stoicism of this devotion to enduring nature set over against fragile, deathbound man, is modified in the essay "Les Amandiers," written in 1940:

> At least I believe that men have never ceased to advance in their cognizance of their own fate. We have not overleapt that fate, and yet we do know it better. We know that we are in a state of contradiction but at the same time that we must reject contradiction and do what must be done to reduce it.[49]

Chastened and enlightened by the agonies, the suspense, and the awful hope of the Resistance, Camus can write in 1946:

> I sometimes doubt if we are to be allowed to save the man of today. But this man's children can still be saved, in their flesh and in their spirit. . . . More than revolt against the gods, it is this long obstinacy that is meaningful for us. And this admirable determination to separate nothing and to rule nothing out, that determination which has always reconciled and will not fail to reconcile again men's sorrowing hearts and the spring-times of the world.[50]

The commitment to death is now in no sense a protective pessimism calculated to guard the human heart against the horror of the absurd that is in death; it is an ethical commitment to struggle for the salvation of man within the limits imposed by death accepted as an ultimate. Such a commitment Camus believes will guarantee man at least against mutilation, against the pointless sacrifice to some idol of a Beyond or a Later On.

A year later Camus has achieved the perfect equilibrium of a balanced revolt, a moderate revolt, tragic and joyous at once, joyous because fully aware of its limits; and he can write of

the great nights of Africa, the royal exile, the despairing exaltation that awaits the solitary traveller. . . . for those who know the lacerations of the yes and the no, of noon and midnight, of revolt and love . . . there is down there a flame that awaits them.[51]

6. Death, a Challenge to the Christian

The evanescence of mortality has often been betrayed by theists who have taken an illicit leap into eternity before the end of time, before the death of the individual and before the genuine eschaton. The most somber of these illicit leaps has been the Nirvana-mentality; but there have been all manner of shadings, down to and including a certain sort of Christian angelism and exaggerated supernaturalism, all the more pernicious because it so seductively responds to the twin simultaneous demands of the heart of Western man: the preservation of individuality and the guarantee of security and a safe haven, even in the midst of the waves of temporality and mortality.

Camus' challenge to take death seriously can only be salutary for the theist. This theist—this convinced believer in an anterior personal Creator who guarantees eternity for the creature; especially this Christian theist, with his firm persuasion that this anterior Creator by his ingress into human history, his grappling at close quarters with death in the Crucifixion, and his triumphant resurrection, has trailblazed immortality for all mortal flesh—must not interpolate this ultimate certitude as a palliative to the terrors and the challenge of genuine mortality.

The past history of Christendom is too full of sad and humiliating examples of the evil effects of such an interpolation. The Christian has too often felt justified in burning man's body to save his soul; and even apart from the excesses of the inquisitorial mentality and its desecration of human flesh, there has been too much evasion of the challenge to build the Kingdom of Christ *on this earth*.

And here is a curious point of contact between Camus and every Christian; even as Camus fights, knowing that he will not succeed in vanquishing death at the end, so the Christian must fight for the establishment of Christ's Kingdom on earth, knowing that the approach to that Kingdom in time can only be asymptotic, that Christ's Kingdom is not of this world. The salutary contribution of Camus is to challenge the Christian, in these circumstances of eschatological hope and temporal despair, to the same high-hearted courage which Camus himself as unbeliever shows in the face of an apparent impossibility.

Dr. Rieux in *The Plague* proposes a kind of religious atheistic ethic in words every theist would do well to ponder:

> . . . since the order of the world is shaped by death, mightn't it be better for God if we refuse to believe in Him, and struggle with all our might against death, without raising our eyes toward the heaven where He sits in silence?[52]

This is the sort of sentence, luminous with genuine meaning, which too many hasty theists pounce upon and parse theologically into absurdity, thus refuting it without benefiting from it. It contains a real challenge to the moral consciousness of the Christian, to his reverence for created freedom and his respect for human mortality: alter it to read "Mightn't it be better for us to refuse to trust exclusively in God and accept the fact of His silence as imposing a grave duty of creative freedom upon His human creatures?" and the lesson is clear beyond cavil or misunderstanding.

Tarrou's awful question: "Can one be a saint without God?" might seem to the theist at first mere flippant blasphemy or else an atrocious misunderstanding. Yet there are hints and indications for the believing Christian: Gethsemane and the agony of the dark hours on Calvary are more than a mere stage script. And every theist tradition speaks somehow of this purifying night of the soul when the creature seems alone, and indeed in one important dimension *is* alone, the Omnipotent Creator having withdrawn the immediate evident support of His power. It is in such situations that the believer must prove his worth. To deny absolutely to humanity any possibility of genuinely independent contribution to personal sanctification is to lapse into a grim and somber heresy of the overriding omnipotence of God. That omnipotence in some mysterious fashion, utterly incomprehensible to the creatures it affects, has managed to order created freedom in such a way that independence of moral action is reconcilable with omnipotence and omniscience.

But the importance of death and the death-boundedness of this life on earth for every man, here assumes absolutely capital importance. For the free creature will simply not mobilize the full, agonized powers of his created freedom if he trivializes into insignificance the curtain that separates him from the life eternal. He will lose both his sense of urgency and his sense of independent responsibility, lying back to wait for God to work and constantly fixing his eyes on a lucid land of promise in which he imagines he dwells somehow already.

The seriousness of Camus' challenge, of his contention that one can truly begin to take man seriously only when one takes death seriously, is pointed up by the whole phenomenon of the death-of-God philosophy and theology of our day. This phenomenon displays to us dedicated and self-professed Christians who claim that God has died. I am persuaded that their motivation is moral rather than ontological. It is not that they see a convincing argument written somewhere in the stars or in man's mind for the contention that God has truly died; it is that they do not see any other way of rousing Christians to their genuine responsibility except by proclaiming the death of God, the demise of the Almighty. When most clearly expounded, this death-of-God theology contends that God had to expose Himself to the implacable consequences of His own entry into the time dimension. In Christ, God truly died and thereafter man, inspired by this appalling sacrifice, was summoned to take up the torch and save the universe and sanctify it.

It is far too easy and pointless for theists to retort that such men are playing fast and loose with the phenomenologically attested fact of the Resurrection. It is banal to remark that they are behaving like rationalists unwilling to accept on principle any violation of the laws of nature such as a resurrection would involve. It is beside the point to allege that they have not appreciated, have indeed forcibly abolished, all *mystery* from the Incarnation and subverted it, rather, into a monstrosity and an impossibility, redolent of initial and preliminary atheism on the part of such temporalizers of God. It is, of course, perfectly true that a god who enters time and dies is a god at best in the pagan Greek tradition and never God of the theist faith. It is equally true that the mystery of the Incarnation resides precisely in the technique whereby God managed to unite really His own divinity personified, i.e., the Person who is divine, who is God, to a perfect humanity, without prejudice to the perfection of either, without prejudice to the infinity, eternity, divine freedom and omnipotence of the Divine Person, nor yet to the created freedom, finitude, and temporality of the human nature taken up into this mysterious union. But the critics of the death-of-God theology are often themselves relapsing into a kind of monophysitism from which precisely these incautious young rebels sought to rouse them. It is this monophysitism that has lain like a long curse over Christian witness for millennia, this pert and superficial loyalty to the divinity of Christ to the detriment of His humanity. Nowhere does this latent monophysitism come into evidence more sharply than in the vulgarization of the death of Christ. If death-of-God theology serves no better purpose than making twentieth-century Christians know for a time at least the utter desolation of the disciples during that three-day lying-in-the-tomb, it will have accomplished a much needed awakening.

Camus himself can be described as the embodiment of the proof that an atheist can be a decent man and that a singularly attractive human personality can be an atheist. He is himself very much the outsider, outside the easily categorized technical limits of any school, outside the fevered madness of so many atheists and theists of our generation who want to save man even against his will, outside the bounds even of clearly defined nationality, for the European Algerian is a hybrid. Above all, Camus is an outsider to the very traditional problematic of atheism: for his atheism stems neither from a fastidious retreat into an epistemological ghetto of subjectivism nor yet from an option in favor of any other god or idol. He wrote to put an end to all idols and recall man to the realities of his situation. Yet neither was Camus a compromising pragmatist, for he knew man to be tormented by questions that transcend the sense-manifold. Camus merely warned against proud and impatient and unsubstantiated answers.

His atheism stemmed from a clear-eyed observation of a mad world, a cruel world, a blind world, an absurd world, wherein he found many human beings carefully avoiding the precious mortality that distinguished them by its presence in them from all inanimate nature and by their knowledge of it from the animals. He urged on man a rebellion moderated by equilibrium and guaranteed in its moderation by the supreme relativizer, death.

7. Plaidoyer for the Mortal

The most terrible indictment of excessively supernaturally oriented theism I have ever read comes from the pen of a horrified and angered Camus. It is also a lesson in the dire consequences of not taking death seriously, befuddled by animadversions of the great eternal life to come, which too often make men of God connive with naked evil. But it would be pointless to cite the terrible little story entire, as I intend to do, if one did not first pinpoint exactly the reason for telling it. For it is a powerful story in its own right; to my mind it is the most powerful single piece of writing a very powerful, evocative novelist has ever written: *but it is a true story.* Like living blood it spills down all over our theoretical considerations to warn us that our object in any such investigation as the one we have here instituted must be preeminently practical or else risk being entirely immoral. The most refined considerations concerning the parameters of creatureliness must be relevant *directly* to the chattering teeth of a frightened boy, or else our pursuits of subtlety are but cowardly evasions of responsibility.

This thing, then, *happened.* That is the first point. Camus tells the story in one of his "Letters to a German Friend," but to those letters he prefaced a powerful declaration: "I should be ashamed today if I implied that a French writer could be the enemy of a single nation. I loathe none but executioners."[53]

This thing has one overriding moral. That is the second point. Nothing is more fatuous or vulgar than to criticize such a powerful explosion of a generous heart with the canons of secondary considerations. The point is not what other considerations may well have entered into the priest's mind in that fatal moment of decision; the point is that they ought all to have been overweighed by one single consideration, the precious quality of a mortal innocent boy. *And they were not.*

The moral has to do with taking death seriously. That is the third point. For this is patently the avenue by which Camus approaches the crisis of the narrative. The story is a kind of parable or paradigm of the cruel compromises effected by one who is not represented as cowardly in every sense, who is not castigated as an active collaborator with the executioners, but who is pilloried as a misguided supernaturalist who proves he is entirely unaware of the value of a beginning human life.

The moral applies to the most convinced theist. That is the final point of supreme importance. The case here presented is an extreme one—that is the privilege and the *modus operandi* of the great narrator, to select a single case that will epitomize in unmistakable colors the much wider, subtler, more complicated problem. Death is that ultimate that gives a human individual an absolutely inviolable dignity; but death is merely the actualization and the paradigm of all the internal parameters of man which we have considered and which could be reduced to the ultimate generic parameter of mobile creatureliness—or to phrase it in a way acceptable to modern atheists as well, mobile fragility. Along every one of those parameters we believe that we have shown how the atheist sins by excess, i.e., by attempting to elevate them to a dignity they do not possess and saddling them with a responsibility they cannot bear; but we hope we have shown equally that the theist sins throughout by defect, by excessive trivialization of these parameters, a trivialization triggered precisely by his misplaced exclusivist adoration of the uncreated Mystery, an adoration which blurs the creaturely dignity and blots out the terrors of created freedom from his eyes.

Now, in the case of death, we have reached the internal parameter that is, to our mind, the most obscure and the most limpid at once. Willingly therefore do we avail ourselves of this stupendous and appalling parable. A few words will suffice to articulate our own divergence from Camus' position on death and to point up our disagreement with much theistic trivialization of death, the supreme terminal parameter of creatureliness. Death is the most human of all the parameters we have thus far treated, for it is the human being who dies. Moreover, death is in him from the very moment of conception and in a very real sense it does bound his horizon. To trivialize death is to trivialize the whole of the creature that is man. If his death is but an incidental transition, then his entire creaturely existence was a phantasmal phenomenon. Whoever believes this is a pathological specimen, quite capable of the blasphemy, the moral cowardice, and the diabolical cruelty of the priest in this story. And the final horror of the tale is this: The priest was not a wicked man, not a renegade to his convictions, only a renegade to humanity. If such be the products theism produces, it is not difficult to grasp the motivation of much atheism. The entire final chapter of this book will be an act of simple reparation to that terrified boy and to the God the theist so wretchedly betrayed. We shall show that faith in God need not produce monsters, that faith in God alone can produce the new humanity longed for by such frightened exiles as that victim of bullets and supernaturalism; but that true faith in God must take God's creation as seriously as God himself takes it.

To his German friend Camus writes:

Let me tell you this story. Before dawn, from a prison I know, somewhere in France, a truck driven by armed soldiers is taking eleven Frenchmen to the cemetery where you are to shoot them. Out of the eleven five or six have really done something: a tract, a few meetings, something that showed their refusal to submit. The five or six, sitting motionless inside the truck, are filled with fear, but, if I may say so, it is an ordinary fear, the kind that grips every man facing the unknown, a fear that is not incompatible with courage. The others have done nothing. This hour is harder for them because they are dying by mistake or as victims of a kind of indifference. Among them is a child of sixteen. You know the faces of our adolescents; I don't want to talk about them. The boy is dominated by fear; he gives in to it shamelessly. Do not smile scornfully; his teeth are chattering. But you have placed beside him a chaplain, whose task it is to alleviate somewhat the agonizing hour of waiting. I believe I can say that for men who are about to be killed a conversation about a future life is of no avail. It is too hard to believe that the lime-pit is not the end of all. The prisoners in the truck are silent. The Chaplain turns toward the child huddled in his corner. He will understand better. The child answers, clings to the chaplain's voice, and hope returns. In the mutest of horrors sometimes it is enough for a man to speak; perhaps he is going to fix everything. "I haven't done anything," says the child. "Yes," says the chaplain, "but that's not the question now. You must get ready to die properly." "It can't be possible that no one understands me." "I am your friend and perhaps I understand you. But it is late. I shall be with you and the Good Lord will be too. You'll see how easy it is." The child turns his head away. The chaplain speaks of God. Does the child believe in him? Yes, he believes. Hence he knows that nothing is as important as the peace awaiting him. But that very peace is what frightens the child. "I am your friend," the chaplain repeats.

The others are silent. He must think of *them*. The chaplain leans toward the silent group, turning his back on the child for a moment. The truck is advancing slowly with a sucking sound over the road, which is damp with dew. Imagine the grey hour, the early morning smell of men, the invisible countryside suggested by sounds of teams being harnessed or the cry of a bird. The child leans against the canvas covering, which gives a little. He notices a narrow space between it and the truck body. He could jump if he wanted. The chaplain has his back turned and, up front, the soldiers are intent on finding their way in the dark. The boy doesn't stop to think; he tears the canvas loose, slips into the opening, and jumps. His fall is hardly heard, the sound of running on the road, then nothing more. He is in the fields, where his steps can't be heard. But the flapping of the canvas, the sharp, damp morning air penetrating the truck make the chaplain and the prisoners turn around. For a second the priest stares at those men looking at him in silence. A second in which the man of God must decide whether he is on the side of the executioners or on the side of the martyrs in keeping with his vocation. But he has already knocked on the partition separating him from his comrades. "Achtung!" The alarm is given. Two soldiers leap into the truck and point their guns at the prisoners. Two others leap to the ground and start running across the fields. The chaplain, a few paces from the truck, standing on the asphalt, tries to see them through the fog. In the truck the men can only listen to the sounds of the chase, the muffled exclamations, a shot, silence, then the sound of voices again coming nearer, finally a hollow stamping of feet. The child is brought back. He wasn't hit, but he stopped surrounded in the enemy fog, suddenly without courage, forsaken by himself. He is carried rather than led by his guards. He has been beaten somewhat, but not much. The most important lies ahead. He doesn't look at the chaplain or anyone else. The priest has climbed up beside the driver. An armed soldier has taken his place in the truck. Thrown into one of the corners, the child doesn't cry. Between the canvas and the floor he watches the road slip away again and sees in its surface a reflection of the dawn.[54]

Men are mortal precisely because they are material. To an examination of that first of man's external parameters we must now proceed.

5

FAITH IN MATTER

The dialectical materialism of the Marxists has often been designated as a secular religion. Gustav Wetter adduces metaphysical reasons for this designation; Leslie Dewart cites psychological ones.

Wetter writes: "Here the higher is not, as such, denied; the world is interpreted as a process of continual ascent, which fundamentally extends into infinity. But it is supposed to be matter itself which continually attains to higher perfection under its own power, thanks to its indwelling dialectic . . . the dialectical materialist attribution of "dialectic" to matter confers on it, not mental attributes only, but even divine ones."[1]

Dewart insists that Marxist materialism, by the very vehemence of its denial of God, sets itself in a different class from the only genuine and consequential atheism evidenced by a man like Heidegger, who considers the very notion of God so preposterous as to be both unworthy and incapable of serious discussion, to be nothing more than the babblings of a madman. Dewart notes that this true and consequential atheism "proceeds from an understanding of being that renders absurd the very possibility of a transcendence that would transcend the transcendence of man."[2] The Marxist anti-theism, on the other hand, is, says Dewart, "above all a *denial* of the existence of God. . . . It is a negative existential judgment concerning an object of thought, God, who is, therefore, at least by implication, allowed the status of a logically possible, conceivable reality."[3]

For Wetter, then, Marxist atheism is a religion because its ultimate metaphysical category has had a set of divine attributes ascribed to it; for Dewart, Marxist atheism is a religion because it involves an ultimate existential self-commitment to ultimate reality.

Both analyses seem to me sound, but neither seems to have noticed the main point about Marxist atheism: this atheism is validly called a religion, I should say, because it confronts man, at the ultimate level, with a primordial reality antedating him historically and presenting itself to him with the take-it-or-be-damned brutishness of a sheer datum; it is validly called a secular religion because this reality is entirely confined to the *saeculum,* this age, radically understood, the space-time continuum; it is entirely immanentized.

1. The Berkeleyan-Hegelian Background

The judgment may not be modified, but the understanding of Marxist materialism will be substantially enriched if the phenomenon of this dialectical materialism is placed in its historical context. And such a positioning will immediately involve some highly embarrassing revelations about theist thinkers. More than two centuries before this dialectical materialism had been excogitated, a Christian bishop and theologian, George Berkeley, had written, in vehement seriousness, a strange outburst which throws a pitiless light on theist attitudes:

> Nay, so great a difficulty has it been thought to conceive Matter pro-duced out of nothing, that the most celebrated among the ancient philos-ophers, even of those who maintained the being of a God, have thought Matter to be uncreated and coeternal with Him. How great a friend *material substance* has been to Atheists in all ages were needless to relate. All their monstrous systems have so visible and necessary a dependence on it, that when this cornerstone is once removed, the whole fabric cannot choose but fall to the ground; insomuch that it is no longer worth-while to bestow a particular consideration on the absurdities of every wretched sect of Atheists.[4]

Berkeley clearly considered his own epistemologization of ontolog-ical status, his *esse est percipi,* to be an effective answer to all athe-ism, a forestalling even of its possibility.

This psychological unhappiness with matter, this radical disinclina-tion to admit any real status to the nonmental or the extramental, reached its pathological climax in Hegel. The Catholic historian of philosophy, Frederick Copleston, generously insists that it would be a gross caricature of Hegel to imagine that there is any question, in Hegel's philosophy "of Nature being unreal or merely idea in a subjectivist sense."[5] But this generosity seems excessive in the light of this same historian's own incisive comments on the key aspects of the Hegelian system. Let me here list only five of the most devastating:

a) ". . . reality is the necessary process by which infinite Reason, the self-thinking Thought, actualizes itself."[6]

b) "Yet it is clear that Hegel comes to philosophy with certain basic convictions: that the rational is the real and the real the rational, that reality is the self-manifestation of infinite reason, and that infinite reason is self-thinking Thought which actualizes itself in the historical process."[7]

c) "If we ask what the Absolute is, we can answer that it is being. And if we ask what being is, we shall in the end be forced to answer that being is self-thinking Thought or Spirit."[8]

d) ". . . we can discern a marked tendency to adopt a Platonic position by distinguishing between the inside, as it were, of Nature, its rational structure or reflection of the Idea, and its outside, its contingent aspect, and by relegating the latter to the sphere of the irrational and unreal."[9]

e) ". . . what Professor Hegel cannot cope with he tends to dismiss as irrational and so as unreal. For the rational is the real and the real the rational."[10]

Since Hegel was not an outright psychopath, even though his system may seem close to being pathologically mentalistic, he had to find some explanation of the apparent spirit-matter or Spirit-Nature dichotomy. He did so by making Spirit radically ontologically anterior to matter and matter (Nature) a mere moment in the life of the Absolute. Nature, matter, for Hegel, was not really real.

This excessive exclusivism in favor of Spirit engendered a violent swing of the pendulum in the opposite direction: whereas Hegel said the Absolute is Spirit, the protestors said that the Absolute is Matter, whereas Hegel said that Spirit is really all there is and matter but a moment in Spirit's dynamic, the protestors said that matter is really all there is and spirit is but an epiphenomenon of matter, a by-product of a certain stage of matter's organization. And it is in this historical context that we must evaluate and appreciate the extreme ontological materialism of the protestors, the Marxists: Marx and

Engels first, and Lenin subsequently and pre-eminently.

Copleston calls Hegel's brilliant tour-de-force of the dialectic "one of the possible ways of satisfying the mind's impulse to obtain conceptual mastery over the whole wealth of empirical data."[11] And Wetter calls Hegelian philosophy "the most complete realization of the romantic urge to incorporate all departments of life and culture into a unitary scheme."[12] Hegelianism is in fact a sorry commentary on the mind's craving not only for intelligibility but for its own native sort of intelligibility. It is this craving that inclines the mind fatally to impose on reality that kind of intelligibility to which the mind is most accustomed. Hegel simply took this bent to its maddest extreme in spiritualistic mentalism. In effect, Hegel mentalized God and imposed upon the Ultimate the laws of procedure of the human mind, impoverished the Sovereign Creator to the status of a Concept operating by logical internal necessity. In Hegel the Absolute Idea has lost entirely its status as a subsistent reality ontologically prior to Nature and the efficient cause of Nature: ". . . there is no room in his system for an efficient cause which transcends the world in the sense that it [that cause] exists quite independently of it [this world]."[13]

In his desire for total yet dynamic real unity, Hegel subsumes all of reality under one supreme category, the dialectically evolving idea. The coequal Divine Persons become stages in a process that subsumes creatures and Creator into one single unidimensional category. Thus, in the Hegelian world-view there is no more room for creation, in the sense of the imparting of being by free decision on the part of Perfect Being; there is only logical deduction, necessary emanation, rendered inescapable by the internal logic of Reality which is Idea and therefore conceptual.

2. Marxist Anti-Hegelian Reaction

Marxist reaction to Hegelian mentalism sought in crude, palpable matter the brute consistency required of a primordial ultimate. The materialistic atheists simply excised anterior thought and grounded everything upon brute matter-in-motion, the only reality left after such an excision from a Hegelian pattern which had already hopelessly blurred the boundaries between Creator and creatures.

The violent Marxist reaction against thought as a radical anterior terminal ultimate was entirely sane, touched the true nerve of the whole business. Unfortunately, their doctrinaire immanentism which confined reality to the space-time continuum warped their vision and prevented them from seeing the transcendent power, Being, of which brute matter is for all that a truer analogue than thought! Indeed, whereas Wetter argues[14] that Marxist materialism has its realism vitiated (and even rendered dangerous to the "the philosophically untutored reader") by its radical materialism, I would contend that the undoubted radical materialism of Marxism must be understood absolutely in its historical context as a reaction against mentalism and that consequently its realism, precisely in its concept of matter, is salutary and illuminating to matter-shy theists.

Wetter in fact himself readily admits that "dialectical materialism, in its present-day official Soviet form, bears a far greater resemblance to the *'forma mentis'* of Scholasticism than to that of Hegelian dialectics."[15] But in his incisive treatment of the implications of the dialectical materialist notion of matter, he is pursued by that skittish nervousness which sees only the anti-God materialism:

And we find in fact that on such a view matter is eternal, infinite in space and time and internal potency of being, that at a certain stage of development it also acquires mental properties, and that it even has a genuine power of creation, so far as it is capable of bringing forth the higher from the lower, the more perfect from the less perfect, a task which would certainly call for genuine creative power. Matter here appears as a new absolute, a new divinity replacing the transcendent Creator-God, and as such unable to tolerate any other sort of deity by its side.[16]

3. The Praise of Matter

It will here be pertinent to cite a lengthy section of Friedrich Engels, *Dialectics of Nature,* to convey something of the flavor of this well-nigh mystical attitude to matter as ultimate and matrix of all that is. This section certainly justifies Wetter's contention that matter is promoted virtually to the status of deity; but surely it does not justify his contention that dialectical materialism is incapable of any salutary effect on theist thought. Indeed, in the section just cited,

Wetter admits that in dialectical materialism the Hegelian concepts are robbed of their idealist meaning and given an interpretation which is simply that appropriate to ordinary common sense. In other words, dialectical materialism is precisely that: substantively anti-idealist materialism, only adjectivally dialectical. The Hegelian dialectic has been forced into service to a Nature accorded a primordial status over against Thought which would have utterly horrified Hegel himself. We shall proceed in due course to show why we believe Wetter's gingerly uneasiness about Marxist materialism to be groundless and precisely what salutary lessons theism can learn from it.

The Engels' peroration of matter runs thus:

> It is an eternal cycle that matter moves in, a cycle that certainly only completes its orbit in periods of time for which our terrestrial year is no adequate measure, a cycle in which the time of highest development, the time of organic life and still more that of the life of beings conscious of nature and of themselves, is just as narrowly restricted as the space in which life and self-consciousness come into operation; a cycle in which every finite mode of existence of matter, whether it be sun or nebular vapour, single animal or genus of animals, chemical combination or dissociation, is equally transient, and wherein nothing is eternal but eternally changing, eternally moving matter and the laws according to which it moves and changes. But however often, and however relentlessly, this cycle is completed in time and space; however many millions of suns and earths may arise and pass away, however long it may last before, in one solar system and only on *one* planet, the conditions for organic life develop; however innumerable the organic beings, too, that have to arise and to pass away before animals with a brain capable of thought are developed from their midst, and for a short span of time find conditions suitable for life, only to be exterminated later without mercy—we have the certainty that matter remains eternally the same in all its transformations, that none of its attributes can ever be lost, and therefore, also, that with the same iron necessity that it will exterminate on the earth its highest creation, the thinking mind, it must somewhere else and at another time again produce it.[17]

4. The Dialectical Defense of Matter

It is precisely this ultimate status of matter which Lenin finds himself compelled to defend in the famous crisis of matter triggered by the nineteenth-century speculations concerning the possibility of reducing matter to a more ultimate electricity or indeed dissolving it altogether. Lenin's reply is contained in his *Materialism and Empirio-Criticism*[18] and it is interesting in the extreme, both for an understanding of the dynamic of Lenin's own thought and for its significance in Marxist materialism's revolt against idealism. Wetter's critique[19] seems to me singularly inapposite. But before dealing with the critique, I must consider Lenin's own articulation and comment on it from my point of view.

Lenin alludes to the "crisis in modern physics" articulated in the book *Valeur de la science* by "the famous French physicist Henri Poincaré." This work, published in 1905, deals with a crisis which may today seem entirely outmoded; but Lenin unerringly argues from the specificities of Poincaré's treatment of the crisis of that day to the generic question involved. Paraphrasing Poincaré, Lenin writes of the specific crisis of that day:

. . . the principle of the conservation of mass has been undermined by the electron theory of matter. . . . The entire mass of the electrons, or, at least, of the negative electrons, proves to be totally and exclusively electrodynamic in its origin. Mass disappears.[20]

Lenin rightly senses that a period of doubt, or at least alarm, had begun already with the electron theory, because tough ultimate matter conceived as the basic fabric of reality was threatening to disintegrate. The hardy ultimate, characterized basically by the mass phenomenon which gave it that brute consistency Marxists thought the ultimate needed, was threatening to dissolve entirely into nonmaterial (i.e., nonmass) realities.

Lenin likewise unerringly sees the chief philosophical danger arising from this shaking of the foundations of matter. If it can be shown that matter (or perhaps, in this context, more accurately, "mass") is not an objective and unchanging reality dictating the very fabric of thought, then mass becomes simply one formulation imposed on a reality that does not any longer possess ontological priority to the human mind; that human mind again acquires ontological ascendency and Poincaré (whom Lenin actually quotes[21]) is justified in saying that whatever is not thought is pure nothing. The mind becomes constitutive of reality and we are back in rampant Hegelian mentalism again.

"The new trend in physics regards theories only as symbols, signs, and marks for practice, i.e., *it denies the existence of an objective reality independent of our mind and reflected by it.*"[22] Thus Lenin sums up the *"essence* of the crisis in modern physics" in a triad of phrases that serve as bridge from the specificity to the generic philosophical problematic: "the breakdown of the old laws and basic principles. . . . *the rejection of an objective reality existing outside the mind.* . . . the replacement of materialism by idealism and agnosticism."[23]

Lenin sees this same danger from another angle of vision, which he describes, citing Righi: "The electron theory 'is not so much a theory of electricity as of matter; the new system simply puts electricity in the place of matter.' "[24] Now, if this can be done so easily, if such an "offense against sacred matter"[25] can be committed with impunity, then matter loses its aura of ultimacy in the ontological order and becomes just one more inadequate word. Nor is the whole business merely a linguistic debate: it is metaphysics which is at stake. For the new idealism coming out of the sciences goes further than merely alleging that the ultimate reality can no longer be adequately described by the word "matter"; it alleges that the basic texture of this reality has been radically misrepresented by the use of that word and by the entire conception of reality which the use of that word implies.

Lenin at once spots and lashes out at the fundamental error he feels this approach to conceal: the argument from the inadequacy, the demonstrable, physically mensurable inadequacy, of one human conception of reality neither means that there is no ultimate reality outside the mind, not yet, nor above all, that the mind can simply play about constructing any pattern of reality it wants to build. The drastically Satanic (if such a term be permitted in the Leninist context) element in such an approach is that it divorces thought from meaningful direct contact with matter (=objective reality) and then reduces that reality to nothingness, leaving thought supreme and alone.

It is here that Lenin makes what Wetter designates as the distinction "between the philosophical and scientific concepts of matter."[26] Wetter admits a certain justification for this distinction; but he then proceeds in most bemusingly imprecise fashion to argue against what he conceives as Lenin's inference "from an intrinsically correct belief in the epistemological priority of matter, to its ontological priority."[27] This whole line of argument brings us to the very heart of the question, to our most basic disagreement with Wetter's critique, and to our own assessment of the cardinal contribution of Lenin's faith in matter to the healthy understanding of ontology. We must first expound with brief running commentary Lenin's actual argumentation, which can usefully be arranged in four main steps. Then we shall deal with Wetter's critique. Finally we shall articulate systematically and in detail our own assessment of the Leninist contribution to a sound ontology, a contribution that could come, in precisely this modality, *only from a materialist.*

Lenin's first statement complex in which we are here interested deals with dialectical materialism's evaluation of the nature and status of scientific theories, and thus is related quite clearly to the specificities of the situation he is discussing in his *topical* plaidoyer; his second statement complex forges outward from this restricted area to the generic *epistemological* question; his third statement complex falls unequivocally within the dimension of *ontology;* and his fourth can only be said to be *theological* in flavor. If we have here considerably rearranged the order of Lenin's exposition, we have not altered his thought. Our rearrangement has been motivated solely by the desire to achieve greater clarity and precision, above all in the dynamic of Leninist thinking on the whole question of matter, and pre-eminently with an eye to Wetter's critique to which we must shortly return.

A. Topical Plaidoyer

On the *status of scientific theories,* Lenin writes: ". . . dialectical materialism insists on the approximate, relative character of every scientific theory of the structure of matter and its properties."[28]

And his critique of the new science in terms precisely of this mandatory relative character of scientific theories serves as a bridge to his second statement complex concerning epistemology. For he charges that these physicists

> . . . threw the baby out with the bath-water. Denying the immutability of the elements and the properties of matter known hitherto, they ended in denying matter, i.e. the objective reality of the physical world. Denying the absolute character of some of the most important and basic laws, they ended in denying all objective law in nature and in declaring that a law of nature is a mere convention, "a limitation of expectation," "a logical necessity," and so forth. Insisting on the approximate and relative character of our knowledge, they ended in denying the object independent of the mind and reflected approximately-correctly and relatively-truthfully by the mind. And so on, and so forth, without end.[29]

Lenin is here quite clearly charging the scientists with a pusillanimous pushing of the good and salutary principle to an extreme at which it becomes insidious. In effect, he is accusing them of a kind of imperialism: observing a trait of their own theories, they haughtily extend this trait to the whole of reality; they mislocate the relativizing principle, transferring it from their theories and the human mind that constructs such theories to reality as such; or, more accurately, they saddle reality with the relativity and radical approximativeness of human theorizing. Unwilling (presumably because of their specialist bias) to admit that they as scientists are dealing with a reality which escapes their conceptualization, which contains elements that will *always* escape that conceptualizing effort, no matter how much science is refined, they totally deny to reality the stability and consistency and immutability at any level which they fail to find in their own theoretical formulations. But this is ultimately to deprive reality of any status whatever and to make the mind indeed not only the measure but even the executive fashioner of all things.

B. The Epistemological Dimension

Lenin articulates a set of *epistemological* observations which, taken globally, amount of an *epistemologization of substance and essence*. It is seductively easy to overleap these strictly epistemological statements and race immediately to Lenin's ontological utterances which initially may seem of far greater importance (even if that importance be later reduced, as Wetter reduces it, to a somewhat flat and obvious common-sense approach, simply restating convictions better articulated by the great Scholastics and masters of traditional realism). But these epistemological statements are there in Lenin's exposition, albeit less clearly delimited and systematically presented than we are here presenting them. Lenin after all was interested in holding the pass against idealism. I do not for a moment suggest that Lenin even consciously adverted in passing to the possible implications or importance of these purely epistemological statements; but they are of absolutely cardinal importance to our own development of that dimension of his insight from which theists can learn, and it is licit to extrapolate provided original texts are scrupulously literally adduced as the basis for the extrapolation:

From Engels' point of view, the only immutability is the reflection by the human mind (when there is a human mind) of an external world existing and developing independently of the mind. No other "immutability," no other "essence," no other "absolute substance," in the sense in which these concepts were depicted by the empty professorial philosophy, exist for Marx and Engels. The "essence" of things, or "substance," is *also* relative; it expresses only the degree of profundity of man's knowledge of objects; and while yesterday the profundity of this knowledge did not go beyond the atom, and today does not go beyond the electron and ether, dialectical materialism insists on the temporary, relative, approximate character of all these *milestones* in the knowledge of nature gained by the progressing science of man.[30]

Previously Lenin has anticipated this cardinal principle, in a section which attempts to cope rather more specifically with the alarm signal "Matter is disappearing," to which slogan Lenin gives a benign interpretation which applies his basic epistemological principle before he actually enunciates it:

"Matter is disappearing" means that the limit within which we have hitherto known matter is vanishing and that our knowledge is penetrating deeper; properties of matter are likewise disappearing which formerly seemed absolute, immutable and primary (impenetrability, inertia, mass, etc.) and which are now revealed to be relative and characteristic only of certain states of matter.[31]

Lenin is here epistemologizing essence against the background of the radically dynamic Marxist materialist conception of ultimate reality. In his third statement complex he will articulate the only statement he feels can be made about this ultimate extramental reality which transcends in every sense the mere knowing human mind, itself a tiny moment in the evolution of that ultimate. But here he is in fact saying: Not only can I not tell you *what* ultimate reality is, I *can* positively tell you that no one can now or will ever be able to tell you what it is. In a somewhat startling reversal of the traditional search for stability somewhere under the agitated surface of apparently constant change, Lenin and Marxism direct man to look, rather, under the illusory surface stability of macro-cosmic objects to find the seething change that is at the heart of things. It is not simply that no adequate *concept* of this ultimate reality, matter-in-motion, has *as yet* been able to be worked out; it is rather that, on principle and a priori, no such adequate concept will ever be able to be formulated. Ultimate reality is of its very nature unconceptualizable. The reason for the approximate and relative character of scientific theories (and indeed of the very *terms* which are the building blocks of those theories) lies not in any merely temporary limitation of man's perceptual machinery which may in time be overcome by refinement of instruments and precision of concepts; it lies, rather, in the *fact* of the radical flux that is ultimate reality.

Our illusory conviction that ultimate reality is even relatively stable or that there is somewhere a core of stability to be discovered if only we can get far enough and deep enough—this conviction comes either from our tendency to take too short-range a view or else from our incapacity to penetrate deeply enough. Whenever the human mind operates, it operates conceptually. It articulates and seems to be able to articulate only in delimited concepts, nounally. And it is this nounalizing tendency that evokes the delimited and contradistinguished concepts that are "essences" in the first place. It is this same tendency that opens the floodgates to despondency when a certain set of these concepts or terms begin to evaporate. This despondency triggers an escape into idealism. Rather than admit the specter of an extramental and amental reality whose innermost character we not only cannot grasp now or in the foreseeable future but will never, on principle, be able to grasp, man is prepared to abolish this objective nature by an intellectual thumbs-down: let it die, so that we may be left with the manipulable and homey atmosphere of pure thought which does obey our conceptual manipulatory operations.

Essentialization has been the bugbear of traditional Western theistic philosophizing and even theologizing. A detailed treatment of the salutary influence of Leninist materialism on this tendency must await the final section of this chapter. For the moment, I am concerned with making Lenin's own position, as I see it, absolutely clear, especially in anticipation of Wetter's critique: Lenin is indeed setting up a sort of concept of matter. Against any high-handed *ad homiem* arguments that such a concept amounts, on Lenin's own terms, to an inconsistency, I would adduce the remarkable insight of Gilson in his remarks about the peculiar problematic encountered by Christian philosophy in its approach to Being or God. The parallelism between Lenin's "concept" of matter-in-motion and this Christian "concept" of God, philosophically approached as *ipsum esse* will not escape the reader. What I intend to make of it will become clear at the end of this chapter. For the moment I wish only to advert to Gilson's advice: since essence, he says, is "proper to the being of creatures, we must give up essence in order to reach to open sea of pure actual existence . . . but we must also keep the notion of essence present to mind so as not to leave it without any object."[32]

Nor am I concerned at this point with the cogency or adequacy of Lenin's ultimate. I am simply concerned to pinpoint Lenin's philosophical concept of matter in the light of and as revealed by his epistemologization of essences; and to correct Wetter's patronizing statements that this concept is "exceedingly broad"[33] and "has nothing to say about matter as such—what it is in itself."[34] In a sense, of course, the latter charge is accurate, but Lenin, I believe, and I myself most certainly, would accept it as a compliment. For it is precisely Lenin's contention that we cannot and never shall be able to say "what" matter is, because it is not a "what." The one crucial statement that can be made about it will be contained in the next set of Lenin statements, an absolutely crucial phrase of which Wetter most bemusingly omits, as we shall be pointing out in due course: an omission which rouses grave doubts in my mind as to whether Wetter has appreciated Lenin's point at all, or at least the clear implications concealed in Lenin's formulation.

In the set of remarks cited above, Lenin is saying that "matter" like "atoms" and "electrons" has traditionally been used unthinkingly by vulgar and mechanistic materialists in a way that betrays an intellectualist or epistemologically exclusivist bias, whatever the conscious intention of the speakers: matter has been held to be a something and therefore immutable. In effect, says Lenin, there are no immutable somethings whatsoever, matter least of all. The quasi-immutability stems from conceptualization and serves well the purposes of practical and theoretical science. I am here reminded of a remark I heard Einstein make in 1943 to the effect that he was always acutely embarrassed when some layman or nonspecialist asked him: "What is an electron?" For, said he, he felt compelled to reply that it was really simply a convenient shorthand term for an indescribably (quite literally indescribably or far too cumbersome to describe) complex process in reality. The undular-granular dualism of the photon causes scientists operating as scientists no great headaches but it may well cause the same scientists twinges of apprehension when they think as philosophizing human beings. The present critical state of the "subatomic jungle" of elementary particles seems to indicate that a breakthrough of major proportions will reveal that all are modalities or manifestations under different energy conditions of a more basic reality *of a different sort,* not merely different as genus from species, but different in the most radical possible sense, so different that virtually a new language will be required in order to speak of it. The theological implications will not escape Scholastic and Thomist readers if we say that Lenin is here pre-eminently describing matter in terms of what it *is not.* Substance and its whole stabilizing dimension "expresses only the degree of profundity of man's knowledge of objects" and the objects themselves are in process of perpetual change. The illusory impression of stability stems solely from the conceptualizing tendency of the human mind, and is an epistemological product. It is this very illusion of stability that evokes the crisis and panic sentiments when further penetration reveals to the mind the relativity of some of these concepts. Reality generally is more complex than man can imagine; ultimate reality is entirely dynamic and absolutely unconceptualizable. There is, however, one statement which can be made about this ultimate reality. It might seem that there are two but we shall be showing that they reduce to one.

C. The Ontological Dimension

Lenin's *ontological* statements, in this work, initially seem to perpetrate precisely the substantivizing fallacy he has been condemning. He insists:

In order to present the question in the only correct way, that is, from the dialectical materialist standpoint, we must ask: Do electrons, ether and so on exist as objective realities outside the human mind or not? The scientists will also have to answer this question unhesitatingly; and they do invariably answer it in the *affirmative,* just as they unhesitatingly recognize that nature existed prior to man and prior to organic matter. Thus, the question is decided in favor of materialism, for the concept matter . . . epistemologically implies *nothing but* objective reality existing independently of the human mind and reflected by it.[35]

Earlier, Lenin asserted:

For the sole "property" of matter with whose recognition philosophical materialism is bound up is the property of *being an objective reality,* of existing outside our mind.[36]

And after a few more quotations and observations, Lenin writes what I believe to be the crucial (and either most misunderstood or most uncomprehended) statements of the entire book:

The electron is as *inexhaustible* as the atom, nature is infinite, but it infinitely *exists.* And it is this sole categorical, this sole unconditional recognition of nature's *existence* outside the mind and perception of man that distinguishes dialectical materialism from relativist agnosticism and idealism.[37]

A little later, he recurs to this point:

The fundamental distinction between the materialist and the adherent of idealist philosophy consists in the fact that the sensation, perception, idea, and the mind of man generally, is regarded as an image of objective reality. The world is the movement of this objective reality reflected by our consciousness. To the movement of ideas, perceptions, etc., there corresponds the movement of matter outside me. The concept matter expresses nothing more than the objective reality which is given us in sensation.[38]

There are obviously two distinct statements here being articulated: the first is the straightforward realist declaration that there is a reality "out there," independent of the act and even of the being of the knower, a reality in no sense created by that act of knowing, nor owing its existence in any sense to the knower; the second is that there is one fact that can be known and articulated adequately by the human mind concerning this ultimate reality, *and that is that it exists.* Lenin's ultimate, philosophical matter, therefore is rather a "that" than a "what." Totally dynamic by its very nature (as every ultimate must be in an atheistic universe in order not to involve the author in hopeless contradictions and inertia difficulties), this reality can never be known as a "what" except with asymptotic approximation. But the human knower can assert validly and absolutely that it exists.

The first statement really reduces to the second and merely specifies it a little. The second is incomparably the more important. Indeed, in order to affirm "unconditionally" (i.e., as not conditioned in any way by the human knower) and "categorically" (i.e., as not dependent on any presence of the knower for its reality) the existence of this ultimate reality, Lenin *must* affirm it to exist independently of the human mind. The key affirmation is contained in the phrase "Nature is infinite, but it infinitely *exists.*" And it is highly significant that Wetter breaks off his quotation from Lenin on p. 288 of *Dialectical Materialism* after the word "infinite," omitting entirely the crucial next four words: "but it infinitely *exists.*"

Wetter's commentary here is also significant: he sees in this Lenin passage nothing but a tactical shift from scientific to philosophical concept of matter, dictated by the science crisis and of dubious value and cogency: "In this fashion Lenin fancied himself to have assured his philosophical materialism against all doubts arising from the further progress of the sciences: the discovery of subatomic particles even supposing that these again should turn out not to be the smallest ultimate constituents of matter—supposing, indeed, the possibility of probing further *ad infinitum*—all this would in no way signify that 'matter has disappeared.' " Such a commentary neglects entirely any real ontological value in Lenin's statement. It emerges simply as an accommodation. Wetter's entire attention is on the increasing comprehensiveness of the notion; he does not advert to the categorical statement: "it infinitely *exists*." I agree with Wetter that "Lenin attempted to revolve the crisis in philosophical materialism . . . by laying down a 'philosophical concept of matter' from a dialectical materialist point of view."[39] And I further agree with Wetter's contention that Lenin's definition could be taken to include even a spiritual being did not Lenin again convert "this realism into an unambiguous materialism, in that he confines the notion of 'reality' to that which affects our sense-organs."[40] But I think there is an element here that Wetter has not properly evaluated at all; and that is Lenin's dogged insistence on the priority of being over thought. The absolutely crucial element in Lenin's characterization of matter (his ultimate) is its extramental anterior *existence*. Is not Lenin here articulating in his conception of matter, the ultimate, far less a rigorously antispiritualist bias and far more an existentialist bias over against idealism of all ilks? Is Lenin's concern not that of protecting at all costs the anterior status of objective reality, the *datum,* the given, the existing-before-perceived, the nonmentally-constructed, the over-against-the-mind-existing-and-mind-affecting, the absolute priority of existence over thought? I believe Lenin's matter is far closer to the theist's God than Hegel's Absolute Idea could ever be. Hegelianism is vitiated from the outset by the priority it assigns to thought over being in the ontological order; Leninism is here *theizable* because it rigorously insists on the priority of being over thought and makes thought derivative of being. I do not for a moment contend that Lenin was a crypto-theist. But I do contend that dialogue can proceed between partners who admit priority of being over thought and then dispute on the nature of being; whereas I maintain that dialogue cannot proceed between partners who admit radical priority of thought over being and then dispute about the nature of that radically anterior thought. At least such dialogue will be sterile and above all entirely untheistic. Christians have misinterpreted John 1:1. "In the beginning was the Word" simply means that ultimate being is thinking being. It does not mean and Christians should not allow themselves to be driven, in pusillanimous terror of materialism, into asserting that it means that the Second Person of the Trinity is really the First!

Indeed it is to Lenin's "theological" utterance that we must now refer in order entirely to explicate the significance of his drastic and trenchant materialism.

D. Theological Implications

This theological statement reads as follows:

Human nature has discovered many amazing things in nature and will discover still more, and will thereby increase its power over nature. But this does not mean that nature is the creation *of our mind or of abstract mind, i.e. of Ward's God.*[41]

Lenin boggles at the notion of creation of the world by our mind *or by abstract mind,* God. This says volumes for the failure or perversion of theistic thought culminating in Hegel. The Hegelian idealism with its curious indifference to actual brute human external suffering (as a mere moment in the infinite) has made Lenin more than cautious, positively hypersensitive, to any introduction of a creation notion which would depress external reality to a mere mind-chimera. He is for the same reason (among others) adamantly opposed to any notion of *abstract mind* (the words are his own, as we have seen), as anterior cause which would merely extrapolate the idealist error to infinity.

That against which Lenin protests, at least in this passage, is a perversion of theist conceptions; but it is a perversion for which theists themselves are responsible. After asserting the total transcendence of God, they proceed to commit two odd and intermeshing errors: they exclude from God in horror any faintest trace of that reality they designate as "matter" and they tend to identify God far too restrictively with another reality accessible to the human being, namely thought. It is more consistent to speak of God as transcending both matter and consciousness and volition, but with matter corresponding in the order to creation more specifically to the First Person, consciousness to the Second, and volition to the Third. It is in the solid contribution of an absolute insistence on the priority of non-mental, premental reality over mental reality that Lenin's most salutary contribution to the theist is to be sought.

E. The Continuing Marxist Materialist Tradition

Stalin develops exactly the same "theological" or "atheological" bias, opposing the notion of God because he associates it with an undue depression of the reality of matter, an undue promotion of spirit conceived and articulated as thinking reality to an untenable position of hegemony. Says Stalin: "The world develops in accordance with the laws of movement of matter and stands in no need of a 'universal Spirit.' "[42] Immediately he appends an Engels quotation containing the phrase "without any foreign admixture." Stalin is protesting against the introduction of a "foreign" transcendent cause to explain the evolution of the universe. And his argument is curiously illuminating. Citing from Marx's criticism of Hegel for transforming the process of *human* thinking "Under the name of the 'Idea' . . . into an independent subject . . . the creator of the real world" and for making the real world into a mere "external phenomenal form of the 'Idea,' "[43] Stalin protests the imposition of thought as anterior to and constitutive of being: there is neither need nor justification for contending that the human mind radically creates (i.e., constitutes out of nothing) the world perceived by the human individual at any point of history; just as little need or justification can be found for positing Universal *Mind* as creator of the perceptible material world which is clearly existent anterior to human knowing of it. The protest against creationism is at bottom a protest against epistemologizing solipsism.

In our own day, the most active Marxist dialoguer with theists, Roger Garaudy, speaks of Marx's "essential discovery" as being that of "a new critical method which seeks outside thought itself the sources and conditions of thought."[44] Again there is this insistence that man is confronted with a reality that transcends him, at least in the sense of not being the mere creation of his own mind. Garaudy proceeds indeed to cite Marx to the effect that "Men make their own history, but they do not make it just as they please . . . under circumstances chosen by themselves."[45] And this assignment of the most radical priority and hegemony to being, existence, over thought, is articulated most drastically in these words: "There is no reflection without a reflected object, while it is perfectly possible for an object to exist without a mirror to reflect it."[46]

There is solid evidence then (of which we have cited only a minute portion by way of sample) that Lenin's insistence on the radical priority of ultimate reality (for him, matter) over thought has been maintained by Marxist-Leninists to this day. Theists seem to take fright at the Leninist notion because of its materialistic bias, totally neglecting its salutary realism and, above all, its anti-idealism, anti-mentalism. Wetter's critique is typical of this fearful and skittish approach, which we would wish to see overcome.

5. Critique of Wetter Critique of Marxist Materialism

The critique has three main points, with two of which we have already dealt in passing and which here need be mentioned only briefly, since they are secondary to and derivative from the main (and most inapposite) critique. The first is the contention that Lenin's philosophical concept of matter has nothing to say about matter as such. This presupposes that matter must be either nothing or an essence, a "what." But this in turn neglects a vitally important dimension of the reality picture as the theist, above all, should see it. This dimension is what might be called the ultimate dimension of created reality in its three reflections of uncreated reality: being, thinking, and willing. In each of these reflecting dimensions as we approach the ultimate level of creation, there is revealed by our empirical investigation and should be enthusiastically greeted by every theist an asymptotic but very real approach to essencelessness, to sheer act. The yen to essentialize all creation at every dimension, however deep, however generic, however close to the nexus with Creator, manifests one of two equally perverse inclinations: the tendency to put creation in its place by delimiting it radically at every level, by making it into a parcel of "whats" the more clearly to enucleate the divine transcendence; or else the abominable tendency to essentialize God himself. Most often this yen is motivated by both inclinations. In fact, the Leninist philosophical concept of matter does have something to say about matter, that it "infinitely *exists*." I enthusiastically agree with Wetter's contention concerning Lenin's divinizing of matter. But I fear Wetter's failure to observe this instance of that divinization stems from his own tendency, shared by so many theists, not to take this same statement really seriously as applied to God!

The second Wetter critique is that the Leninist philosophical concept of matter is "exceedingly broad." In the first place, this would surely be what one might expect of the concept which is supposed to articulate the ultimate. But there is here also the consideration that *in effect for Lenin this concept is a pseudo-concept.* Ultimate reality precisely resists all conceptualization.

It is Wetter's third critique which is the really basic one, and which provides the perfect bridge to my own conclusions about the Leninist faith in matter as salutary for all theists. This critique is expressed as follows:

"There is one final objection to be raised against the use made by Lenin and the Soviet philosophers of the philosophical concept of matter. If it implies matter to be that which exists independently of consciousness and acts upon our sense-organs, this independence and priority of matter in regard to consciousness can be understood in two different ways: firstly, as an *epistemological* priority, in that the material world is not created by the knowing consciousness (of man), but conditions the latter; secondly, however, as an *ontological* priority, in that the being of matter (Nature) presupposes no consciousness of any kind (such as an intelligent first cause outside it), but on the contrary, itself gives rise to consciousness out of its own being. Now both Lenin and the Leninists infer, from an intrinsically correct belief in the epistemological priority of matter, to its ontological priority, which constitutes an obvious misuse of the "philosophical concept of matter."[47]

This critique is a curious mixture of basically and generically correct conclusions and extremely dubious implicit links in the chain of reasoning, or indeed in the *forma mentis* of the critic. Wetter observed just a few pages previously that the realist claims of materialism are unjustly pushed to such an extreme that "Anyone who rejects idealism as a theory of knowledge is subpoenaed as a crown-witness for materialism, and arguments tending to prove the existence of a reality independent of the knowing subject are seized upon without further ado as arguments in favor of the materialist thesis as such, though this entails an assertion about the *nature* of objective reality, and does in fact proclaim it to be exclusively material."[48] This objection cuts both ways: the a priori dismissal of the realism of materialism for no other reason than that it is materialist can entail or manifest an attitude to ultimate reality which is just as biased in the other direction. And it is precisely this anthropomorphic bias I believe Leninist faith in matter can help to correct in the theist. Wetter speaks explicitly in his critique of an intelligent first cause outside matter. This seems to be the only alternative he admits to a Marxist mindless, will-less anterior terminal reality, matter-in-motion. Such an absolutely dichotomizing approach seems to me to concentrate too bewitchedly on the specificity of the fully developed Marxist ultimate in the context of the whole Marxist philosophy, and to pay far too little attention to the logical internal dynamic of the Leninist ultimate, as that ultimate is articulated in the passages we have cited. However crudely antispiritually the Marxist philosophy may develop when it thrusts into the realm of morality and sociology, its neat epistemologico-ontological underpinning remains not only realist but healthily corrective of idealist essentialization. For Marxism keeps stubbornly insisting on a primordial epistemological and ontological ultimate over against man, compelling man and demanding a creative response from man.

Christian theists should not be so horrified at the mindlessness and will-lessness of this primordial ultimate not to see the importance attaching to Marxism's insistence on the *existence* of that ultimate, not to realize that Marxists are uniquely bent, by their whole worldview to assert and be sensitive to the assertion of a real extramental ultimate within the space-time continuum. And this is drastically salvific for idealism-besotted theist thought. To put it crudely: intellect and will can be superimposed on stark primitive being recognized as a real ultimate; but if intellect and/or will be reified in the essentialist universe, being can by no means so easily, if at all, be sub-posited or slid in under them. Rather, we are much more likely to end with the Hegelian Absolute Idea or the Schopenhauerian Arbitrary Will.

Wetter's "intelligent first cause" is a kind of paradigm of the unsound ontologico-theological ambiguities, or downright mistakes, into which theists can so easily allow themselves to be driven by an overreaction to materialism. Such a phrase seems to indicate that the most proper and basic characteristic of the Creator is intelligence. This in turn leads to an expunging from the Creator, not only of any materiality (crude or most subtly refined), but even of the analogue and Prime Cause of matter in the dimension of the sheerly transcendent. God is converted into a sheer intelligence, planning creation in His theoretical intellect and then creating it by His practical intellect. Granting that all conversation about the sheerly transcendent must necessarily limp, this still seems to me to be deliberate and quite unnecessary hobbling of that conversation. The most serious consequence of this too exclusive and restrictive intellectualization and anthropomorphic spiritualization of God is the emergence of an insoluble and dangerous problematic concerning creation itself, both the act and the resulting reality.

The Marxists avoid any question of creation problematic by positing initially mindless will-less matter-in-motion as eternal. It is surely not unduly difficult (though quite extraneous to the present purpose) to indicate the insufficiencies of this ultimate as a vehicle of explanation of the evolution of the cosmos to our day. But the traditional theist approach, virtually down to our own day, seems to have attacked the Marxists on the wrong ground, because the theist attack has been mounted against the mindlessness and will-lessness of the Marxist ultimate in such a way as to imply that a mind and a will, even in the transcendent Creator, are the constitutive and basic characteristic; for the wrong reason, because the theist attack on matter-in-motion as an ultimate too readily lends itself to a crypto-idealist perversion and furthermore is attacking Marxist materialism precisely at the point at which it is strongest and sanest, namely, the point of its dogged insistence on the real independent existence of a nonmental reality.

6. Take Matter Seriously

It is an encouraging sign to observe such straws in the wind as the Conference at the University of Notre Dame (from September 5 to September 9, 1961) on "The Concept of Matter." This conference has been reported in great detail in an excellent publication of the University of Notre Dame Press.[49] It is not to our purpose here to enter into any of the vast number of detailed clarifications and controversies which this Conference brought forth. Suffice it to note that this sort of approach, "taking matter seriously" even as Whitehead advised theologians to take time seriously (a remark to which we shall be recurring in the next chapter), is more desirable than any premature and unjustified crowing over dematerialization in recent scientific developments.

A. The Dangers of Nothingness

The key difficulty encountered by theists who degrade matter is an odd one indeed: degraded matter revenges itself upon them, as it were, by assuming, with the inevitability of conceptual logic, a kind of reality that militates against the very total sovereignty of God which matter's degradation was supposed to ensure. For if matter be defined radically and restrictively as entirely alien to God, then the creation problem is drastically complicated. Creation becomes an event, not centered any longer circumscriptively within the dimension of being. A kind of (perhaps infinitely subtly conceived) cosmic dough or gossamer is introduced, into which God brings order and form, and thus makes beings. This has two drastic disadvantages: it sets up a kind of something, however amorphous, over against God, as a medium between the ineffably pure One and the manifold; it favours a kind of discrete, transcendental, direct action in the creation of individuals, bypassing any notion of an education out of previously supremely disposed matter. Even Teilhard, for all his consequential evolutionism, takes refuge in a kind of nothingness, at least, over against God, with which manifold the Creator "grapples." The nothingness to which Sartre gives such prominence must be utterly expunged from the theist (and even the atheist!) over-all world-view, as devoid of any consistency whatsoever, except in the formal conceptual order of the human mind. The act of creation must be explained (so far as any mystery can be) entirely within the dimension of being. Creation amounts, then, to an admittedly mysterious supreme pleromization of Spirit, with matter amounting simply to the dimensional parameter of this pleromized Spirit. Then begins the long march, which in due course will give rise to free, intelligent, conscious material beings. The pleromization, in the initial moment of creation, was incomparably more drastic than it is in today's highly convoluted and individualized cosmos. Yet, by an odd paradox, surely inescapable or at least understandable in the circumstances, the very drastic intensity of the pleromization of Spirit in the moment of creation entailed a drastic inhibition of individualization: and the earth was without form and void. If God, in His native habitat, transcends the present degree or level of pleromization incomparably in the direction of sheer, centered unity, the created universe in the first instant of creation transcended the present degree or level of pleromization incomparably in the direction of diversity and uncenteredness, trembling at the very edge of being, reduced to the absolute degree of lack of consistency it could reach without slipping into nonbeing. This means, more strictly, simply the ultimate degree of lack of centeredness it could reach: we have here attained to an absolute limit!

B. Creation as Pleromization

This clearly positions the creative act within the realm of being, admitting no faintest breath of nothingness into the picture. On this view, in this dispensation and dimension of creation that is the space-time-matter continuum, we do not have a drawing up of nonexistent essences into existence; rather, we have a radical and total pleromization of Spirit, i.e., an operation remaining entirely within the realm of being. It is an inanition, an emptying, a kenosis, in comparison with which the Incarnation is comparatively mild. But it is God, and God alone, who is operative. This pleromization in no sense whatever touches the sheer supercentered Being who *is* eternally. But it begins a cosmos (one of an infinite number, in all probability) which can evolve into a clamorous multitude sharing in the feast of being. And it signs the cosmos with the indelible and discoverable mark of God! Surely the Being who can be sheerly trinitarian, without violation of His serene immutability, can, in a supreme act of love, pleromize integrally his sheer act of being so that the many may eventually come to join the Three-in-One!

There is much talk in theist circles about the creation act as a kind of overflowing. This figure is unfortunate in the extreme, for it instantly conjures up the notion and even the picture of a non-God area *into* which the overflow spills. The notion of pleromization conjures up no such picture. It speaks, rather, of an act immanent in God, not as eternally triune, but certainly as being. Creation is firmly tethered to being. Matter is made to appear what I am persuaded it really is, a parameter of Spirit in the spatio-temporal continuum, at once productive of and subsisting in and as that dimension-complex that is the space-time continuum. Spirit is now not infinitely refined reality, defined by the appallingly privative term "immaterial." Rather, Spirit is the eternally unfettered, the eternally and radically free, the genuine instance of the Sartrean *pour-soi*. Spirit voluntarily pleromizes with the consequent materialization that this entails, pleromizing with an end in view, the gradual eduction out of this total pleromization of free created material beings to share in the act of sheer being.

C. Matter and God

Matter thus emerges in its authentically passive feminine role, vis-à-vis the actively masculine operation of the Creator God, in the basic cosmologico-sexual paradigm elaborated by Henry Miller. The deification of matter with which Marxist materialism is rightly charged should serve as a salutary corrective and warning to theists: with due deliberation and caution in the choice of expressions, a nexus must be articulated between matter and God.

The notion of matter dithyrambically described by Engels makes matter as such the explosively, immutably, and executively dynamic substrate of all change, indeed of all occurrence. It saddles matter with a burden that matter cannot bear.

Lenin's articulation, on the other hand, designates matter as a "that" rather than as a "what," articulates as the only statement

that can properly be made about matter the contention that "it infinitely exists." Within the Triune God himself, the approach to the
creation problematic I have suggested would lead back the strand of
creation—neither to a planning intellect nor yet to a deliberate will,
in the final analysis but, rather, to the sheer act of being itself. According to the biblical account, when God began to reveal himself
historically to His Chosen People, He taught them a First Name,
which might be rendered in English: "I am the being One." Later,
intellect (the Logos, the Incarnate Son) and will (the Holy Spirit)
are to come into their own in the revelation in time of this immense
God. But it is surely no accident that His First Name was "Being."
To this most intimate, ultimate, mysterious, and too often neglected
or uncomprehended Name of God, peculiar in a special way to the
First Person, there would correspond, in the order of inanition, that
reality which possesses (for creatures or creation, the *creatura* can
possess, in contradistinction to God, who is) neither actual intellect
nor actual will, but simply the most primordial Name of God, here
evoked in the dimension of creation as a constitutive parameter,
namely being. This absolute ultimate in the temporal order of creation would, throughout the entire dynamic of creation's history, ex-
hibit a strange dual face: relatively minimal stature and dignity, combined with derivative supreme dignity. Indeed the test of man's own
equilibrium of realistic humility would reside in his reaction to this
strange ultimate: he could either mistakenly deify it and thus fall into
the error of radical materialism; or he could excessively degrade it
and thereby fall into the equally hideous error of spiritualistic, antimaterialistic idealism. Moreover, the latter error would be more dangerous than the former: for matter, even matter-in-motion, cannot
indefinitely sustain this sort of worship from thinking man; whereas
man's own mind, thinking power, spiritual efficacy, is far more seductively able and inclined to arrogate to itself the worship due to God
alone.

I do not suggest that any of the considerations I have myself
articulated from a theistic point of view in this chapter were present
either consciously or subconsciously to Lenin or have been present to
any other Marxist. I do contend that there is a deeper meaning in the

historical moment of the emergence of Marxist materialism than has been generally admitted or comprehended by theists. Precisely because, at least to a great extent in reaction against Hegelian mentalism, they put their ultimate faith in matter, it has been given to Marxists to observe and articulate, albeit not always or perhaps indeed ever realizing the implication of their statements, certain vital truths about matter, above all the specific clues that matter, rightly understood and appreciated, can give us to God.

The most precious of these clues is that matter is an antipode (*not* the antithesis) of God. Of it as of Him, the only thing that can properly be articulated by unaided human thinking is "that it infinitely exists." And this, in the case of matter, in two senses: matter exists supremely, solidly, totally and integrally, for it is paradoxically so close to nonbeing that this existing is the only "operation" (used here in an analogical sense) it can perform (its very weakness is its strength; it is too starkly simple in the created order to admit of composition and the resulting fragility, and for this precise reason it is ultimately unconceptualizable); and, again, matter exists, in the created order, in the closest analogy possible to God's "way" of existing sheer and simple as himself. Plants and animals and mortal men are incomparably more complex and for that very reason more actually contingent, more subject to the terminal mortality Camus affirms as the most basic datum of human life. Matter, as human knowers encounter it, is so simple as to give palpable evidence that it comes straight from the creative act of God. Matter might even be described as creation sheer and simply ultimate. And there is a further mystery here at which I can only hint: this drastic and ultimate simplicity and passivity that is matter somehow accompanies and pervades the more complex subsequent stages of evolution up to and including man. Woe to man if, in the pride (legitimate within bounds but fatal if allowed to get out of bounds) of his higher development, he ever forgets this absolute root of his creatureliness! The key feature of that higher and more complex (but for that very reason more fragile) development is man's intellect, theoretical and practical, his intellect and his will. I cannot stress too strongly the importance of seeing Marxist materialism in context, as an immediate reaction to

Hegelian mentalism. I would now bluntly assert my own conviction that Marxist atheism is, on the one hand, the most consequential expression of shamanistic insistence on the autonomy of the space-time manifold; and, on the other hand, a most violent reaction against the essentializing mentalism of Hegelian idealism. Marxist insistence on the primordiality of matter is certainly not crypto-theism in any sense; but it does present a cast of mind, in the area of the science of being, ontology, which is more in tune with Christian theism's insistence on being as the most primordial act of God, the First Person of the Trinity, than is any Hegelian essentializing mentalism, or Schopenhauerian voluntarism.

7. The Importance of De-Epistemologization

Man is, notoriously, distinctively a knowing being. Therefore the temptation is very strong indeed to sickly o'er with the pale cast of thought the whole of reality, to make certain assumptions—or perhaps it would be more accurate to say to assume a certain posture—on the basis of which he is so limited, so confined, and so trammeled within the epistemological dimension as to be unable at all to come into direct contact with the most basic, the most primordial, the richest and most fruitful of all realities, Being himself. Being is neither a secondary attribute, power, or quality added to something more substantial than itself, nor yet a totality along the lines of a squamous amorphous generalized mass. Being is an act, pure Act, an action, a verbal reality.

The epistemologizing tendency of man throughout history has issued in all those forms of idealism which have trammeled man not only into not being open to verbal being, but further and more seriously have inclined man to equate being with intelligibility, rationality, or an idea. This trend reached its ultimate acme in Hegel. The radical Marxist materialist rebellion against this impermissible epistemologization of being issued in a drastic drive to take into account an element of human experience which is most difficult to conceptualize but equally irresistibly present to the human experiencer. Marxists located the ultimate reality in matter-in-motion, that brute datum, nonmental, eternal and implacable, devoid of all anterior consciousness. I am persuaded the Marxists were trying to express and assert a certain cast or hue or dimension of reality which they considered absolutely primordial, prior to thought entirely.

The supremely salvific influence of Marxist faith in matter is its salutary depression of man's faith in mind, which invariably turns out ultimately to be *his own mind*. For no other reality so effectively and fatally shuts man off from God as precisely his own intellect, theoretical and practical. Marxist faith in matter may appear at the end almost Stoic in its necessitarianism; but I believe this attitude can more easily be redeemed than the attitude of the proud mentalist. For Being as pulsating, ebullient, supremely powerful Act is neither a passive, quiescent, splayed out background from which beings emerge by some mysterious process of emanation; nor yet is Being a stable What, pinpointable in some empyrean, into meaningful relationship with which creation can be brought only by subtle mental gymnastic. Being permeates all that is. Being is He who is every way (*omnimodo*). But this does not mean that the pleroma, the many, the manifold, the restless temporal process, is an illusion. And both the ontological nexus between creation and Creator and the pledge of the real autonomy of the pleroma is provided more adequately by the notion of ultimate matter to which Marxists direct our attention than it is by any idealist elucubration.

Yet matter chosen as absolute ultimate seems to render genuinely atheistic hearts uneasy. Its apparent infinity and infinite divisibility pose a nameless threat to man's total autonomy and even to his yen for firm ground under his feet. Therefore a drastic reaction occurs, not merely and chronologically not primarily against Marxist materialism alone but against the very notion of the Infinite (mindless or suprarational) in favor of an ultimate finitude answering to man's own self-admitted and self-cognized finitude. This revolt in favor of finitude as ultimate has been notoriously powered in Western thought by Friedrich Nietzsche.

6

FAITH IN FINITUDE

Nietzsche is the prophet and proponent, in the final analysis and at the deepest level, neither of the Death of God nor of the Superman as God's successor, nor even of the Will to Power, but of *finitude*. No man has yet written more poignantly and incisively, more lovingly or more illuminatingly, of finitude than has this brilliant and sensitive German, who fought a running battle with madness for many years and succumbed in the end.

Of the monumental quality of Nietzsche's self-assigned task and the true dynamic of his search, Hollingdale has written a succinct and pithy articulation:

> It seems improbable that any man could have accomplished the task Nietzsche set himself, which was nothing less than a total reorientation of the European mind. The final effect of his life's work is one of failure. Yet it is a failure only by the impossible standard that Nietzsche himself set. . . . He inaugurated a search for naturalistic values to replace moral values based upon supernatural sanction, but he did not complete it: it is still going on and may well continue to go on for at least two or three centuries more. To regard Nietzsche's solutions as final and not provisional would be to trivialize the problem with which he grappled: not one man alone, but generations of men are required when the aim is to reverse the moral judgment of millennia.[1]

The fulcrum of Nietzsche's entire articulation of a new vision of reality which is to serve as the basis for his "transvaluation of all values" is precisely finitude. Much has been written on the Nietzsche problem and vast numbers of critical works have been devoted to his four basic notions: Death of God, Superman, Will to Power, and Eternal Recurrence. It is, of course, this last notion which encapsules and undergirds Nietzsche's defense of finitude. And although this

Eternal Recurrence notion has been treated from many angles, I believe it has not yet been systematically approached from the point of view of its relation to the Nietzschean faith in finitude.

James Collins has touched on the crucial nexus between Eternal Recurrence and finitude in the following remarks:

> Nietzsche charges that God has been made the great objection against existence and the destroyer of the innocence of becoming. Outside the courtroom, this means that his original hypothesis imprints the trait of self-sufficiency upon temporal existence and finite becoming. . . . The result was a substitutional situation in which Nietzsche willed passionately that the great ring of natural becoming should support all our meanings and values.[2]

We shall here devote ourselves to a systematic and detailed examination of Nietzsche's faith in finitude as revealed in the dynamic and the content of his own articulation of the notion of eternal recurrence.

Two prefatory considerations must precede our examination, in order that it shall emerge as a sympathetic and fruitful inspection of the ultimate object of faith of this tormented genius, precursor and predictor of our own modern age, who "by diagnosing the spiritual state of his own day . . . was able to prophesy that of ours."[3]

We must first note and evaluate the curiously ambivalent texture and status of the idea of Eternal Recurrence in Nietzsche's own thinking, as nearly as this can be sympathetically interpreted; and in the light of this, we must specify quite exactly what we shall be understanding throughout this chapter by the term "finitude."

1. Eternal Recurrence—Fact or Option?

The cumulative commentaries of four distinguished Nietzsche interpreters will best serve to center the problem of the curiously dual status of Eternal Recurrence in Nietzsche's thought. Crane Brinton writes a somewhat devastating evaluation of the origin of the notion in Nietzsche:

> Nietzsche's grand and much-prized conception of the "Eternal Recurrence"—which he considered absolutely unique, snatched from the pure air of the Engadine—has much in common with notions prevalent in

Eastern philosophy and theology, in Stoicism, and even in modern mathematical speculation. Yet we cannot say absolutely that he took it from any of these sources. He read much, if rather desultorily, in translations of and commentaries on Indian and Persian philosophy. The name, at least, of Zarathustra he proudly borrowed from the East. Greek philosophy he knew very well indeed. Of modern mathematics he knew very little. It seems likely, then, that he built the Eternal Recurrence out of confused memories of his reading, fused together in the ecstasy of poetic composition. . . . Nietzsche's concept of the Eternal Recurrence is an unrefined mixture of oriental speculation on metempsychosis, old European striving for a metaphysical absolute, and misunderstood theoretical physics of the late nineteenth century. . . . Abandon, as we must, any system of theism, of belief in a creator, and we have only this endless and almost unbearable Becoming.[4]

Otto Manthey-Zorn says of Eternal Recurrence in Nietzsche:

. . . the idea reveals itself frankly as a regulative principle which he needs for the basis of his teaching, if, as he insisted that it must, his teaching is to function independently of an arbitrarily creating and directing God; if life is to explain itself or man is to accept it as he must, and thereby have the opportunity to make it the more truly itself by sublimating that which he is. The idea also, so he believes, protects him against a mechanistic interpretation of life in which nature itself merely substitutes for God.[5]

Hollingdale comments:

The objections to this theory as it stands are no doubt many, but they are unimportant from our point of view, because it is doubtful whether Nietzsche ever seriously considered them. What interested him was the consequence that would follow *if* such a belief were true, or were thought true. (Nietzsche, however, was convinced that it *was* true.)[6]

And Collins notes:

Nietzsche's positive doctrines of the superman and the eternal recurrence of the same events were his deliberate substitutes for theism. His aim was to make a godless existence endurable and meaningful, through an artistic overevaluation or "poetic lie" about the temporal world, and thus to divert the human tendency to transcend nature. In his myth about temporal becoming, there can be gods or particular manifestations of the will-to-power but no transcendent God; there can be a sempiternal cycle of recurring events but no distinctive eternal existent.[7]

All four commentators, of course, stress the substitutional character of Eternal Recurrence in Nietzsche's vision of reality. Eternal Recurrence is the necessary alternative to a Creator-God. But all four stress equally strongly the fact that the Eternal Recurrence and all that it implies represent in some sense an *option* on Nietzsche's part: "Abandon as we must . . . theism . . . and we have only this" (Brinton); ". . . a regulative principle which he needs for the basis of his teaching" (Manthey-Zorn); ". . . the consequence that would follow *if* such a belief were true or were thought true" (Hollingdale); ". . . deliberate substitutes for theism . . . an artistic overevaluation or 'poetic lie' about the temporal world . . . to divert the human tendency to transcend nature" (Collins).

This quality of option, not only in the Eternal Recurrence notion, but in the entire thrust of Nietzschean philosophizing, is of paramount concern to us here, in the interests of a sympathetic understanding of the heart of the Nietzschean atheistic revolt. That heart lies in the fact that Nietzsche's was a spiritualist, as opposed to a materialist, revolt against God. The materialist revolt may have many psychological and moral overtones; but its core, like its ultimate, as we have seen in the preceding chapter, lies, rather, in the epistemologico-ontological dimension. The materialist simply maintains that matter-in-motion suffices and that there is no need for or proof of any further assumption. The spiritualist rebel goes much further. His revolt is basically psychological and pre-eminently personal-moral. Not only need this God not exist: He *must* not exist. What God? The God conceived and purveyed as the existent Eternal Infinite.

The same optional dimension is present in the whole exposition of the Death of God (anterior corollary to Eternal Recurrence):

God is dead! God remains dead! And we have killed him![8] . . .
It is now no longer our reason but our taste that decides against Christianity.[9]

We should, however, advert to Hollingdale's important parenthesis, informing us that Nietzsche himself believed Eternal Recurrence to be true. This gives us a key to an interpretation of the ambivalent texture and status of the Eternal Recurrence notion in

Nietzsche: Nietzsche is himself and pre-eminently represents a whole subspecies of the human race, the primordially practical, the anti-theoretical, the men who are not willing, not concerned to sit in passive contemplation, who elect rather to create truths and values themselves. In our age, the age Nietzsche foresaw and perhaps substantially helped to form with his own dicta, the age of mass communications and mass propaganda, the age of a rewriting of history so drastic as to create indeed, in some sense, a really new truth (if only in the sense that the misinterpretations engendered by the misstatements themselves become at least facts of history), it is certainly unwise to belittle or ridicule the executive-creative power of the human will. Nietzsche, the poet, looks at reality with a gaze that is simultaneously contemplative and active. He sees that reality is grounded in and shades off into mystery, the challenging penumbra of our momentary sense impressions and experiences; and, rejecting trenchantly one description or deciphering of the message, he excogitates another and presents it as a battle slogan: So it *must* be! So it *shall* be, for Dr. Friedrich Nietzsche will have it so!

It is thus that Nietzsche's fanatical faith in finitude must be understood, if we are to understand at all his intention and his significance, his self-appointed task and the cause of his tragedy. It is otiose and pointless to criticize the fairly obvious inadequacies of his vision, for that vision is not intended to be an exhaustive scientific articulation for theoretical consumption but, rather, a highly and nervously practical slogan for executive endeavor. Before we examine the dynamic and content of Nietzsche's vision of Eternal Recurrence, we must endeavor to pinpoint our understanding of *finitude* in this context and its relevance to Eternal Recurrence.

2. Finitude—Fulcrum of Finite Freedom

Our first clue comes from Hollingdale:

Nietzsche is seeking to minimize the importance of *ends*, of *purposes*, and of *actions* and maximize the importance of *states of being*. If everything is eternally repeated, then there is no purpose or end in existence, and all who look for one are doomed to everlasting disappointment. The concept of purpose becomes meaningless. But the opposite concept is invested with infinite meaning: not what I *do*—my purpose—but what I *am*—my state of being—is what counts for me. It is as if one were on an unending sea journey. The destination is immaterial, since it is never reached; but whether one is seasick for much of the time is very material: it is really all that matters. Every moment is repeated infinitely; therefore every moment is of infinite significance—and no one moment can be more significant than another. It is the supreme repudiation of the "historical" outlook—in which it does not matter whether one is prostrate the whole of the journey, because reaching the destination is what counts. . . . if "God is dead," then the end of humanity lies within itself. There is no "beyond," there is only a "here and now"; therefore this "here and now" must be endowed with the greatest possible significance. By this chain of reasoning Nietzsche is led away from purpose and to state of being as the meaning of life: to the doctrine that every moment is an eternity, and every individual must become a God.[10]

This points up a consideration of crucial importance for a proper understanding of Nietzsche: Eternal Recurrence is relevant, in the final analysis, to individual human beings more than to the more generic and amorphous course of nature. If you insist on starting from the phenomenological continuum, restrictively all-embracing so far as human beings are concerned—and Nietzsche does so start, in that strange and indissoluble mixture of description and option—you will inevitably, by the very internal dynamic of the human knower, be pushed as knower, thinker, and speculator to the innermost nucleus of that continuum, *the present moment*. This I-as-*I*-am-here-and-now-as-creature answers to God-as-He-is-in-His-eternal-Now as abyss answers to abyss, as one extreme to another. The creature in the event-moment has a kind of supreme analogy to God, because this creature is, in a certain deep sense, once again, like matter, the exact and extreme antipode of God.

We shall later be seeing the clumsy and almost impishly inconsistent articulation of the consequences of finitization of the ultimate in the realm of cosmology. But far more important, from Nietzsche's position, is the extreme and drastic finitization of the ultimate in terms of consciousness and executive willing. What does the Superman really want? Certainly not mere physical enjoyment (one finds in Nietzsche that super-Puritanical antisexuality and even antialcohol-

ism so typical of the Extreme Rightist), definitely not simply the
sadistic pleasure deriving from his exercise of power over his infe-
riors; not even the delights of noble fame. Basically he wants *more
Being*. And this more-being wish is a power-drive, pushing the finite
individual into a virtually hysterical but exhilarating fight and perpetual battering against the limits of his own finitude. Brinton is
waspish here again, but he articulates crisply the crucial point of
Nietzsche's ethic, an ethic which can only be properly interpreted
poetically, since it is a poetic vision in the first place: "We must
struggle to attain the pure heights on which alone so stark a doctrine
as that of the Eternal Recurrence can be endured. We must put off
softness and take on hardness. We must give up the little hopes and
cherish the great hope of hopelessness."[11]

The sea-voyage metaphor utilized above by Hollingdale permeates
the whole of *The Joyful Wisdom*. One brief section is supremely
relevant to our present purpose:

> In fact, we philosophers and "free spirits" feel ourselves irradiated as by
> a new dawn by the report that the "old God is dead"; our hearts overflow
> with gratitude, astonishment, presentiment and expectation. At last the
> horizon seems open once more, granting even that it is not bright; our
> ships can at last put out to sea in face of every danger; every hazard is
> again permitted to the discerner; the sea, *our* sea, again lies open before
> us; perhaps never before did such an "open sea" exist.[12]

Finitude, in the Nietzschean context, must not, on pain of distortion and misunderstanding, be conceived in an exclusively or primarily mathematical or cosmologico-material sense. It must be interpolated into the ontological dimension and framework. It is in this
sense that the eternally recurring Superman answers to the Eternally
Present God as abyss to abyss; it is in this sense that finitude is, like
matter-in-motion, such an antipode to God as to reveal, at another
level and in another dimension, one of his basic characteristics.

The cosmological conundrum, which we shall be treating in due
course, is but a pale analogy of the ontological conundrum: finite will
issuing from finite being is doing nothing less than to attempt to
batter against its own finitude, that finitude which is at once its greatest torment and the only protection of its total autonomy. Grant for

an instant the Infinite and Infinitely Present Being with His Infinite Will (i.e., executive power), and, for Nietzsche, the finite will, manifestation of finite being, is immediately and unavoidably reduced to the status of puppet or slave. For God as Infinitely Present Infinite Will is, for Nietzsche, precisely the "spider deity" of Collins' description; and Collins is unerringly right in his conclusion: "A realistic theism can only add that the death of such a notion of God is well deserved and can serve to clarify what the living God does not mean . . . and to bring out clearly one way of distinguishing God from the world which a historically enlightened theism cannot support."[13]

But it is the other side of this coin of Nietzschean faith in finitude that we would here examine. The brilliant, terrifying, and exhilarating probing into and articulation of the full meaning and implications of finitude conceived as an ultimate—that is what interests us here.

The infinite matter-in-motion of the Marxists would be as intolerable to Nietzsche as the Infinitely Present Infinite Will of God of the theist. Each would trammel, though in antithetical ways, the supreme freedom of the conscious human existent, whose glory is his shame, whose tormenting challenge of finitude is his only guarantee of hegemony. Nietzsche is perfectly legitimately considered the founder of existentialism in the most drastic and deepest sense: for he has confused existence with being, *existentia* with *esse,* or more accurately has promoted existence—that most tenuous and megalomaniac of all human concepts, signifying legitimately only the technique whereby, in a mystery surpassing human understanding, Perfect Being enables finite creatures to share in his Infinite Act of Being—to the status of ultimate being, than which there is and *shall be* no greater. But in so doing, Nietzsche teaches theists more than the merely negative truth that the true and ultimate freedom of individual conscious created being cannot be assured in the absence of the Infinitely Present Infinite Will of the Creator. He teaches the theist also the positive wisdom of the necessity of taking finitude seriously.

In Nietzschean terms this means that if *existentia,* the act of finite existence, would elevate itself to the status of the ultimate reality, then the only issue can be endless recurrence, endless *repetition.* Infinite, unbounded Will has the capacity for infinite newness of executive decision, even as infinite being has the capacity for infinite newness of existence. But he who would at all costs avoid Being, with His power of Unbounded Newness, will have to put up with and reconcile himself to the repetition that is bound to occur when the finite exhausts its power.

3. Dynamic of the Eternal Recurrence Notion in Nietzsche

We are now ready to trace the dynamic and content of the Eternal Recurrence notion through the three Nietzschean works in which it bulks largest. The dynamic of the development of the notion is as important as its progressively articulated content. For Nietzsche is clearly himself and in his created characters terrified of the idea. If I were asked to put a finger on the one most trenchant and most important contribution of Friedrich Nietzsche to modern thought and modern man, I would unhesitatingly identify it as the furious and impassioned protest against the trivialization of finitude.

In the separate treatise, specifically dedicated to the Eternal Recurrence, a treatise intended as an introduction to *The Joyful Wisdom* but not printed with that work and only published among the Posthumous Works, Nietzsche appends to a somewhat cumbrous and even ludicrous pseudo-scientific explication of the doctrine of Eternal Recurrence a highly poetic conclusion, in which he speaks of the fact that the Superman of the future will finally attain to a genuinely fearless insight into and acceptance of Eternal Recurrence "somewhere between golden ice and a pure heaven."[14] This treatise in fact we shall consider as the initial stage of the development and articulation of Nietzsche's notion of the Eternal Recurrence.

The second work, in this dynamic, is *The Joyful Wisdom,* published in June, 1882. The third is Nietzsche's best-known work, *Thus Spake Zarathustra,* the chronology of whose composition is more important to us than the chronology of the publication: Part I was written in the brief space of ten days, in February, 1883; Part II was written in the same length of time, in the last days of June and the first days of July, 1883; Part III was written in Nice in January, 1884; Part IV was written in the autumn and winter of 1884-1885. It should further be noted that *The Joyful Wisdom* as published in 1882 contained only four books. The fifth was added in the 1886 edition, and we shall therefore consider it as representing chronologically the latest stage in Nietzsche's articulation of Eternal Recurrence.

A. Pseudo-Scientific Prologue

The first stage, the highly dubious pseudo-scientific essay, need not detain us long; nor would it be rewarding to enter into much detail on its thoroughly unacceptable scientific reasoning. But there are some vital hints about finitude in this mishmash of undigested physics:

> The world of energy suffers no diminution, otherwise in eternal time it would have weakened and disappeared. The world of energy suffers no point of rest, otherwise that point would have been reached and the clock of life would be standing still. The world of energy never comes into balance, it never has a moment of rest, its force and movement are the same for every period of time. Whatever condition this world can attain, it must have attained, and not once, but an infinite number of times.[15]

Our interest here is exclusively in the ontological, not the strictly cosmological dimension. But one clarification must be made forthwith. There is no creation-moment or creation-parameter or creation-element in Nietzsche; therefore the time of which he speaks is in no sense a creation and certainly least of all in any sense a scaffolding or roadway or riverbed along which energy-matter flows. Time is internal to that matter-energy continuum with which Nietzsche begins; and in a certain very real sense created by it. Thus it is less than accurate to speak, in Nietzsche, of infinite time, and totally mistaken and false to speak of eternity as positive timelessness. What we have is, rather, indefinite time, a creation of the unending interplay of finite energy and finite matter. The finitude must be protected at all costs in order to guarantee against the autonomy-destructive incursion of any would-be autocrat, whether infinite matter-in-motion or the Creator God. And the price that must be paid is crystal clear. The time-creating motion possible to finite energy playing upon finite matter must be circular or cyclic. This truth comes out in the uncanny poetic symbol Nietzsche uses in this same section of his treatise on the Eternal Recurrence:

Your whole life will always be turned over like an hourglass and will run out again and again—with one great moment in between, until all conditions from which you arose will come together again in the cyclic motion of the world.[16]

The hourglass, by its very physical shape, recalls and evokes the purely mathematical symbol of infinity. Its perpetual inversion indicates poetically the only fashion in which finitude can function in the long view. Nietzsche proceeds indeed to specify this with almost incredible blatancy:

. . . and then you will find again every pain, every joy, every friend and enemy, and every hope and error, and every blade of grass and ray of light, the whole interrelationship of all things. This ring, of which you are a particle, will shine forth again and again.[17]

Nietzsche will tolerate no comforting compromise. Imperiously he demands that man shall face the stark fact of finitude and its implications. The very finitude that guarantees man that total autonomy and radical freedom from the specter of "supernatural" intervention involves an acceptance of repetition. Finitude accepted as ultimate can indeed guarantee finite man that the ultimate texture of reality is no more powerful than himself; but the finite ultimate necessarily produces and entails Eternal Recurrence rather than eternal and infinite dynamism.

Well does Ernst Bertram say: "We experience all eternity *only* in the form of the Dionysian moment; we say Yes to all eternity only in the Yes to the justifying, to the fateful moment of the Faustian verse[18]—that is the radical conclusion drawn by Nietzsche's eternity-craving will . . . the boldest elevation of his Socratic individualism into Platonic metaphysic. The platonist in him welds the golden moment to Zarathustra's nuptial ring of rings, the Ring of the Return."[19] Finitude is nowhere more perfectly epitomized than in the transience and evanescence of the moment. And Nietzsche's faith in finitude as ultimate reality is expressed in his contention that each "golden moment" calls to the ultimate "Ring of the Return" as abyss to abyss.

B. Nihilistic Articulation

In *The Joyful Wisdom,* the progressive clarification of the notion of Eternal Recurrence assumes the aspects of a fugue. It is a poetic enucleation and we cannot expect scientific precision or consistency of sequence. It is a counterpoint of terror and exhilaration, of rebellion against order and acceptance of necessity, of exaltation of the strong individual and his ultimate confrontation with the supreme horror of Eternal Recurrence. We may usefully note these stages:

i. A fragmentary staccato announcement in negative terms:

> The general character of the world . . . is to all eternity chaos; not by the absence of necessity, but in the sense of the absence of order, structure, form, beauty, wisdom, and whatever else our aesthetic humanities are called. . . . Let us be on our guard against saying that there are laws in nature. There are only necessities: there is no one who commands, no one who obeys, no one who transgresses. . . . Let us be on our guard against thinking that the world eternally creates the new. There are no eternally enduring substances; matter is just another such error as the God of the Eleatics. But when shall we be at an end with our foresight and precaution! When will all these shadows of God cease to obscure us? When shall we have nature entirely undeified! When shall we be permitted to *naturalise* ourselves by means of the pure, newly discovered, newly redeemed nature?[20]

Laws must be avoided because they presume a lawgiver. Even order and design must be avoided because they imply a designer. Indeed even eternally enduring substances must be renounced in this ruthless march to genuine nihilism.

ii. A preliminary affirmation:

> *Amor fati:* let that henceforth be my love! . . . *Looking aside,* let that be my sole negation! And all in all, to sum up: I wish to be at any time hereafter only a yea-sayer![21]

This *amor fati* is the willing and exhilarated acceptance of the un-God behind the gods; having abolished by an act of intellectual negation all those principles (pre-eminently the Personal Deity) that might give meaning and design to reality, Nietzsche is left with the ineluctable conclusion that any meaning that is to be imposed must come from the truly unfettered, unshackled, but also orphaned and evanescent will of man, or more accurately of the Superman.

iii. The forthright but extremely poetic enunciation of the principle:

What if a demon crept after thee into thy loneliest loneliness some day or night, and said to thee: "This life, as thou livest it at present, and hast lived it, thou must live it once more, and also innumerable times; and there will be nothing new in it, but every pain and every joy and every thought and every sigh, and all the unspeakably small and great in thy life must come to thee again, and all in the same series and sequence—and similarly this spider and this moonlight among the trees, and similarly this moment, and I myself. The eternal sandglass of existence will ever be turned once more, and thou with it, thou speck of dust!"—Wouldst thou not throw thyself down and gnash thy teeth, and curse the demon that so spake? Or hast thou once experienced a tremendous moment in which thou wouldst answer him: "Thou art a God, and never did I hear anything so divine!" If that thought acquired power over thee as thou art, it would transform thee, and perhaps crush thee; the question with regard to all and everything: "Dost thou want this once more, and also for innumerable times?" would lie as the heaviest burden upon thy activity! Or, how wouldst thou have to become favourably inclined to thyself and to life, so as *to long for nothing more ardently* than for this last eternal sanctioning and sealing?[22]

This astonishing prose poem will occasion perplexity only to those who persistently refuse to recognize in Nietzsche the poet. The ultimate question being asked by the demon is not: Will you agree theoretically to the objective truth of Eternal Recurrence? but rather: Will you accept *practically* this notion? Nay further: Do you positively want, will it? Can you say Yes to it without reservation, and make it the very fulcrum of your practical action? The finite in its highest form, incipient Superman, is being tested in heart and reins as to his own acceptance of and willingness to place his faith in his own finitude. "This last eternal sanctioning and sealing" is nothing else than the most fateful decision of an age, of our age, the decision to face a universe radically and totally deprived, by an act of human will, of any ultimate executive power except man's finite will and finite being, recognized as finite and recognized as ultimate.

Theists all too often commit two reprehensible errors and injustices: out of false and laggard reverence for God and his power, they lightly overleap the finitude of man, a genuine ultimate in its own order; and they trivialize the courage of the radical spiritualist atheist, of whom Nietzsche is the prototype, who faces with sober courage the world in which he is an utter orphan, the world in which, while implacably and trenchantly admitting and proclaiming his own finitude and the finitude of the ultimate texture of reality, he yet rises to the challenge and strives to wrest meaning from, or impose meaning upon, this chaos.

Indeed the very next section of *The Joyful Wisdom,* the mysterious and pregnant last section of Book IV, the final book of the original manuscript, the section bearing the ominous title *Incipit tragoedia,* articulates this courage and introduces the hero of the next work we shall examine. Not only does it introduce Zarathustra, it sketches the entire cycle that is Zarathustra: initial rejection

> When Zarathustra was thirty years old, he left his home and the Lake of Urmi, and went into the mountains;

lofty and theoretical contemplation:

> There he enjoyed his spirit and his solitude, and for ten years did not weary of it;

the crucial change of heart:

> But at last his heart changed,—and rising one morning with the rosy dawn, he went before the sun and spake thus to it: ". . . Like thee must I *go down,* as men say, to whom I shall descend. . . . Lo! This cup is again going to empty itself, and Zarathustra is again going to be a man." Thus began Zarathustra's down-going.[23]

The last word, *Niedergang,* has always been a *crux interpretum:* there is at least a three-way play on the word: setting of the sun; physical descent from the mountain; and the overtone of perishing, fall, collapse, sinking. In short, Zarathustra, who has absorbed from the sun, his "God," the highest wisdom, knows that this wisdom ineluctably implies a rhythmic cycle of rising and falling, the supreme tragedy of finitude, with which he has made his peace, nay more, to which he has given his enthusiastic allegiance.

C. Nightmare Affirmation

In *Thus Spake Zarathustra*, the idea of Eternal Recurrence is introduced as an almost nightmare-vision for Zarathustra, growing out of the ideas of the Superman and the Will–to–Power, whose ultimate undergirding it has always been. Toward the end of Part II, in the section "The Prophet," Zarathustra has a nightmare about Eternal Recurrence, and in the last section, "The Stillest Hour," he has a second nightmare. The sailors told him his *alter ego* had been crying: "It is time! It is high time!"; and now his "stillest hour" mercilessly repeats:

Then, voicelessly, something said to me: *You know, Zarathustra?"*
And I cried out for terror at this whisper, and the blood drained from my face; but I kept silent.
Then again, something said to me voicelessly: "You know, Zarathustra, but you do not speak!"
And I answered at last defiantly: "Yes, I know, but I will not speak!"
Then again, something said to me voicelessly: "You *will* not, Zarathustra: Is this true? Do not hide yourself in your defiance!"[24]

At the beginning of Part III comes the poetic articulation of the doctrine itself:

"Behold this gateway, dwarf" I went on: "it has two aspects. Two paths come together here: no one has ever reached their end.
"This long lane behind us: it goes on for an eternity. And that long lane ahead of us—that is another eternity.
"They are in opposition to one another, these paths; they abut on one another; and it is here at this gateway that they come together. The name of the gateway is written above it: 'Moment.'
"But if one were to follow them further and ever further and further; do you think, dwarf, that these paths would be in eternal opposition?"
"Everything straight lies," murmured the dwarf disdainfully. "All truth is crooked, time itself is a circle." . . .
"Behold this moment!" I went on. "From this gateway Moment, a long, eternal lane runs *back:* an eternity lies behind us.
"Must not all things that *can* run have already run along this lane. Must not all things that *can* happen *have* already happened, been done, run past:
"And if all things have been here before: what do you think of this moment, dwarf? Must not this gateway, too, have been here—before?

"And are not all things bound fast together in such a way that this moment draws after it all future things? *Therefore*—draws itself too?

"For all things that *can* run *must* also run once again forward along this long lane.

"And this slow spider that creeps along in the moonlight, and this moonlight itself, and I and you at this gateway whispering together, whispering of eternal things—must we not all have been here before?

"—and must we not return and run down that other lane out before us, down that long, terrible lane—must we not return eternally?"

"Thus I spoke, and I spoke more and more softly: for I was afraid of my own thoughts and reservations.[25]

Immediately thereafter, Zarathustra hears a dog howl, follows the sound, and finds a shepherd writhing on the ground, with a heavy black snake hanging out of his mouth. Zarathustra himself tries to tug the snake loose from the shepherd's throat, but to no avail.

Then a voice cried from me: "Bite! Bite! Its head off! Bite!"—thus a voice cried from me, my horror, my hate, my disgust, my pity, all my good and evil cried out of me with a single cry.[26]

The shepherd bites the snake loose and spits its head far away. He springs up, laughing, the truly transformed Superman.

Eternal Recurrence has been accepted; as Hollingdale succinctly sums up: "the shepherd is a vision of himself wrestling with and overcoming the repugnance he feels towards his own theory."[27]

Toward the end of Part III, the animals echo and develop further the Eternal Recurrence theme:

"O Zarathustra," said the animals then, "all things themselves dance for such as think as we: they come and offer their hand and laugh and flee—and return.

"Everything goes, everything returns; the wheel of existence rolls for ever.

Everything dies, everything blossoms anew; the year of existence runs on for ever.

"Everything breaks, everything is joined anew; the same house of existence builds itself for ever. Everything departs, everything meets again; the ring of existence is true to itself for ever.

"Existence begins in every instant; the ball There rolls around every Here. The middle is everywhere. The path of eternity is crooked."[28]

This outburst of the animals contains two of the most important explications of Eternal Recurrence: "The same house of existence builds itself for ever" and "The middle is everywhere."

The first phrase banishes all thought of emergent evolution, which Nietzsche would consider but another of the childish Fool's Paradises built by cowardly men to replace the God they have killed. It is not the *house* of existence which builds itself forever; it is the *same house* of existence which builds itself forever.

The second phrase, "The middle is everywhere," explicates the Faustian reference to the moment, that reference that is well-nigh an incantation. The middle, the mid-point, the fulcrum, which Nietzsche likes in another context to call "the noon hour," is precisely "every instant" in which "existence begins." The instant, the moment, paradigm of finitude, has by an act of utterly autonomous finite will been raised, by God-destroying man, to the level of ultimate reality. For ultimate reality in a universe of Eternal Recurrence is that single moment of willing activity which incorporates individual conscious man into the great dance of Eternal Recurrence.

That Nietzsche is implacably trenchant in forcing himself and his readers to face the full implications of this choice emerges clearly a few lines later:

"The man of whom you are weary, the little man, recurs eternally" —thus my sadness yawned and dragged its feet and could not fall asleep. . . .

"Alas, man recurs eternally: The little man recurs eternally!

"I had seen them both naked, the greatest man and the smallest man: all too similar to one another, even the greatest all too human!

"The greatest all too small!—that was my disgust at man! And eternal recurrence even for the smallest! that was my disgust at all existence!

"Ah, disgust! Disgust! Disgust!" Thus spoke Zarathustra and sighed and shuddered; for he remembered his sickness.[29]

A superficial reading of the immediately subsequent sections of *Thus Spake Zarathustra* might lead the unwary reader to suppose that precisely at this point Nietzsche effects that noble but pathological act of will which sets Superman over against these little men and gives a kind of maniac hope that the dark side of Eternal Recurrence can be overcome. Indeed Nietzsche does summon the Superman to conquer the herd's littleness, stupidity, and cowardice. But "The Intoxicated Song," which closes Nietzsche's articulation of Eternal Recurrence in *Thus Spake Zarathustra,* gives the lie to such facile interpretations. This broken, staccato section, full of strange metaphors, pictures and fragmented cries, may indeed indicate and have been a product of a human mind not far from madness. But there is a very closely knit logic in the development of this song and it gives us the final clue to Nietzsche's over-all doctrine of Eternal Recurrence: the Higher Men, the Supermen, are commanded to sing Zarathustra's Roundelay:

> O Man! Attend.
> What does deep midnight's voice contend?
> "I slept my sleep,
> And now awake at dreaming's end:
> The world is deep,
> Deeper than day can comprehend.
> Deep is its woe,
> Joy—deeper than heart's agony:
> Woe says: Fade! Go!"
> But all joy wants eternity
> Wants deep, deep, deep eternity![30]

Nietzsche's own poetic gloss of the crucial last three lines reveals the secret:

Did you ever say Yes to one joy? O my friends, then you said Yes to *all* woe as well. All things are chained and entwined together, all things are in love;

if ever you wanted one moment twice, if ever you said: "You please me, happiness, instant, moment!" then you wanted *everything* to return!

you wanted everything anew, everything eternal, everything chained, entwined together, everything in love, O that is how you *loved* the world, you everlasting men, loved it eternally and for all time; and you say even to woe: "Go, but return!" *For all joy wants—eternity!*

All joy wants the eternity of all things, wants honey, wants dregs, wants intoxicated midnight, wants graves, wants the consolation of graveside tears, wants gilded sunsets, *what* does joy not want! it is thirstier, warmer, hungrier, more fearful, more secret than all woe, it wants *itself:* it bites into *itself,* the will of the ring wrestles within it.

it wants love, it wants hatred, it is superabundant, it gives, throws away, begs for someone to take it, thanks him who takes, it would like to be hated; so rich is joy that it thirsts for woe, for Hell, for hatred, for shame, for the lame, for the *world*—for it knows, oh it knows this world!

You Higher Men, joy longs for you, joy the intractable, blissful—for your woe, you ill-constituted! All eternal joy longs for the ill-constituted.

For all joy wants itself, therefore it also wants heart's agony! O happiness! O pain!

Oh break, heart! You Higher men, learn this, learn that joy wants eternity,

joy wants the eternity of all things, *wants deep, deep, deep eternity!*[31]

The finitude in which Nietzsche puts his faith has revealed its ultimate face; its end is its beginning. He who begins from the bewitching moment wherein, and wherein alone, resides the unassailable total autonomy he craves must face the fact that, if his vision be true, everything is given once and for all, and everything is finite. The noblest and most powerful, the most robust and most exhilarating that this finite, this finitude can produce is at every instant, in the great ring, inextricably linked with the smallest, the most petty, the most painful, the most horrible. We are standing at the antipodes, at the level of willing, of the Eternally Present Willing of the eternal God. That true, eternal, infinite Will can indeed "make all things new," can indeed promise finite man an unending fountain of ever new delights, but at a price Nietzsche is not willing to pay (perhaps, indeed, feels that there is no point in paying, since there is no God there). The ambivalence persists to the end but it does not really matter what Nietzsche himself believed, for his contribution is in the dimension of willing, not of understanding. At the ultimate goal of his ruthless search he is faced with a mystery, even as the theist is faced with a Mystery. To the Mystery of the Infinitely Present Eternal Will, the finite human will epitomized in the instant answers as abyss to abyss. The only medicine for this mortality, the only antidote to this finitude, is exuberant acceptance, not the pallid, quiet, sad acceptance of the ascetic Stoic, but the exhilarated, deliberately joyous, yea-saying of the Superman.

In the fifth book of *The Joyful Wisdom,* there are three enormously poignant and extraordinarily significant fragments which sound forth as a finalization of the ultimate Nietzschean vision:

> *Has existence then a significance at all?*—the question which will require a couple of centuries even to be completely heard in all its profundity. . . . [32]
>
> Once more the great horror seizes us—but who would desire forthwith to deify once more *this* monster of an unknown world in the old fashion: . . . [33]
>
> . . . *the great seriousness* . . . commences, the proper interrogation mark is set up, the fate of the soul changes, the hour-hand moves, and tragedy *begins.* . . . [34]

Is Nietzsche in fact going that one fatal step beyond the evanescent moment? Or is there at least in his approach and thought a dynamic, a bias, a fatal gravitation toward that lethal ulterior step? Kurt Reinhardt, in his Introduction to *The Joyful Wisdom* has highly sobering remarks on this question:

> If "God is dead," then "nothingness" is spreading. This means that *Nihilism,* "the uncanniest of all guests," stands at the door. . . . And thus the "death of God" means the resurrection of the self-responsible, self-determining individual, whose "freedom-toward-Nothingness" turns at its outer limit into the freedom of willing the "Eternal Return."[35]

Reinhardt has, of course, unerringly espied the approach from afar of that uncanny guest that is to come to full status in Jean-Paul Sartre. But I think that an evocation of Nothingness, that darkest and most terrible of all human concepts, is unjust in the delicate balance of Nietzsche's own thought, whatever its intellectual inconsistencies. At the end of his Introduction, Reinhardt indeed cites Nietzsche's own answer to the question of whether his is truly a Joyful Wisdom:

> Anguish, privation, destitution, dark midnights, adventures, daring risks and failures are as necessary for you and for me as their opposites; or, to speak mystically, the path to one's own heaven leads always through the lusts of one's own hell.[36]

And Reinhardt concludes in four trenchant words: "Joyful wisdom? *Incipit tragoedia!*"[37]

4. The Love-Knot of Joy and Tragedy

This, I believe, is to overlook precisely the fact that in Nietzsche's faith in finitude, joy and tragedy are inextricably interlinked. It is also to neglect his own anticipatory delight in a sort of spirit who "could bid farewell to every belief, to every wish for certainty, accustomed as it would be to support itself on slender cords and possibilities, and to dance even on the verge of abysses."[38]

Nietzsche's vision, of course, by no means so dominates our modern world as does Marxist materialist atheism. But there are signs of the time, and there is an internal dynamic in human thought itself, which makes it highly plausible to assume that the Nietzschean questioning must come, is coming, is already upon us. It is no use, long-range, for mortal man to console himself with the Fool's Paradise of emergent evolution. Nor will his own trenchant intellect allow him to. Brinton is implacable but perhaps more perceptive than he realizes when he writes: "There is something abstractly, noisily—yes, and coldly—intellectual about Nietzsche's work that makes it almost unadaptable to the religious needs of ordinary men. His excitements, his transportments are cerebral; his absolute a little squirrel running frantically about the cage of Nietzsche's mind."[39]

It is perceptive of the entire tragedy of Nietzsche to realize that his was indeed a cold and probing brain, albeit allied to a warm and tormented heart. The tortured prophet saw, with appalling clarity, something from which too many modern atheists, agnostics, and simply modern technocratic men are trying to hide behind barricades of pseudo-ultimates and shibboleths of common sense. It is something from which theists too often hide behind the invocation, the lulling evocation, of the supreme Uncreated Mystery.

Nietzsche sees that the man who would dethrone God must replace God and therefore take upon himself the ultimate burden of the cosmos. But this is a cosmos which, by his own act (whether of deliberate volition or perceptive understanding, it matters not), he has undeified, so that he has none of the tools God has to start with. The Superman must attempt by an act of will to impose the meaning of Eternity and Infinitude on that which cannot support it. He can do this only by an act of acceptance of what is, a joyful yea-saying to chaos and the primordial force that surges through endless cycles. He has not even the hope of extinction. Again and again he will return; again and again the wheel will turn, this truly awful wheel whose middle is everywhere, this serpent with its tail in its mouth, this serpent that bit into the shepherd's throat, this serpent of hopeless finitude which bit into Nietzsche's brain, which he could not in real life spit out and which drove him mad.

It is highly significant that Heidegger, who claims that Nietzsche is the philosopher "in whose light and shadow everyone today thinks and reflects with his 'for him' or 'against him,' "[40] should himself write: "To conservation as the guarding of Being corresponds the shepherd who has so little to do with an idyllic sheepwalk and nature mystique, that he can only become a shepherd of Being to the extent that he remains a 'stand-in' for Non-being."[41] To Heidegger, obviously, the shepherd picture in *Thus Spake Zarathustra* is much more than a mere pastoral frill; it pertains to the essence of man's assignment; but the outcome is compromised from the outset, for the serpent of nothingness from which man would protect Being as a Good Shepherd, that very serpent is already in man's own mouth, biting deeply into his throat. Man's own evanescent, *essentially, structurally and constitutively* evanescent becoming is all that stands between Being and the void in the Nietzschean world. The deepest curse of man is that he can neither bite the serpent out of his mouth nor even die of its venom. This is the fully articulated horror of Eternal Recurrence, of finitude set up as ultimate.

5. The Finite Hero

Fabro well pinpoints the crucial Nietzschean contribution to modern man and modern thought:

Nietzsche is quite firm on one point: after the elimination of transcendence, it would be a new error, worse than the first, to make man into the new God, the Absolute. No, man is a finite and limited being and it would be madness to conceive of him as infinite. In the wake of the suppression of God and of the values associated with transcendence, man has a free field; he becomes the creator of new values. But man's creative activity is a finite activity. . . . This makes it quite understandable that the Will-to-Power should have its meaning and foundation in its own self-actualization as a Will-to-Nothingness, inasmuch as the essence of the Will-to-Live is a "willing-of-nothing(ness)," a refusal to tarry or jell, a trenchant insistence on being in process of becoming and on willing the becoming in its totality as a perfectly welded chain of necessity (*amor fati*). . . . the real importance of his thought, in the deepest sense, lies not so much in its having been the occasion of such phenomena of atheistic degeneration as Titanism, absolute aestheticism, National Socialism and the like. It is to be found rather in the fact that Nietzsche called the modern mind to a definitive reckoning, implacable and inexorable.[42]

Man the shepherd of Being, therefore, with the snake of his own ineluctable finitude biting into his throat, must attempt finitely to will a whole set of new values, the only values that can save him from the loping shadows of nothingness—or so he thinks! In effect it is something worse than nothingness, something very akin to the Christian notion of Hell, which Superman-shepherd faces: the perpetual laceration of his infinitude-craving soul by willed finitude: "Divinity without immortality defines the extent of the creator's freedom. Dionysos, the earth-god, shrieks eternally as he is torn limb from limb. But at the same time he represents the agonized beauty that coincides with suffering."[43]

Here again there is an ambivalence and perhaps a sort of counterpoint in Nietzsche: the fulcrum of his formless cosmos shifts bemusingly from the center of the willing finite conscious creature into the formless flux of becoming itself and back again to man. It is as if man cries to his new "god," that Dionysos Nietzsche set up against Christ and all other transcendent invaders from the Beyond, and this Dionysian god cries back: I am as weak, as helpless as you. Löwith even speaks of the World as nature representing in Nietzsche itself a Will to Power willing itself and speaks of all Nietzsche's doctrines as "part and parcel of the single drive for a 'new betrothal' with the world, from which we had been divorced in the wake of the victorious campaign of Christianity against the pagan worship and veneration of the cosmos."[44]

We cannot neglect the final curious ambivalence noted by Colsins[45] and Jaspers[46] in Nietzsche's attitude to God and Christ. Fabro allows that "Nietzsche's campaign against religion and Christianity" may well have been "the result of a 'psychic trauma' and that Nietzsche's denial of God hid a deep religious feeling, a feeling that had been played false and frustrated and was seeking to vent its outrage in this proclamation of the Will-to-Power as the fullness of life."[47] This trauma again may have been multidimensional and have been sustained of Christian misbehavior; the deeper one of misguided the scandal of Christian misbehavior; the deeper one of misguided Christian asceticism of the rigorist type; and a score of other levels. But surely the deepest level is precisely the theistic refusal to take finitude seriously.

Ignace Lepp remarks that a psychologist would be most inclined to interpret Nietzsche's colossal hate for Christianity as a sign and symptom of a disappointed love, which in its day had been as burning as the subsequent hate.[48] And indeed in *The Antichrist* Nietzsche clearly expatiates against not only Christ, but God as well as "the declaration of war against life, against nature, against the will to live! God—the formula for every slander against 'this world' for every lie about the 'beyond'!"[49] Again in *The Joyful Wisdom*, he cries: "The Christian resolution to find the world ugly and bad has made the world ugly and bad."[50] And so, at the end, in this area once again, we find Nietzsche, as throughout, speaking with two voices: warning theism solemnly against trivialization of finitude and warning atheists equally solemnly against evasion of its ultimate face and implications.

As the Marxist materialist, with his ultimate of matter-in-motion, contributes to the theist a valuable positive insight into the creation problem, so Nietzsche with his implacable contemplation of finitude, in which he puts his faith, provides that same theist with a valuable negative insight into creatureliness. It is not fun playing God! The man who would attempt it must be a Nietzschean Superman, or else he is a gull, a cheat, a really dangerous madman who can wreak havoc in the real universe. If he accepts finitude, like Nietzsche he will go mad and one may well suppose that God will be merciful. However, the man who individually or collectively would play God without drawing the most radical consequences from his own demonstrable finitude, is lightly taking on a heavier burden than he can bear. Finitude is the dimension of passivity, of weakness, of evanescence, and of utter openness. It is the hallmark of creatureliness. It cannot create perpetual newness, it can only perpetuate its own repetition. It does not possess the very thing that rings so centrally in Nietzschean striving: power. The fragile created will, evolutionary product of matter-in-motion, is ontologically less worthy of worship than matter-in-motion itself. But if neither the ultimate stuff of creatureliness nor yet the point-instant fulcrum of conscious creatureliness can aspire to the status of ultimate, there is only one reality left which might. That is time, the internal thrust of creatureliness at the deepest level, the antipode of eternity, of the Eternal Logos, even as matter-in-motion is the antipode of Perfect Being, and finitude coagulated into and epitomized by the created will is the antipode of the Great Eternal Will, the Spirit of God, the Holy Spirit.

Time as a candidate for the ultimate will be considered in the next chapter. A final word here on a question which arose earlier but could not be treated before the end of our exposition and which we therefore elected to raise only now: Why does Nietzsche not settle for finite time?

It is, of course, first because he aspires to make the finite the eternal—the eternal, however, which shall still be finite, and therefore guarantee the radical autonomy of the created will. This sort of eternal can only be Eternal Recurrence. It would therefore surely be juster and more accurate to say that Nietzsche does not so much reject finite time as, rather, deprive time itself of all meaning. Of the very essence of time, as we shall see in the next chapter, is a forward movement, at least on the ontological level, from less being to more being, from before to after, from a past then, through a present now, to a future then. To admit such a time is to uncoil the serpent and to deal a death blow to true finitude as ultimate.

6. The Importance of Finitude

In the light of the sacrificial holocaust that was the tragic life of Friedrich Nietzsche, any theistic trivialization of finitude or God's infinity emerges as a shabby and despicable performance. The very concept of infinite must be purged of the anthropomorphic accretions that have often reduced it to little more than the indefinitely greater than the finite in the finite's own dimension. The infinite is not the unbounded in the sense of the indefinitely large; it is the unbounded in the sense of a reality existing in such a way that bounds are meaningless. This statement must be trenchant, not only and indeed not primarily, in the physico-cosmological dimension but, rather, in the ontological dimension. The true God is not simply He who is perfect Being in the sense of the unbounded whole of being; the true God is He who is *intensively* so powerful as to know no limitation. This is the only alternative the human mind will accept to Nietzsche's ring of Eternal Recurrence, of finitude made manifest. This is He who can sustain the onrushing but not recurrent tide of created being; and His infinity must be recognized by theists most frankly in the most ticklish dimension of all, the dimension of Will. How that can be reconciled with true human freedom, we have already discussed in the chapter dealing with the modern philosopher most devotedly obsessed with human freedom, Jean-Paul Sartre.

Finally, we must here pass in detailed review the message of the ambivalent voice of Nietzsche speaking to all men of the unacceptability of Being and the impotence of Becoming.

The theist has reason to listen because his traditional picture does lend itself to abuses. And these begin right in the very creation notion itself. As soon as Platonic cookie-cutter essences are set up as having some sort of anterior consistency over against God, the eternal First Principle is already betrayed and his creation with him. And each member of the creation who is rational and possessed of at least apparent executive power is reduced to the status of having to conform to something supremely worthy of scorn and contempt, a code of behavior dictated by an implacable impersonal *nature* with which not only he himself but even his Creator has been saddled.

It is against this kind of slavery to essences that Nietzscheanism represents the flaming revolt. Small wonder that modern existentialists invoke him so often as precursor. He himself saw prophetically an age approaching in which the existent and existence itself would get loose of these chains of essences and rage freely.

In fact the God who is condemned to create a cosmos that imposes anterior restrictions on him is not God. For such anterior restrictions presupposes once again a kind of prior consistency in the order of essence which no creation can possibly possess.

But the Nietzscheans are mistaken too; I believe their mistake, which is a profound one, consists in a confusion of the moral and the ontological orders and levels, a confusion to which spiritualists (Nietzscheans and their too strident theist antagonists, the Puritans and standpatters of every Christian age) are all too prone. To act as if ontological structure were in itself trammeling of human freedom, indeed of created freedom as such, is to act insanely. To act as if a creature were per se a moral offense, i.e., that it is wrong of God to create, that He should only beget, is to commit the fallacy of wishing the impossible, the absolutely and totally impossible, the inherently contradictory. Pleromization is the only way in which multitude, manifold, can truly come to pass by an action of the One alone, an action presupposing no faintest anterior collaboration on the part of the created, much less any imposition by that created reality of conditions upon the Creator. And pleromization entails, not anteriorily but posteriorily its own de facto conditions. And the deepest of human wisdom consists in working within these conditions, loving matter precisely for its inertia, grasping as far as possible the laws which express simply the factual fabric of this pleromized being in operation and then using them creatively. Herein lies perfect freedom for the creature. But, of course, one cannot do this effectively unless one loves matter: one must not regard matter as a stumbling block or creaturehood as a monstrosity a priori!

However, the second step is as vital as the first. Once the situation has been grasped, there must be creative manipulation, not mere dumb passive acceptance. It is this that theism must avoid like the plague and still more avoid making God seem to be commanding such a dumb passive acceptance. The deep rhythms of creaturely existence and the mounting tide of universalizing love are one thing; the cramping staticizing moral precepts, incautiously specified and even individualized and numbered and then falsely and mistakenly eternalized, are quite another. Such precepts so purveyed, far from ensuring salvation, will wreck the evolution of the cosmos if they are slavishly adhered to when their day, their constellation is past.

7. Salvation From Essences

The mention of salvation provides the perfect bridge to the second dimension of Nietzsche's message. When he speaks in his fiery rebel voice, he is summoning mankind in its noblest members to an implacable war against all manner of cramping codes and restrictive essences. But, because he has leapt too far in the direction of sheer being for any creature safely to tread the path he treads, he soon begins to speak in his somber voice and articulate the hopelessness of this very striving for the salvation that would consist in man dictating his own values and then living them and so realizing his inmost self!

There is a strange strain here in Nietzsche, a strain by no means untheizable, by no means ignoble. It recurs in many science fiction tales of our day; and such tales are the pre-eminent present-day vehicle of satire and prophecy. It is the motif of the space wanderer, whose unusual motivations seek their only conceivable and possible gratification and fulfillment among the dark uncertainty of outer stars. But because Nietzsche is vowed to finitude, this initially laudable thrust slackens off, even at its moment of apparently supreme tension, into a mere listening to the seductive song of the mother of being! There can surely be no question that a psychological element here plays a powerful part, the desire to escape from the restrictive paternalism of the theological god to the all-permissive, all-seducing, serenely amoral Mother, who smiles sadly but permissively upon all her heroic sons. But this Mother is no mother at all; eventually she is helpless. She is not the nourishing fertile womb which brings forth heroes within herself. She is closer to the *Belle Dame sans Merci*. She lies beyond prime matter, in the very dimension of creatureliness or becoming itself. The dark swirling primordiality into which Nietzsche the myth-maker and myth-lover was persuaded man must retreat or into which he must stride by the frenzy of the dance cannot give the power man craves.

It is an odd symptom of the whole Nietzschean trend that it

should protest most violently in the realm of essences against exactly that which it exalts in the world of existences. In the realm of essences, Nietzscheanism protests violently against staticized natures in the name of total freedom for the existent; man the heroic individual is not to be saddled with or paralyzed by unchanging essences. In the realm of existences, on the other hand, Nietzscheanism loudly defends the absolute independence and consequent metaphysical closedness of each individual existent, and deprecates any love-relation between existents as namelessly threatening to their independence. This apparent contradiction in the Nietzschean stand gives us a valuable clue to a fuller understanding of the ontological and ultimately theological problem involved.

Baldly stated, the problem is to find a First Principle who is not cramping or cramped, not impotent like that Nietzschean goddess, the Mother of Being, yet not trammeling of creaturely freedom by his omnipotence. The problem is to redeem finitude without destroying personal freedom. And out of this study of Nietzsche can come already the foreshadowing of an answer which must be much more thoroughly developed in the final chapter: the key lies in the First Principle who is Love, who is superabundantly and even explosively open, whose interior life is loving, i.e., relatedness, and whose prime action *ad extra* is loving creation. This is the fertile God, the all-powerful God who yet guarantees human freedom. In himself, He *is* Loving; in His primordial creative act He loves.

I was privileged recently to speak with the present leader of the Sufi movement, Pir Zade Viliyat Inayat Khan. He told me a moving story of two theologians discussing the best articulation of creation. The one maintained that the believer had to be told that God so desired to know himself that He created that believer in order that God might have an object, in a sense become in the believer an object, so that He might know himself. The believer was then to be urged to become worthy of being the object of God's own knowledge. "No," quietly remonstrated the Sufi theologian. "Say, rather, God so loved you, believer, that He willed to become object to himself, i.e., create, so that you might be. Love therefore and become worthy of the love of the God who loved you so much."

7

FAITH IN TIME

With Samuel Alexander, we encounter a problem of interpretative justice which has not presented itself in the case of any of the thinkers we have thus far inspected. For up to now we have been dealing with thinkers who either profess outright atheism or who do not deal expressly with the God-question at all, whereas Alexander constantly uses the name of God and himself describes his system precisely as an effort to supplement the popular religious notion of God with a notion more sufficient for the theoretical needs of the philosopher:

> Primarily God must be defined as the object of the religious emotion or of worship. He is correlative to that emotion or sentiment, as food is correlative to appetite. What we worship, that is God. This is the practical or religious approach to God. But it is insufficient for our theoretical needs. It labours under the defect that so far as religion itself is able to assure us, the object of religion, however vitally rooted in human nature, however responsive to its needs, may be disconnected with the rest of the world. God may be but an ennobling fancy, a being whom we project before us in our imagination, in whom to believe may sustain and inspire us and have its own sufficient justification in its effects on our happiness, but to whom no reality corresponds which can be co-ordinated with familiar realities of the world.[1]

Yet Alexander himself frankly admits that he intends to define God in terms of something more basic than God himself:

> . . . from the metaphysical approach, God must be defined as the being, if any, which possesses deity or the divine quality; or, if there are more Gods than one, the beings which possess deity. The defect of this definition (which is only apparently circular) is that the being which possesses deity need not necessarily, so far as the bare metaphysical description goes, be the object of religious sentiment. It has to be shown that the

being which possesses deity coincides with the object of religious passion and is its food.[2]

And Alexander proceeds to set his own course unequivocally by the compass of this more ultimate something:

Abandoning the attempt to define God directly, we may ask ourselves whether there is place in the world for the quality of deity; we may then verify the reality of the being which possesses it, that is of the Deity or God; and having done so, we may then consult the religious consciousness to see whether this being coincides with the object of worship.[3]

In a corrective specification, intended to contradistinguish his own position from Lloyd Morgan's emergent evolution, Alexander writes, in his Preface to the 1927 edition of *Space, Time and Deity,* a set of statements which neatly identify the tantalizing ambivalence of Alexander's whole position on God:

I do not say, as has been thought, that God never is, but is always yet to be. "What I say is that God as actually possessing deity does not exist, but is an ideal, is always becoming; but God as the whole universe tending towards deity does exist. Deity is a quality, and God is a being. Actual God is the forecast and, as it were, divining of ideal God."[4]

Fabro gives high praise to this effort to articulate a new sort of Einsteinian theology: "The originality of Alexander's conception lies mainly in his reiteration of the Spinozan paired attributes of Being, with the substitution of Time for Thought as the drive-powering process. This substitution is intended to avoid both the impasse of rationalism's static Absolute and the idealist reduction of God to Absolute Mind, a reduction that makes thought the point of departure, whereas it is only one of the points of destination, albeit the highest. . . . Everything flows from the nisus (push, striving, impulse) which Time impresses upon Space. . . . The great drawback is that, in this system, deity as such never becomes real. That is the drawback that Whitehead strove to eliminate with his notion of the bipolar God."[5]

The judgment of Hartshorne and Reese, themselves avowed panentheists and sympathetic to Alexander, may well be considered clinching:

The result is a conception of God which . . . hovers between reality and unreality. Alexander himself in writing seems to waver between a traditional and an empirical view of what one means by "possible". Since his deity is conceivable, it would seem to be possible; since observation directs otherwise, it seems impossible that the deity described can ever be a reality. A luminous possibility is advanced, which we are then told is not really possible. In this form the view satisfies only partially, and perhaps does not satisfy at all, man's religious propensities.[6]

Our aim in these pages is to listen to Alexander's own articulation and its supplementary development by Alfred North Whitehead, whose writings have had such a profound influence on Protestant theology in our day. We shall not cavil at Alexander's use of the name "God"; we shall show that his own creative ultimate is Time, in which he squarely places his whole faith. We shall see what vital insights he brings to theists. Only then, in the light of all this, shall we register our own caveat against the use of the name "God" in Alexander's system. And this caveat will be based, not on an arrogant moral judgment of propriety, but on a modest but firm demand for linguistic accuracy. "God" as used by Alexander simply does not correspond to "God" as used throughout the theistic tradition: in that sense his system is a-theistic.

1. An Einsteinean Dynamic Metaphysic

Alexander is especially exciting as a thinker because of his effort to base a metaphysical system on recent scientific discoveries and specifically to build into that system the great unifying tenet of Einstein, namely Space-Time. Macquarrie in fact calls Alexander's philosophy "one of the greatest efforts in recent times towards a comprehensive metaphysical system";[7] and Metz has a meaty summary of Alexander's selective genius: "Alexander takes over Hume's empirical philosophy but not his scepticism; Spencer's evolutionary philosophy but not his agnosticism; the theory of knowledge of New Realism without halting at it; and the physical theory of Relativity but not without a speculative evaluation of it and a subordination of it to his own system."[8] Alexander himself once wryly remarked, with the modest humor so characteristic of him, that the Epstein bust of him presented to the University of Manchester might well be remembered as "the bust of a professor, not otherwise now remembered, except as an ingredient of the ferment which the earlier years of the 20th century cast into speculation."[9]

His *Space, Time and Deity* in fact represents the published version of the Gifford Lectures which he had been invited to deliver at Glasgow in 1916-1918, "thus having an opportunity to present the whole sustained metaphysical view which he had been gestating."[10] The Lectures were published originally in 1920; it is highly significant that it should have been found feasible and desirable to reprint them again in 1966. After a considerable period of eclipse, Alexander is coming back into his own; and one reason is certainly the current wave of death-of-God speculation, indirectly inspired (though certainly not sired) by Whitehead, who in turn wrote gratefully: "I am especially indebted to Alexander's great work."[11]

It entirely transcends our present purpose to probe into the imposing over-all picture of reality Alexander presents. We are here concerned to isolate and study in detail his ultimate, Time, in which he places his faith. And the first crucial point he stresses is that Space and Time cannot be separated in the ontological order of reality; Space-Time is a unified whole and the ultimate matrix of all reality: "Space or Time only exists with the existence of the other.[12] . . . Space-Time is the matrix of all empirical existence."[13]

Within this Space-Time matrix, Time is the mind and Space the body. Alexander immediately forestalls any tendency to anthropomorphic projection:

Time is the mind of Space and Space the body of Time. According to this formula the world as a whole and each of its parts is built on the model with which we are familiar in ourselves as persons, that is as union of mind and body, and in particular as a union of mind and brain. But as this may lead to the misapprehension that we are the standard and exemplar of things, the statement is better made in the reverse and truer form that we are examples of a pattern which is universal and is followed not only by things but by Space-Time itself. In any point-instant the instant is the mind or soul of its point. . . . In Space-Time as a whole the total Time is the mind of total Space.[14]

And he pursues this point further in a section which begins to reveal his conception of the creative function of Time:

> Rather than hold that Time is a form of mind we must say that mind is a form of Time. . . . Out of the time-element . . . the quality mind as well as all lower empirical qualities emerge, and this quality mind belongs to or corresponds to the configuration of time which enters into the space-time configuration which is proper to the level of existence on which mind is found.[15]

We may very summarily point up three subsequent levels of development issuing from the Space-Time matrix "under the guiding hand of Time": matter, life, and mind. In his discussion of the first of these levels, Alexander clearly posits Space-Time as anterior to matter:

> Space-Time . . . is the stuff which receives determination in the qualities it assumes as its complexity of grouping develops in Time. . . . Space-Time, though the stuff of material things and of all other things, is not material. . . . it is anterior to . . . matter. . . . there is no reason to regard matter . . . as other than a complex of motion, that is made out of the original stuff which is Space-Time.[16]

Precisely in this connection we begin to zero in on Alexander's equivalent deification of Space-Time (or more accurately his adumbration of a Creator-creation mutual embrace at the constitutive level) and on a curious and exciting parallel in Alexander's presentation to our own contention, in the chapter on Lenin, concerning the deep though antipodal correspondence between matter-in-motion and God. For Alexander writes:

> . . . neither Space nor Time are mere relations between things or events. . . . they are themselves entities or rather Space-Time is an entity. Of the familiar types of existents, material existence is possibly closest to Space-Time.[17]

In a thoroughly fascinating follow-up, Alexander gingerly deals with what in theistic terms would be the creation-mystery, what we have already called the technique whereby Perfect Being enables finite created existents to share in Perfect Being's own perfect and infinite simple act of being:

> If it is asked further by what steps it is that mere motion under the guiding hand of Time leads to the emergence of the material complexes of

motion which we find in the world of things; how a specific motion like that of light is generated, with constant and maximal velocity, and how atoms come into existence as combinations of electrons with or without the distinctively material nucleus, with relatively constant constitutions; I can only reply that I do not know, and that it is not for the metaphysician to say, in the absence of indications from the physicist himself. Yet it is difficult to refrain from hazarding conjecture by way of asking a question. And so I dare to ask if there may not be in these ages of simpler existence something corresponding to the method pursued by nature in its higher stages, of natural selection. . . . Whether that is to say, nature or Space-Time did not try various complexes of simple motions and out of the chaos of motion preserve certain types.[18]

In a vital note dealing with the question of whether all forms of existence must, on his hypothesis, have always existed (the Nie-tzschean conundrum), Alexander at once highlights the crucial impor-tance of the total merger of Space and Time, and within this merger the primordial creative capacity inherent in Time, a capacity of which Alexander speaks poetically but with scientific precision:

Since the instants of abstract Time are homogeneous, the conclusion is drawn that in an infinite Time everything which can happen has hap-pened. But this overlooks what is essential to Time, that it is creative: that something comes into being which before was not. . . . But the deeper cause of the misunderstanding is that Time . . . is taken apart from Space. There is no such thing as a Time which subsists alongside of Space. There is only one reality which is Space-Time. . . . We are dealing with patterns as traced out in time. But to arrive at a higher or more complex order of finite existence *takes time*. Time is taken in the abstract, separated from Space, and accordingly things in the real stuff of Space-Time are emanci-pated from the history of their becoming. But when we think of things as generated in time out of the fundamental stuff, they have all of them a history. The time which has elapsed down to man is infinite, but it is an infinity which has been occupied with the generation of certain forms, and will be occupied with the generation of other forms. Though Time is infinite, experience as registered in historical records tells us that in times before the birth of man there was no man. That pattern had not yet been traced which is the condition of the emergence of human mind. The same reality of Time which has evolved the various forms of finite existence leaves room for still higher births. Except for the belief that development is finished with the highest thing we know, there is no ground for the doctrine of cyclical periods of the world's history, a cataclysm followed by a fresh beginning, such as are supposed by many philosophers, from Heraclitus and Zarathustra and the Stoics down to Nietzsche. On the contrary the notion of a fresh beginning vaguely assumes the finitude of Time, which in reality has no beginning or begins at each moment indifferently. Real Time hints, by analogy with the past, the movement towards higher empirical qualities of existence. On this is founded the possibility of understanding deity.[19]

Descending beyond matter, then, Alexander seizes on Space-Time as the real anterior matrix and in this matrix pinpoints and highlights the truly creative force, Time, which renders process possible. This is, without doubt, the most exciting external parameter that we have yet encountered. Beside it both Marxist matter-in-motion and Nietzschean finite cyclic recurrence show up as crude and dead. One senses in Alexander's creative-Time notion a genuine insight, however insufficient it may prove to be. J. A. Gunn has most revealing remarks on the nature of this insight:

> In Alexander's view, Space-Time is "the stuff of things." The evolution of the Universe is due to the restlessness of Space-Time and, indeed, to its creativeness. . . . For Alexander Time is spatial because it cannot exist alone. What Bergson regards as a weakness and error in our representation of Time, Alexander regards as a vital and essential truth. . . . Time . . . is the abiding eternal principle of impermanence.[20]

2. Immutability and Dynamism

We can most enthusiastically agree that precisely in pointing up the radical instability of the universe of our empirical experience as anterior to and deeper-rooted than merely matter, Alexander has articulated a tremendous insight. The universe is unstable, not in function of the parameter of matter (which indeed explains the manifold but does not give the ultimate clue to the instability) but, rather, because of its *temporality*. Alexander has shown that temporality is the absolutely and generically indispensable parameter and presupposition for any *coming into existence*. It should be noted that, with Alexander's Space-Time notion, we are far beyond and in a much deeper-lying and more unified field than the traditional notion of time as a kind of line between an initial and a terminal point. Within Alexander's Space-Time unified field, Time is the *creative* agent. It is the element in the picture which makes possible both a coming into being and an evolution with an overriding direction, i.e., a thrust that can only be described, albeit inadequately, as a motion upward to ever greater degrees of complexity.

Every theist may be grateful to Alexander for bringing clearly into the light the profoundest riddle of empirical reality in the widest sense: not its apparent duality of mind and matter; not even the apparently mysterious curtain that descends on its beginnings; but its essential instability, an instability that is indispensable to any explanation or even conception of evolution, freedom, and a real (i.e., a non-Nietzschean) future.

In his attribution of instability to the discrete whole that is the universe, or more accurately Space-Time, Alexander takes an unwarranted step; or at least elects to adopt a stance that is not the only possible one. What if this instability lay, rather, in the relation of creation to creator? Then we would have hold of (without, of course, being at all able to *explain*) the very creative nexus itself. Matter, we have said, is the parameter of initial pleromization of the Eternal Infinite Act of Being; the instability inherent in temporality would, on the suggested reading, be a parameter still more radical: it would be the line along which creation received, not its manifoldness and multiplicity, but its very createdness: to be created would be to be rendered unstable. And as the total manifold would be the utter obverse of the simplicity of God, so would this utter instability be the radical obverse of God's eternity.

Even as matter-in-motion is the parameter whereby the simplicity of God's act of Being (or of God, Act of Being) gains purchase in the (or as a) manifold, even so would the point-instant be the parameter whereby the Eternity of God, Act of Being, gets purchase in or as the radical *historicity* that is evolving creation. Creation would have to be regarded here again not as the palpable opposite of a highly impalpable God, stagnating in a static eternity. Rather, creation would properly be described as uneternal and unsimple, a drastic, radical, voluntary denial of the eternity and simplicity of God, so that the pleroma might be. The creative act would not be an imparting of a quantifiable commodity, being, to creatures who previously did not possess it; it would, rather, be a voluntary abandonment of eternity and simplicity so that creatures might be.

And it may well be that, though all metaphors are inadequate when used to describe God, the fountain is less inadequate than the circle. The bugbear terror of a mutability of God arises only from our persistent tendency to conceive of God's eternity and simplicity as a basically already quantified commodity which cannot be denied or abandoned without some kind of prejudice to God's perfection. If all the divine attributes are conceived, rather, in terms of power, then the creative act is no longer a hemming of the infinite, nor yet a splitting of the simplicity but, rather, a dimensionalization of the power. And if the banal but legitimate question be now asked: How, on this reading, do you preserve the identity of God?, the answer must be trenchantly along the same lines: This identity has been likewise conceived entirely too quantifiedly and even mathematically. The immense Power-Source who is the Anterior Tripersonal Creator is neither hemmed from without nor split from within by dimensionalization. Nor is it all cogent to warn that this view involves a conception of God as existing via a finite or at least finitized act of existence. *What* exists is the pleroma! And for all we know, there may be and most probably are, an infinity of other pleromas resulting from other dimensionalizations of the power. Nor must this dimensionalization be conceived as a channeling of the power into pre-existing dimensions but, rather, as a neat act, the creative act. We can really glimpse or imagine it at all contentually only in our own Space-Time continuum: here it is not so accurate to say that the creative act produces the point-instants; it is more illuminating to say that it *is* the point-instants. For in the point-instants we have surprised surely that elemental nexus that is constitutive of the instability that unfolds as Space-Time history.

The precise problem with Alexander's creative Time is that it lacks any such power-source as we have just posited. And creative Time truly regarded as absolute ultimate has one fatal flaw, so far as the satisfaction of man's longings and requirements are concerned. We could of course dilate at length on the curious flight of Alexander from nouns to *adjectives* rather than verbs, which latter we have above suggested would be an improvement over nouns in ontological vocabulary. Verbs express pure act; nouns, delimited act; but adjectives precisely utter qualities which demand a subject. But it is not really this "qualification" of reality in Alexander, not really this strange *nisus* rendering qualities more substantial than substances, which is the crucial flaw. Rather, it is what Whitehead himself unerringly put his finger upon when he writes:

> The ultimate evil in the temporal world is deeper than any specific evil. It lies in the fact that the past fades, that time is a "perpetual perishing." Objectification involves elimination. The present fact has not the past fact with it in any full immediacy. The process of time veils the past.[21]

3. Whiteheadian Rescue Operation

Whitehead sees that Alexander's creative Time, while indeed crucially important, is not entirely a positive phenomenon. Though admittedly essential to *Process,* it is destructive of *Reality.* For even as it builds a future, it consigns a past to oblivion or at least to a minor degree of immediate presence. Whitehead therefore feels that what is needed is a whiff of eternity somehow brought into Time itself. And he brings it with his dipolar God notion.

Whitehead writes succinctly and penetratingly of the supreme and final religious problem in these terms:

> The culminating fact of conscious rational life refuses to conceive itself as a transient enjoyment, transiently useful. In the order of the physical world, its role is defined by the introduction of novelty. But, just as physical feelings are haunted by the vague insistence of causality, so the higher intellectual feelings are haunted by the vague insistence of another order, where there is no unrest, no travel, no shipwreck: "There shall be no more sea." This is the problem which gradually shapes itself as religion reaches its higher phases in civilized communities. The most general formulation of the religious problem is the question whether the process of the temporal world passes into the formation of other actualities bound together in an order in which novelty does not mean loss.[22]

Whitehead's negative critique of two great religious attitudes must be most enthusiastically approved by anyone conscious of the true specificities and deepest roots of the religious problem of our day.

Whitehead identifies the first attitude as "Buddhistic" and the second as "the fallacy that has infused tragedy into the histories of Christianity and of Mahometanism." The first attitude, he says, considers the temporal world as a "self-sufficient completion of the creative act, explicable by its derivation from an ultimate principle which is at once eminently real and the unmoved mover."[23] The second attitude Whitehead describes as "The doctrine of an aboriginal, eminently real, transcendent creator, at whose fiat the world came into being and whose imposed will it obeys."[24]

The former attitude would, Whitehead feels, reduce the world to a purely patterned, quasi-mechanical apparition of an ultimate static deity. The latter attitude does indeed introduce a kind of dynamism but makes it revolve upon the fulcrum of the ruthless *moral* energy of the One, to the exclusion of any real active collaboration on the part of the many.

Whitehead sees a third possible religious attitude, of which he writes in moving terms and which he derives from the Galilean origin of Christianity:

> It does not emphasize the ruling Caesar or the ruthless moralist or the unmoved mover. It dwells upon the tender elements in the world, which slowly and in quietness operate by love; and it finds purpose in the present immediacy of a kingdom not of this world. Love neither rules, nor is it unmoved; also it is a little oblivious as to morals. It does not look to the future: for it finds its own reward in the immediate present.[25]

This Galilean love notion adumbrates a quiet poignant sort of collaboration between deity and creation with some sort of specially immediate and intimate ingress of the molding deity into the time flux and a consequent location of the meaningful divine and human activity in the present moment, which has now been redeemed of its transience by the presence of the divine ground of permanence who in turn had been robbed of (or had voluntarily abandoned) his unmoved ruthless security of eternity to collaborate with the transient.

When, in this connection, Whitehead begins to speak of the dipolar God, his initial statements can again be welcomed most enthusiastically by anyone concerned to see properly implemented in ontology the contention that God exists all ways (*omnimodo*). "God," writes

Whitehead, "is not to be treated as an exception to all metaphysical principles, invoked to save their collapse. He is their chief exemplification."[26]

This statement is certainly susceptible of the interpretation that would make its meaning identical with our own contention that God is not a reality beyond being but the intensive fullness of being, that creation must be explained entirely within the framework and dimension of being. But Whitehead chooses, rather, to push the principle in another direction, thereby denying anterior fullness of conscious actuality to God:

Thus, analogously to all actual entities, the nature of God is dipolar. He has a primordial nature and a consequent nature. The consequent nature of God is conscious; and it is the realization of the actual world in the unity of his nature, and through the transformation of his wisdom. The primordial nature is conceptual, the consequent nature is the weaving of God's physical feelings upon his primordial concepts. One side of God's nature is constituted by his conceptual experience. This experience is the primordial fact in the world, limited by no actuality which it presupposes. It is therefore infinite, devoid of all negative prehensions. This side of his nature is free, complete, primordial, eternal, actually deficient, and unconscious. The other side originates with physical experience derived from the temporal world, and then acquires integration with the primordial side. It is determined, incomplete, consequent, "everlasting," fully actual and conscious.[27]

This basic notion of the anterior insufficiency of reality in God, a notion which Whitehead seems to feel essential to a protection of freedom and novelty, soon develops into or gives rise to a new sort of ultimate, in whose grip both God and man find themselves as fellow dipolar realities:

God and the World stand to each other in . . . opposed requirement. God is the infinite ground of all mentality, the unity of vision seeking physical multiplicity. The World is the multiplicity of finites, actualities seeking a perfected unity. Neither God, nor the world, reaches static completion. Both are in the grip of the ultimate metaphysical ground, the creative advance into novelty. Either of them, God and the World, is the instrument of novelty for the other.[28]

Whitehead's crucial error seems to me to be the apparently psychologically conditioned concern to depress the anterior reality of God so as to protect the genuine reality of creation. The result is that White-head's God is not quite full-blooded enough to sustain theism. Yet this Whiteheadian God is substantially more full-blooded than Alexander's; or we must, rather, say that Whitehead's over-all reality-picture and his location of source of the power-drive that powers the cosmos (part of which he locates in God, part in creation, and part in the creative advance into "novelty") is substantially more satisfying than Alexander's. For in Alexander, the dipolarity comes from the fact that God as individual is in process with man of trying to bring about deity, an eternally future face, a kind of ever advancing forward rim of the evolving cosmos; whereas, in Whitehead, God and man are trying to articulate the full power of the creative urge, itself unconscious to be sure, but definitely anteriorly eternal, always there.

Yet, though the creative urge, presumably the subject of the creative advance into novelty which Whitehead chooses as his "ultimate metaphysical ground," is indeed eternally anterior to God and man and anteriorly eternal in the most radical sense, God himself, "like all actual entities," is very much in process and anteriorly (or "primordially") "deficient in actuality." Macquarrie points up what might usefully be termed Whitehead's temporalization of God and highlights that element in Whitehead which has most contributed to the emergence of a death-of-God theology: Whitehead, says Macquarrie, is at pains to ". . . bring God into time so that he becomes to some extent a God who is 'on his way,' so to speak, a God who in one way or another is not yet complete in his perfection, a natural God rather than a supernatural."[29] And he stresses the crucial weakness of this approach, a weakness inherent precisely in its greatest strength: "A God who is not or is not yet completely perfect, may indeed stir in us genuinely religious feelings of love and aspiration but can he evoke that deep awe and reverence . . . which is surely at the heart of religion?"[30] Collins reiterates this weakness and goes on to stress Whitehead's impermissible extremism in his initially laudable drive to achieve rapprochement between God and creation:

> Whitehead fails to note that the bipolar theory can be criticized not only from a one-sided or monopolar standpoint but also from the stand-

point of a deliberately *non*-polar approach to God. . . . . Whitehead's procedure of building his account of the human structure into a prototype for all actual entities is just as unwarranted in the study of God as in the study of nature. In a universe of analogous causes, the validity of one's description of finite things need not depend upon injecting all of their elements into the divine nature.[31]

Whitehead might well reply that this is precisely the mystery element in the ultimate wherein he places his faith; and that his vision is a nobler and tenderer one than the mere power-worship of traditional theistic religions. Precisely by taking Time seriously, he has replaced the Caesar-God by the Suffering Christ, to whom each successive moment of advancing Time is copresent and in whom it is eternalized. We may indeed at this point usefully report Whitehead's magnificent peroration in which he apotheosizes Alexander's elusive ultimate within the framework and dimensionality of the over-all Whiteheadian vision itself:

There are thus four creative phases in which the universe accomplishes its actuality. There is first the phase of conceptual origination, deficient in actuality, but infinite in its adjustment of valuation. Secondly, there is the temporal phase of physical origination, with its multiplicity of actualities. In this phase full actuality is attained; but there is deficiency in the solidarity of individuals with each other. This phase derives its determinate conditions from the first phase. Thirdly, there is the phase of perfected actuality in which the many are one everlastingly, without the qualification of any loss either of individual identity or of completeness of unity. In everlastingness, immediacy is reconciled with objective immortality. This phase derives the conditions of its being from the two antecedent phases. In the fourth phase, the creative action completes itself. For the perfected actuality passes back into the temporal world, and qualifies this world so that each temporal actuality includes it as an immediate fact of relevant experiences. For the kingdom of heaven is with us today. The action of the fourth phase is the love of God for the world. It is the particular providence for particular occasions. What is done in the world is transformed into a reality in heaven. And the reality in heaven passes back into the world. By reason of this reciprocal relation, the love in the world passes into the love in heaven, and floods back again into the world. In this sense, God is the great companion—the fellow sufferer who understands.[32]

It seems to me, however, that the question is not so much one of emotional acceptability as of capacity for intellectual explanation and satisfaction. Or say, rather, that the emotionally acceptable God-notion must still be squared with the intellectually acceptable God-notion. Alexander and Whitehead are on the track of a singularly important discovery. But the discovery that God is involved in Time, and Time is most intimately related to the Creator-God, must not blind the human searcher to the fact that a real transcendence of Time, a transcendence involving atemporal actuality, is essential to a God-notion that is to provide an intellectually acceptable answer to Faust's question: Tell me, *who* made the world?

4. Time, the Parameter of Creaturehood

The salutary realization to which Alexander and Whitehead lead the theist is the awareness that Time, too, can in a sense be called a creation of God, or more accurately, we feel, Time can be called the very parameter of creaturehood, and hence of the creative act, the pleromization of the Simple Perfect Act of Being in the dimension of historicity, even as matter-in-motion is that pleromization in the dimension of multitude. Time is accorded an ontological status analogous to that accorded matter by the materialist Marxists; Time, like matter, is de-epistemologized. The term "matter-in-motion" is a shorthand expression for the *fact* that the One creates the many, initially the radical and utter manifold. The term "Time" is a shorthand expression for the *fact* that this manifold *is created to have a history.*

We suggest that the whole problematic can be approached in a different way, using precisely the insights of Alexander and Whitehead. Begin with eternity or the eternal as more real than temporal creatureliness; *but* derive creatureliness totally from the eternal via a radical initial pleromization in *our* universe (leaving open the question of possible other dimensional pleromizations) and then build up the rational out of the material as an interiorizing complexification which at *a certain point in Time* (the irreversible forward line of motion) produces thought and freedom. Freedom is an ultimate in its own dimension and perfectly adequate to account for (though of course not to explain) the emergence of evil within a closed universe, i.e., a universe in which the Creator in no sense mixes eternal nothingness with His being or even negates His own being to start things going.

The creative power can most adequately be expressed in human terms as the ability to dimensionalize the sheer simple act of being that is himself, in a sense to fractionalize, thereby bringing about an entirely new radical dimension of reality, creaturehood. This utterly generic dimension as contrasted with the pandimensionalism of the Eternal Simple God may be any one of an infinite multitude of dimensional pleromizations. We are legitimately concerned solely with two such possible dimensionalizations of God's Act of Being, to wit, the one that produced our spatio-temporal universe and possibly the one that produced the "angelic" world. We cannot know what was the nexus in the act of angel-creation, but we can strongly suspect that in our universe temporalization and radical materialization were indivisible and inseparable. This pleromization of the Act of Being involved absolutely nothing exterior to God. What it brought into the picture was *not* God existing now by a finitized act of existence, but simply a finitization of His Act of Being which was and is the pleroma. The numerator of a fraction is in no way whatever altered or restricted in its own dimension as numerator by the pleromization of the denominator; it is only the denominator that is absolutely restricted by that unity that *overlies* (not underlies) it: that is what it means to be a creature.

5. The Past Recaptured?

The irreversibility of Time is held by modern science to have a genuine meaning, at least within systems that can communicate with one another.[33] Is the colossal effort of the greatest of modern Time-novelists, Marcel Proust, then merely an artistic fantasy? For his effort is directed to nothing less than the conquest of Time. The overall title of his great work loses its key meaning in the accepted English version. This English title is an inspired rendition but it only very indirectly articulates what the French title clearly proclaims. Proust is concerned with more than the *Remembrance of Things Past*. He is concerned with the *Search for Time Lost*. And the English title must be taken in its wider Shakespearean context to evoke the key to an understanding of Proust's drive and of its ultimate metaphysical pessimism: "When to the sessions of sweet silent *thought,* I summon up remembrance of things past. . . ." When Time Lost is summoned up by thought, then and then only can Time Past be rendered Time Present. Well does Howard Moss remark: *"Remembrance of Things Past* is its own self-sealing device. Circular in structure, its end leads us back to its beginning. The word 'Time' embedded in the first sentence of the book rings out grandly as the last word of the novel and brings us once again to where we started."[34]

As catalyst Proust does indeed choose the impressions of those human senses farthest removed from conscious thought and most akin to animal senses:

> But when from a long-distant past nothing subsists, after the people are dead, after the things are broken and scattered, still, alone, more fragile, but with more vitality, more unsubstantial, more persistent, more faithful, the smell and taste of things remain poised a long time, like souls, ready to remind us, waiting and hoping for their moment, amid the ruins of all the rest; and bear unfaltering, in the tiny and almost impalpable drop of their essence, the vast structure of recollection.[35]

But it is the power of thought which enables man to transcend time by effecting connections, juxtapositions, and interpretations that play fast and loose precisely with the most hallowed characteristic of Time, its chronology. The famous social scenes so liberally strewn throughout the huge Proustian work "are literally time-stoppers. . . . make us aware of time in a special way by confusing us as to duration and speed. Hundreds of pages go by at which the activities of one evening are described."[36]

And this tampering with Time assumes, early in the work, a sad and noble status: the Combray steeple of his childhood is evoked, says Proust, by a chance passer-by pointing at some belfry as he responds to the adult Proust's request for directions; and this adult Proust is left standing

> for hours on end, motionless, trying to remember, feeling deep within my self a tract of soil reclaimed from the waters of Lethe slowly drying until the buildings rise on it again; and then no doubt, and then more uneasily

than when, just now, I asked him for a direction, I will seek my way again, I will turn a corner . . . but . . . the goal is in my heart.[37]

Moss admirably pinpoints the dynamic and deepest significance of Proust's work in his concluding remarks:

> *Remembrance of Things Past* is a gigantic disappearing act in which the magician vanishes along with his magic in the service of illusion. He does so to prove to us that the illusory is real. By the time we reach the end of *Remembrance of Things Past,* Swann and the Duchesse de Guermantes, upon whom so much time and elucidation have been expended, are revealed at last for what they are. Two human beings in the boyhood of Marcel Proust he once conceived of as gods. Now the true god, the writer, paying homage to the deities of his childhood, secreting their lives from within himself, confers upon them a genuine immortality.[38]

Yet the very serenity with which the artist can operate is bought at a truly horrible price. The artist's emancipation from Time's chronology, an emancipation which enables the artist to effect the very remaking of the real world, stems ultimately from the fact that the artist, like every man, is utterly alone. Milton Hindus justly notes: "For Proust, the individual exists irremediably alone! No real tie is possible between him and any of his fellows."[39] And the brief section of Proust he cites in support of this contention is clinching evidence:

> The bonds that unite another person to ourself exist only in our mind. Memory as it grows fainter relaxes them, and notwithstanding the illusion by which we would fain be cheated and with which, out of love, friendship, politeness, deference, duty, we cheat other people, we exist alone. Man is the creature that cannot emerge from himself, that knows his fellows only in himself; when he asserts the contrary, he is lying.[40]

One further bemusing stage remains in our delving into Proust's world and vision: after we have absorbed the artistic capacity to play with Time, the psychologization of the most precious essences of things and the drastic metaphysical solipsism that leaves no place for love save as a pathetic illusion, we find that at the deepest level Proust is claiming, after all, to articulate something not only about psychological time but about objective Time itself:

When the bell tinkled, I was already in existence and, since that night, for me to have been able to hear the sound again, there must have been no break of continuity, not a moment of rest for me, no cessation of existence, of thought, of consciousness of myself, since this distant moment still clung to me and I could recapture it, go back to it, merely by descending more deeply within myself. It was this conception of time as incarnate, of past years as still close held within us, which I was now determined to bring out into such bold relief in my book.[41]

There is indeed a strange reciprocal interaction and mutual actualization in progress between the self and Time. For the same individual who holds past years so close within him is himself spread out in Time: the last words of the novel describe

men . . . as occupying in Time a place far more considerable than the so restricted one allotted them in space, a place, on the contrary, extending boundlessly since, giant-like, reaching far back into the years, they touch simultaneously epochs of their lives—with countless intervening days between—so widely separated from one another in Time.[42]

And Hindus is entirely justified in his judgment that Proust

succeeds in communicating to us the very feeling of Time itself as a palpable medium which gives an iridescence to the most commonplace experiences immersed in it, somewhat after the way which the earth itself has of transforming into colorful and arresting objects any ordinary bits of glass that have been buried in it for thousands of years . . . memories recalled after many years had passed were commonplace no longer. Something magical had happened to them. They were transmuted as if by alchemy, and, simply from having lain imbedded for so long in the mysterious caves and recesses of the mind, they came forth once more into the light of an unfading day, completely emblazoned and covered with the golden imagery of his genius.[43]

Thus, at the end, after many a courageous and hazardous turn, we have basically *an artistic rather than a moral creation,* indeed an artistic edifice thrown up in despair of any meaningful moral effort. I do not for a moment here intend to restrict moral effort simply to restrained, controlled, "moral" as opposed to "immoral" behavior. Moral effort at its deepest level is a concreative activity, that builds the future of self and community, society. For its exercise it necessarily requires that Time shall be very real, irreversible, and part and portion of the very fabric of the moral agent. Moral effort presupposes likewise that the individual agent possesses and represents a focus of reality at once independent of Time and immersed in Time: the independence is required for Time-mastery, the immersion for the meaningfulness of successive endeavor.

6. Time, Vehicle of What Freedom?

Jean Guitton has some exciting speculations on man in Time which serve admirably to focus the insights of Alexander and Whitehead against the background of the new dimension of a positive, meaningful eternity, at once fulfillment of and menace to the temporal being:

Therefore time is necessary for the edification of an eternal spiritual person. The attribute of time is to flow, its essence conservation. Biological time is merely the image of historical time; its beginning, its prime, and its decline have no subsistence and so their final office is to act as symbols. In the animal order, individuals are the servants of life, which uses them to maintain its form. This is why the moment between fecundation and corruption tends to grow shorter, at least for the male who, even if he grows old, does no more than outlive his acts of love. It is quite otherwise in the spiritual order, where the word "life" points to something altogether unlike that self-enclosed movement and obscure drive. The temporal spiritual life is the conservation of what has been in what is, which is necessary if one is to move forward toward what will be. But since, as we have seen, what will be, in the last analysis, is eternity, the future being only its image, then time must be conceived as the preparation for a life of a third order. The biological rhythm is not abolished in the spiritual life; no more can consciousness and memory, however sublimated one may imagine them, disappear in this third form of existence. I will say, further, that if one strips time of any notion of flight or of *alea*, either contingency may still continue or persist, for nothing forbids us to conceive of a pure and substantial progress that eternally adds good to good and better to better. The supreme office of time is to prepare for each conscious being organs of vision and of life that cannot mature in our current existence but that will immediately begin to function so soon as a propitious sphere of operation is offered them, just as the organs of the embryo wait throughout their uterine existence for effort, space, and mobility in order to become active. Temporal reality—which goes by the name of history and memory, of trial and merit—comprises the stuff of these spiritual organs of eternity that have no function in what we call life. We have no words to denote them, any more than an embryo endowed with intelligence and consciousness could name or even conceive of the purpose of the still unformed apparatus that is silently modifying him without being immediately useful to him, but that later will be his tools of communication and equilibrium. Someone may object that no tool will be needed to adapt to eternity and that any intervention will be useless and therefore should be rejected. But without an analogue for what biology calls the body—or at least without the subsistence of our consciousness and consequently without the persistence of what has been in time—how could the finite being offer that unresisting opposition to the infinite being which it needs in order to enjoy the presence of the infinite without being absorbed in it:[44]

We may therefore agree with Herbert Dingle that "all the real problems associated with the notion of time are independent of physics."[45] And with G. A. Whitrow in his contention that there is "a profound connection between the temporal and contingent aspects of the universe."[46]

Without accepting all his other conclusions, we can say that Satosi Watanabe has articulated a profound insight when he writes:

We are told that space provides room for being and time provides room for becoming. We can accept this adage provided that we interpret the word "becoming" properly. Becoming is not changing, it is fulfilling, it is achieving, it is taking the form which a thing has been intended to assume. Becoming has intent, yet it has no plan. If the entire future development is mapped out already, and if we are shown every day a small fragment of it, then it is not becoming. Becoming is making of the yet-unmade. Becoming is constant death and constant rebirth. It is a simultaneous destruction and creation. Thus becoming implies creative action, pregnant with purpose, fortified by volition and, above all, nurtured with freedom and guided by knowledge. . . . Space is the vehicle of determination and being, time is the vehicle of freedom and value.[47]

And we can most enthusiastically subscribe to J. L. Russell's opinion that Teilhard's "synthesis of the Biblical Hebrew-Christian view of linear time moving towards a climax with the scientist's insight into the innate capacity of matter to complexify would seem to provide a richer and more fruitful context for Christianity than did the static, structureless view of history which dominated Western thought during the Middle Ages and for so many years afterwards."[48]

Friedrich Kümmel provides us with a further crucial insight when he writes:

Time is traditionally described as a *fragmentation* of successive vanishing moments; one can, however, just as logically assert the *integrity* of time based on the inner correlation and coexistence of its parts. *Only the two definitions taken together can fully describe the nature of time.* Since, however, as we have seen, they are contradictory, there is no question of there existing only one form or aspect of time but a variety of time structures and their corresponding modifications. . . . That time as succession could hold the attention of philosophy for such a long period in the history of thought, is not surprising. Time as flux, with its essentially destructive power, is always confronting man, whereas the positive "sustaining" time, being largely immanent to him, remains always partly hidden. It is not easily externalized or abstracted for its very inwardness constitutes a necessary precondition of the free form of life which is realized within it.[49]

Finally a waspish but perceptive materialist supplies us with the master key, though we intend to use it differently from the way in which he does: *"The world is not extended in time so that in a fraction of time there is only a fraction of world and in no time there is no world at all. Incessantly changing, the world is wholly present all the time."*[50]

7. The Revenge of Creatureliness

Unquestionably, Alexander's preoccupation with Time and his effort to articulate a whole Time-based metaphysic stems not only from a laudable attention, in the long shadow cast by Einstein, to a much neglected phenomenon which in Alexander's day was being fitted into a broader unified field, Space-Time, and therein endowed with a new and concrete reality. Alexander's effort and preoccupation amounted to and was motivated by much more than simply the tendency to take Time more seriously than it had been taken in the heyday of Platonic and Platonizing Christian metaphysics; the preoccupation and the effort stem likewise from a gradual shift in attitude from cosmic optimism of a specially facile and superficial sort to a cosmic pessimism of a restrictive and unjustified sort as man comes more and more to regard the whole evolution of the Space-Time continuum as a result of impersonal forces, only entropically directional at all and tending to reduce man to a fragile status. Parsons' crisp and trenchant statement just cited epitomized this attitude carried to its logical materialist extreme. And here we must note the curious and ironic revenge of neglected creatureliness upon the ruthlessly autocratic theism that so manhandled it. Precisely the new real status conferred on Time by modern science exacts the toll of a drastic relativization and even depression of Time itself. When the effort is made to impose on this most basic parameter of creatureliness the full weight of divine responsibility, we are, at least initially, left with a radically stagnant world. However much it changes in respect of the relative position of its components, it is precisely "wholly present all the time." Indeed we have here simply a variant of Lenin's "Nature is infinite but it infinitely exists."

Still psychologically open to the theist tradition, Alexander endeavors to issue out of this impasse by wrenching Time to a genuine creative status, making it a truly forward-driving power, so that the universe may have a new, true dimension of motion, the drive into genuine novelty. But the deepest fulcrum of this new dimension is precisely human intelligent and in the widest sense *moral* action and effort. This is what Kümmel sees and says so well. Sustaining Time, what might even be called redemptive Time, is internal and immanent to the *free* form of life that, in our Space-Time world, is man.

Teilhard's insight, as articulated by Russell, is precisely that man cannot be considered a total sport, nor yet held to represent a drastic and utter discontinuity with the past of the Space-Time universe. In a certain real sense, all of that universe moves in men into the dimension of freedom, attains to hominization. Watanabe is therefore entirely right in calling Space the vehicle of determination and Being and Time the vehicle of freedom and value. But in Teilhardian terms, Time is anteriorly coterminous with Space: and so, from the outset, the entire Space-Time continuum, which Parsons in one sense rightly says to be "wholly present all the time" is, from its first instant, driving toward actual freedom and value.

Whitrow is therefore profoundly right in stressing the intimate connection between the temporal and the contingent aspects of the universe. The most basic contingent aspect is precisely the *creatureliness* of that universe of our experience. And so we arrive at Dingle's position that the real Time-problems are independent of physics or, as we would say, *meta*-physical. Teilhard's constant reproach to modern scientists was that they were seeing only the outside of the web of being, neglecting the inside, interiority. Precisely from this neglect stems their pessimism, for sustaining Time is an inward phenomenon. It is not illegitimate to take the leap Parsons so deplores from physical to psychic, even to spiritual, *if the facts used come from a balanced over-all inspection of the universe of which man is an undeniable part and if these facts warrant that leap.*

The real problem is that a further leap is mandatory, from intelligent but fragile and evanescent man to Eternal God. Otherwise metaphysics will be replaced by ethics as the basic science and onto man's shoulders will be shifted the intolerable burden of making the universe meaningful. This was in fact the effort of Jean-Paul Sartre, whose *Being and Nothingness,* as we have seen, makes sense at all (but then eminent) if it be read as an ethics rather than as an ontology. There is a real "before" and "after" and the watershed is the irreducible mystery that is a free act of creaturely choice. On the other hand, this act of creaturely choice must be seen against the sustaining background of the eternal God in whom there is no "before" and "after" even though there is maximum dynamism.

It is because theists have trivialized into total insignificance the human contribution by exalting falsely and in the wrong way the supereminent power of the eternal God, that death-of-God theologians have felt compelled to tear down the whole fabric of theism and compel God to come into Time and be subject to Time in His redemption of the world. God, they implicitly aver, must know and taste the great relativizer, death, ultimate terminal of a distinctively temporal process, in order to achieve meaningful moral action. The Christian theist may indeed agree that the Incarnation was indispensable to a redemption not only of man but of Time itself. But such an Incarnation as expounded throughout the entire Christian tradition, presupposes the creation! The Creator descends with such power precisely because He is Creator; creation needs redemption and is capable of it precisely because it is created and, we would add, temporal. The constant tenet of the unredeemable status of Satan and his angels is most intimately connected with their atemporality. Though admittedly not eternal, they yet transcend, to their everlasting bane, the very Time that is the vehicle not only of created man's imperfection and consecutive repeated effort, but also of his redeemability.

We believe Whitehead, despite all the possible reservations about his over-all position and approach, to have come very close to expressing the real picture here when he writes that God and the world (note well, the entire world and not just man as a sport in an alien cosmos, the entire world hominized in man) are the instrument of novelty for each other; and when he insists that the ultimate nexus of interaction is a love-flow, the love in the world passing into the love in heaven and flooding back again into the world. God, we may say, is indeed an instrument of novelty for the world in two senses, first as its Creator, imparting to it the anterior novelty of existence, and second, as its Redeemer and Sanctifier, imparting to it the terminal novelty of perfection despite the imponderable of human freedom, nay employing that *very created imponderable as parameter of this perfecting action.*

Against both Alexander and Whitehead, we would maintain that a meaningful love relationship can exist only between two fully constituted personal beings. The mystery with which theists must more adequately grapple is the mystery of the possibility of the two anteriorly constituted beings, one of whom depends ultimately upon the other as Henry Miller maintains and yet can relate to Him freely (which Miller denies), and can in a tremendously real sense defy that Other.

We cannot here too strongly stress the importance of Teilhardian vision of man as the hominized cosmos and not merely a lonely sport on the horizons of an utterly alien universe. We hold that it is no accident that Scripture writes not "God so loved man" but "God so loved *the world*"; nor is it any accident that St. Paul should speak so glowingly of the whole of creation groaning in travail waiting for the appearance of the perfect creature. When man acts morally, when man operates in the moral dimension, he does not cease to be an immatered spirit. His act of will, his act of love, is a material act, involving his own body as well as his soul. And an absolutely crucial element of this material act is precisely its Time-intinctedness. Thus, even the laudable and edifying notion that God in forgiveness can cause the past to cease to be in some sense, must never be pushed too far. Every present of material time-intincted man is full of and inseparably linked to the past because he is a temporal creature. Time must be moved by a sane metaphysic from its entirely outward status as mere measurement or mere line of advance, empty riverbed or spiral scaffolding to its true status as co-constitutive of the complex phenomenon that is the hominized spatio-temporal continuum. But it must not be moved further onward and upward into a co-constitutive or constitutive parameter of God himself. If it is, Time the Redeemer degenerates into Time the fatalistic Tyrant, tyrannizing even God.

Time in its dimension, like the electron in its dimension, can most usefully be described as a shorthand expression for the complex phenomenon of creatureliness seen in function of its historicity. Its ambivalence derives from the very cachet it imparts to the evolving cosmos or more accurately from the complex character of that evolving cosmos of which the phenomenon articulated as Time is one indispensable element. This cosmos is a pleromization of the Eternally Simple and Really Infinite. Therefore the cosmos represents at its anterior terminal a total inhibition, not only of simplicity but even of personality and actual consciousness. But this cosmos is intrinsically temporal; it is created to thrust forward to ever greater complexity of compresence of those very parts outside of parts that issue from its material pleromization. And this forward thrust is asymptotic: never will the creation, the *creatura,* attain the total simplicity and absolute compresence from which it sprang. That would involve a reabsorption into the Creator. Furthermore, this forward thrust itself introduces a new dimension (I would not, indeed, rule out the possibility of its introduction of a multitude of dimensions; but there is one with which we are here vitally concerned); moreover, this new dimension, the dimension of conscious created freedom, does not abolish or destroy the preceding dimensions but remains in constant creative tension with those preceding dimensions, notably the obvious dimension of exteriority accessible to the natural sciences. It is at the levels preceding actual and active free conscious intelligence that the temporality of the cosmos operates destructively; it is at the level of free conscious intelligence that this same temporality, now hominized, operates sustainingly and even redemptively. It is man, not God, who combines within himself as his bane and glory, the two operations of temporality. The key, then, to a proper grasp of the riddle of time's ambivalence lies not in a temporalization of God but in a taking seriously of man, the crossroads creature, not only a taking seriously of man's real freedom but likewise a courageous facing up to man's immatered status, that element of man's situation against which Sartre so horrifiedly rebels. Man must be held to be incapable of a radical and unmixedly free act (even a creaturely act of this sort) not because of any suspected necessity of preserving God's sovereign power, but because of the empirically recognizable fact of man's materiality. On every occasion on which man coils for the leap into perfect creaturely freedom, he drags with him the whole inertia of the material pleroma. And this because of the temporal nexus linking him to the very dawn of creation.

All of the parameters selected by the atheists here considered have led us back to that mysterious dawn. Beyond it lies the blazing Light to which I now direct the attention of all who have shared this dialogue.

8

FAITH IN GOD

In the beginning God created the heaven and the earth (Gen. 1:1). . . . In the beginning was the Word and the Word was with God, and the Word was God. . . . And the Word was made flesh and dwelt among us (and we beheld his glory, the glory as of the only begotten of the Father) full of grace and truth (John 1:1, 14). . . . And I saw a new heaven and a new earth: for the first heaven and the first earth were passed away: and there was no more sea. . . . And I heard a great voice out of heaven saying, Behold, the tabernacle of God is with men, and he will dwell with them, and they shall be his people, and God Himself shall be with them, and be their God. And God shall wipe away all tears from their eyes: and there shall be no more death, neither sorrow, nor crying, neither shall there be any more pain: for the former things are passed away. And he that sat upon the throne said, Behold I make all things new. . . . And He said unto me, It is done. I am Alpha and Omega, the beginning and the end (Rev. 21:1, 3-5a, 6a).

The entire gamut of Christian pictures of reality is summed up in these three sections of Scripture. It is patently a creational view, but that is not its most important or distinctive characteristic. That characteristic is to be sought, rather, in the comprehensiveness attributed to God, the Creator but also the Goal. I would unhesitatingly say that the single most potent, important and distinctive sentence ever written by a theist is that compendium of theism which articulates God's proclamation: *I am Alpha and Omega.*

Plastic likenesses always limp in their effort to portray ultimate reality; but, with this warning, the picture is useful that portrays God as enveloping creation. At the outset, He launched it on its restless, unstable, historical way; at the end He welcomes it back into eternity where there shall be no more sea. Every moment of its restless voyage is copresent to God's eternity, precisely to His eternity rather than to

His "eternal now," a highly infelicitous expression, well-intentioned but already anthropomorphizing. The reality of creation derives entirely from the reality who is God. There is no external nothingness, however poetically conceived, with which the Creator grapples. Yet the reality of creation is really distinct from the reality who is God. On the other hand, the nexus between creation and God is so intimate that the distinction is a genuine mystery.

The effort of visual or optic adjustment we must here beg of the atheist, if only for the purpose of real empathetic understanding of what we would articulate, involves a total inversion of standards of reality whereby all that is initially considered by man most real and solid shall be dissolved into a restless and essentially unstable *dependency* of the genuine reality. Yet the modern atheist should here be aided somewhat by the disturbing discoveries of modern science concerning apparently solid material reality. It is here that we can most usefully begin.

Matter, then, apparently solid and everlasting, dissolves into an inherently unstable ebullience incapable of supporting even its own evolution, much less of explaining it; matter reveals its true face as a sort of stagnating coagulation of a reality more terribly unfamiliar to human eyes, energy pure and simple. Finitude, the apparently crucial parameter of genuine identifiable (precisely because *bounded*) reality, dissolves into nothing more than a dimensionalized drag on the genuine reality, Infinity. Time, apparently the crucial parameter of meaningful adventurous consecutive development, dissolves into a kind of stagnation of the truly dynamic reality, eternity; for Time, though indeed permitting and enjoining adventurous and even terrifying development, yet splays that development out so that its successive stages refuse to be grasped meaningfully by any human being, at least as equally meaningfully and brilliantly copresent. Freedom as man knows it, apparently the indispensible prerequisite of responsibility and dignity, reveals itself as precisely created freedom, an opening onto chaos, because powerless in function of the being it powers, a being radically incapable of total vision and therefore prone to partial and distorting thinking and consequent action. The most palpable of all apparent parameters of human activity, manufacturing potential, manipulative operation on matter, reveals itself as incapable of sustaining the entire human being precisely because of the openness of that being, his craving for more being and a different sort of completing union that can be effected by his creative-manipulative nexus with matter. But the moment one seeks in human sexuality that conjunctive parameter, it in turn reveals itself as opaque and insufficient, if invoked within the exclusive dimension of interhuman relationships. For the satisfier turns out to be another ultimate solitude who can procure even the pseudo-satisfaction of the lover only by a surrender that annihilates the beloved. But death at least remains. Yet this ultimate parameter of creatureliness, this apparently final absurdity of a universe of brute facticity, reveals itself as incapable of stilling an imperious longing of the human individual and the human genus, the longing for meaningful immortality. Hence, in place of a reality bounded by the material, finite, temporalized, factually free, productive, self-perpetuating, mortal entity (not only the human individual but the very complex that is the cosmos itself, considered as certainly material, finite, temporalized, even factually free in the sense of being radically open to new faces and advancing rims of development, productive, self-perpetuating yet entropically mortal), there emerges a reality actualizing in sheer untrammeled being the brute persistence of matter, actualizing as infinite the supreme identity partialized by finitude, actualizing as eternal the dynamism splayed out by temporality, actualizing sheerly the freedom endangered by dimensionalizing thrust, actualizing as creator the productivity palely reflected in manufacture, actualizing drastically the self-giving imperfectly realized in sexuality, actualizing Life as the Living God standing over against the supreme creaturely terminal of death, guaranteeing as Life-Giver that "there shall be no more death."

1. The Mystery of the Triune God

In this new perspective, God reveals himself pre-eminently as Triune Loving Creator. In these three words is revealed the pith of the God in whom the Christian theist places his faith. Christianity is not to be thought of as an overriding single revelation. It must be integrated into the total revelation-fact that is cosmic history. And there is one overriding salutary truth which Christian theism can and must learn from the Semitic theistic traditions of Judaism and Islam.

This is the truth that God is One. The Trinity is an early constituent of the Christian tradition and I contend that its pluralizing thrust is an indispensable corrective to the pantheism-inducing dangers of monolithic monotheism. Yet even the reality which is the doctrine of the Trinity can be mistakenly regarded. One can start from the absolutely flat fact of the three and try to show how they are one. This mistake in approach seems to me to characterize the recent exciting essay in theological speculation of Herbert Richardson.[1] For such an approach reduces the pivot of unity to a highly abstract and only very weakly explosive *principle* or indeed brute fact of coexistence.

The God who is to sustain creatures, redeem creation, and achieve reconciliation in the Omega Point must be one by a stronger power than a simple brute fact. He must be one in being. His act of existence must actualize all the thrust of created unities and infinitely more as well. But such a One will be explosively one. His unity will derive from His Being, along the quasi-parameters of infinity, eternity, supreme freedom, utter productivity, and total self-giving.

At this precise point we have arrived at a definitive crisis of theistic articulation, where the slightest admixture of anthropomorphism is fatal. If this Being whose unity derives from his being is conceived or articulated anthropomorphically, even in the subtlest terms, then insuperable difficulties are immediately encountered and thus strictures of the atheists of our age become entirely cogent. We hold entirely with the theistic legitimacy (abstracting from any questions of historical textural interpretation) of the reading of John 1:3b-4a as "what was made, in Him was life." In the Eternal, infinite God, that community in identity which is the poignant ideal and desperate need of modern man, which has been dimly adumbrated in all ages as a *desideratum,* is actualized by the very power of His Being. Human words boggle here; but we must nonetheless forge forward and say: God is Three not in virtue of a brute fact of ontological diversity in unity; rather, He is Three by virtue of an explosive internal act. Certainly the cautious theologians can insist that this act is eternal:

we insist that it is nonetheless an act. They can retort that the act is indivisible from the being; we retort that the Being cannot be articulated in abstraction from the act. And the act can be expressed in human terminology only as an Act of Love, the Act that *is* Love. The Supreme Being *is* supremely in that He loves: loves, not as a secondary afterthought but as the internal dynamism of His Being! A God who is and then loves, however subtly and supratemporally this state of affairs may be expressed, can only engender demiurges and compromise the absolute primacy of love. Being, the ontological ultimate, is expansive, is explosive. This is the deep relevant meaning of the Trinity, of the Triune God. But His infinity guarantees that the explosive character of His Being shall not erupt necessarily into a falling shower of relatively impotent sparks. The great Infinite Act of Being can face himself and love himself. All of the explosiveness of what we can only articulate as the initial thrust is answered entirely by the responsive thrust. *And the Word was God.* Yet the divine dialectic can never be exhausted safely by duality. Duality is the sign of contradiction. The deepest secret for us mortal creatures is that the two thrusts encounter each other not in tension but in a reality we can only attempt to describe as a Person.

Every nontheistic evaluation of reality sees behind the curtain of cosmic motion and human striving an ultimate, great, entropic peace. A thrust (mysteriously in all conscience) erupting into action gradually exhausts itself, and that is the end. Perhaps the end is another beginning; but each beginning is ultimately discrete and there is certainly no persistence of consciousness. The theistic evaluation of reality sees, rather, behind the curtain of cosmic motion and human striving, behind the entropically cursed thrust of cosmic motion and the recurrently frustrated human yen for immortality, a dynamic One who *is* trinitarianly: whose act of being which is His constitutive essence can only be described (not defined) as a diastole of exuberance engendering a systole of answering flooding-back, the rhythmic interchange spirating a sigh that is neither the yen for perfection nor yet the grasping for external nourishment that is our poor anatomical analogue but, rather, a thrill of sheer love. To our atheist listeners, we would say that at the moment he has realized this mystery the theist has broken through to the staggering conviction that *ultimate reality is alive!* Nay more, that ultimate reality is the fountainhead of that precarious defiance of entropy in the spatio-temporal-material universe that we, with mingled fierce loyalty and despairing uncertainty, call life.

"And Adam knew Eve his wife" (Gen. 4:1). This is the Eve of whom Adam had already said: "This is now bone of my bones, and flesh of my flesh: she shall be called Woman, because she was taken out of Man . . . and they shall be one flesh" (Gen. 2:23a, 24b). But here we are already in the familiar dimensions of human spatio-temporal reality; yet the analogy is not equivocity. It must only be turned right side up. It is not that man out of his ecstasy excogitated an impossible dream of God. It is that God out of His infinite ebullient goodness created a reality that would eventually reach the stage of such articulation. In the Ultimate Reality, the event is quite other. Being explosively present to himself knows himself, and the Word is with God and the Word is God.

The knowledge of every Adam in this dimension is a transitory ecstatic touching of the solitude that is every Eve; and the product is a third existent, namelessly and solitarily distinct from both. Not so in Ultimate Reality. As the knowing was unobstructed and utter, so the breath spirated is no lonely infant isolated by the rigorous laws of spatio-temporality and creatureliness; that breath is internally as the thrill of Being utterly and unobstructedly present to himself. We mortals tend to call this *Will*. But again the whole picture must be set right side up. For us, willing is a tendential act, a reaching out and grasping after the not yet actual. In God, Will internally considered must rather be the actual thrill of consent to the awareness that He is. Here again we must rigorously expunge anthropomorphism: we do not intend to say in our preceding articulation that the Will of God is an actual thrill of consent to an awareness of His Being, which awareness can be in any sense separated from that Being or even ontologically ordered in numbering sequence *after* that Being and therefore somehow consequent to it. Rather, we wish to speak of a thrill of consent to the awareness *which* God is.

God *is* in a fashion to which matter, not man, is the analogue; God *knows* in a fashion to which sex, not intellection, is the analogue; God *wills* in a fashion to which frisking and purring kittens, not laboring and longing man, is the analogue.

The Triune God is Three because Being is explosive; He is One because Being is Eternally Infinite. And this Triune God is Loving. It is not merely that He does love (himself or creatures, even before their creation), nor even that He is *Love*. Again we must avoid substantives like the plague, for their function is delimitation, the crucial parameter of creaturehood not Creatorhood. No, God is loving. Only when the Name of the Third Person has been spoken has the true meaning of the First or Second Person been articulated. Were God's *Being* not Loving, then His diastolic thrust would be indeed that entropic debilitation incumbent on matter; were His Knowing not Loving, then the systolic response would be the tensional clash of antithesis and thesis purveyed by Hegel. Were God's Being not Loving, then the course of the universe would indeed be the somber spectacle of recurrent deaths; were God's Knowing not Loving, then the course of the universe would indeed be the conflict-powered march to perfect self-possession which is the horror of the Hegelian universe. But the diastolic thrust who is God is Loving, the expansiveness of Being richer than the heat of the proto-atom; the systolic response who is God is Loving, untrammeled and unafraid and unconflicting because an awareness of the total lambent power and goodness of Being. And therefore (again *not* consequently) the thrill of consent who is God is Loving, immanent and powerful as the rhythm who spirated it.

We have again arrived at a crucial point in our exposition. The atheist listener may now politely exclaim that we have done yeoman work at subtilization but have succeeded in nothing more than writing poetry. We have adduced not a shred of proof. We have answered not a single one of the conundrums posed by human existence, knowing, and desire. We have regaled a summer's afternoon with a pleasant myth but we have convinced no one not already susceptible to a perhaps novel articulation but for all that an articulation of familiar hopeful poetry.

We now unhesitatingly say to the atheist listener: We ask you to consider the ramifications of our vision, if once the secondary problems (real indeed but still secondary) can be resolved. We draw attention deliberately to our cardiac analogy and we cite the passionate words of Browning:

> The very God, think, Abib, doest thou think?
> So the All-Great were the All-Loving too!
> So through the thunder comes a human voice
> Saying: O heart I made, a heart beats here.[2]

You have not *proved* that matter-in-motion is absolutely ultimate, nor that finitude in repetition closes the circle of our hope, nor that time alone can be a potent Creator, nor that the perilous freedom of the for-itself is irremediably pitted against an anterior and ultimate sliminess, nor that productive manufacture in its widest sense is all that man can expect, nor that the yen for self-surrender must be satisfied temporarily with the uneasy ecstasy of sex and ultimately with a surrender to the great passive Mother, nor even that man who raised so many grave mounds in defiance of death must indeed succumb to death in the end.

Consider therefore a moment the ramifications of our vision of the Supreme Being who is Loving. And confront Him with that boy with the chattering teeth, about to be cut off from the land of the living and abandoned to the terrifying fog in which he is utterly alone, that infant to whom we promised this chapter would be an act of reparation. I believe every atheist we have here considered would agree on the appropriateness of this challenge: Lenin because of his hatred of fascist oppression and his consistent devotion to the greatest possible fullness in the only life there is; Nietzsche because his poet's eye would see in the act of condemnation a total betrayal of his own notion of the Superman; the Time-worshippers because they would deplore the arrogation by certain temporal creatures of the destructive-creative-but-ultimately-benign action of Time; Sartre because his angry compassionate eyes would see yet another in-itself being sucked down into the sliminess of the for-itself; Miller because he would lament the joys this boy might have known and the agonies of remorse his killers must experience; Camus quite simply because he hates to see any human being, especially a young and innocent human being, die or to see men arrogate to themselves the right to play vicar of death, the terrible but ultimately benignant relativizer. If each actor in that drama, nay if even the theistic priest, had been thoroughly and operatively convinced of the fact that Ultimate Reality is Loving, would the tragedy have taken the course described in the powerful act of accusation? Perfect Love, even in human beings, casts out fear. What, then, would a human being be capable of achieving when he is convinced that this fragile and inconstant human love is but a pale reflection of the Loving that is Ultimate Reality? Nay, I dare to press further; if the ultimate background of all our striving is a mindless will-less reality, or some species of primeval and ultimate slime, or merely the hard crystalline stagnant fact that we are here for a while, *is that boy worth saving?* Or say, rather, will the priest, beset with a hundred calculations of personal prudence, thrust unerringly to save him? But if, on the other hand, that priest at least and those soldiers at most know that beyond all the vicissitudes of their strivings beats a heart who is Loving, will they not then value that life with reverent terror? If they do not, they have simply not understood in all its dimensions what it means to say that this Triune Loving God is *Creator*.

2. The Twinning Mystery of Creation and Freedom

Virtually every problem that arises at the crucial crossroads of the *freedom-problem* really derives from a foreshortened or distorted notion of *creation*. The Genesis account says: "In the beginning God created *the heaven and the earth*" and every succeeding "act" of "creation" is represented rather as a formation or an eduction or a fashioning. Because theists have been nervously unwilling to tolerate the notion of global creation and successive evolution, they have neglected impermissibly the secret of matter and the dynamic of evolution as parameter of the divine action on and in creaturely evolution. Once grant, for a moment, the global-creation notion, and the whole gamut of subsequent problems takes on quite a different complexion.

A great modern theist document eloquently and even, perhaps, to some theists, startlingly, articulates the need consequent upon the global-creation notion to take matter seriously:

> . . . man is one. Through his bodily composition he gathers to himself the elements of the material world. Thus they reach their crown through him, and through him raise their voice in free praise of the Creator.[3]

It would surely be impossible more drastically to articulate man's integral nexus with that matter which in man raises its voice in free praise of the Creator.

But the instant man's material nexus and parameter is fully recognized, a sane interpretation of human freedom will be based on the realization and admission that man exercises freedom not only as a created being, but also as a material being.

Of almost equal importance to a proper grasp of the freedom-problem is a sound and sane persuasion of the fact that man exercises freedom *in time*. Man is a temporal being, who, along the parameter of interiorizing complexification of the material pleroma is asymptotically approaching the perfect freedom of God. The temporality of man's freedom is of vital importance for a proper grasp of events and prescriptions which might otherwise be gratuitous stumbling blocks.

Man the individual is time-tincted and can only be grasped in his entirety when his temporality is taken seriously. Similarly the human genus is a temporally evolving entity whose temporality deserves equally serious consideration. We have already indicated one important conclusion: the norms of conduct fitting for the individual at an early stage of the evolution of the genus are simply no longer fitting when the genus has reached genuine actuality and the individual has been integrated into the new actuality. But these are considerations oriented much more to the future and, perhaps, the more distant future. The forcing of the threshold of the new mankind was always regarded by Teilhard as an urgent and imperative necessity of our day, but he certainly did not envision the emergence of this new mankind as an event likely to occur in our own century. While I have presumed to modify somewhat this very long-range perspective of Teilhard's, by reference to the phenomenon of acceleration of progress, evolution and human development in our own decade, I would not wish to be read as saying that the new mankind is drastically imminent.

Even as Scripture tells us that the kingdom of God does not come by observation and warns us against sterile mathematical calculations, so it must be said that it is more important for every individual to labor toward the realization of this new mankind than to attempt to deduce the degree of imminence of its appearance. Yet here again the freedom-conundrum raises its head. It is entirely mandatory that the free human being realizes the dramatic extent to which he can impede the realization of this next stage of cosmic evolution on our planet. Being enveloped in a greater power, the power of the triune Loving Creator-God, does not reduce to nothing man's real creative freedom; rather, it dramatically intensifies it, for if, on the one hand, man drags with him the beloved fragility of matter, he at the same time participates in the creative freedom of God himself.

3. The Twinning Mystery of Freedom and Sin

But there is a further consideration flowing from the noble status of temporality in man's evolution. This consideration is critically applicable to man's past and present. Precisely because man is a temporal creature and exercises his freedom in Time; precisely because time is ontologically irreversible and genuinely concreative, *man's exercise of freedom can and should intensify through Time.* The radical power to defy the Creator or to collaborate with Him in imaginative adventure is, to be sure, present from the moment of the emergence of the first truly free creature. But, even assuming perfect cooperation on man's part, the intensity of the exercise of his freedom should naturally depend on the point-instant in the Time-dimension at which man finds himself. Knowledge, the contradistinctive feature of man's being, is essential for the proper exercise of freedom. As the one increases, so should the intensity of exercise of the other. Thus, there is nothing contradictory in the picture of a Loving Creator aiding incipient knowing man by very strict and detailed prescriptions and leaving maturing man more and more to his own resources in the applications of generic norms. Actions can certainly be inappropriate and harmful at a certain point and beneficent or at least harmless at another. It would be cruel madness to allow a ten-year-old total freedom from all prescriptions in the styling of his daily life; it would be equally cruel madness to impose these prescriptions on a thirty-year-old. Human parents usually find the perfect balance particularly hard to come by: they err on the side either of excess or of defect. It can be assumed that a Loving Ominiscient Creator-God would not make either error. This consideration ought to reassure those timid theists who see the people of God rushing to perdition because certain time-honored prescriptions have now been made no longer mandatory though still highly recommended. Indeed the only sort of person who could still have difficulties after such a reflection is the one who either believes passionately that humanity will never grow up *or who does not want it to.*

A God who is Loving neither needs nor wants to hobble his creature. To introduce such notions is hopelessly to distort the reality we have just enunciated concerning Ultimate Reality as Loving. A "law of God" is never an arbitrary whim geared to the practice of an autocratic power. Such a "law" is always a flat articulation of the very fabric of reality. No atheist seems to object to the dreadful trammeling of human freedom resulting from the "law" that if you leap out of a high window in your natural state you will fall to your death on the ground below. The "moral laws" are of course more subtle but their origin is analogous: they stem from the very fabric of created intelligent volitional entities, taken separately and taken in interrelation.

A final consideration of phenomenological history must here be interpolated, however, in order to assure a sane and balanced grasp of the freedom problem: man has already defied his Creator! The reality of what the theist calls sin is not disputed by any intelligent commentator of the modern scene. Too much evidence speaks for the fact that something is amiss in man. This already perpetrated defiance has, of course, engendered a nameless disturbance of the cosmic harmony, brutalized man, and dulled his ear to the voice of God. But here again it should be emphasized that man's sin is and always has been more than simple personal disloyalty to a Loving Creator: it is and always has been a defiance of and attempted rebellion against the very fabric of *man's own reality*. The Creator cannot, without violating the very freedom of the creature he deigned to create in slow rhythmic stages out of the pleroma, prevent the dire consequences of such tampering on the part of that creature with its own being. When, out of the compounded hell of their own multifarious and millennial sinning, human beings scream angry resentment at the Loving Creator, they would do well to meditate the courage and the unbounded love of a Creator who was willing to risk all this precisely so that man might be free.

4. The Mystery of the Incarnation

Yet there is a way in which the Creator who pleromized His own Act of Being in a total kenosis can come to grips with the problem of sin without infringing the freedom of His wayward creatures. He can descend into the dimension and reality of their very created, free, intelligent, volitional nature to show that nature how it can be co-operatively united to Him and to repair the rent already made by man's sinning. This mystery, utterly unfathomable to the human creature, involved a deification of humanity beyond man's wildest dreams. Henceforth the glory of God is bound indivisibly to that one possible mode of reception of being which is the only sensible thing that can be meant by "human nature." As the first kenosis involved a prodigal pleromization, so the second kenosis involves a restrictive identification.

This God Incarnate is come not to explain but to suffer and to redeem. The Incarnate God, having animated a free and genuine existent human nature to walk the whole way of union with God, has gloriously reanimated that existent human nature in the strictly spatio-temporal, material event that is the Resurrection. In the light of all three events, Creation, Incarnation and Resurrection, and in their light alone, can the still agonizing problem of human freedom be usefully posed.

Sartre has exclaimed that if God exists, Sartre is not free. Our response is that if the God Sartre envisions existed no one of us would be free. It is otherwise with the Triune Loving Creator, Incarnate and Risen. The problematic of freedom is illuminated by the fact of Loving. Being himself, utterly and unobstructedly present to and consenting to himself, is utterly free: free, because no barrier interposes itself between His Being and His Will. Man, whose dramatic and imperiled emergence from prehuman reality Sartre has so masterfully portrayed, is the most total antipode in our cosmos of this Free God. For between man's being and his will there is interposed the barrier of man's materiality, finitude, and temporality; man is dependent on a long line of heredity and an often apparently hostile environment and, worse still, on his own often imperfect and destructive acts; man's knowledge is fragmentary and often emotion-tinged, so that he can abuse his own reason to his own perdition. Yet this being has been granted freedom of action. Wars and exploitation, the long agony of ideology-motivated prisons, Dachau and Belsen in our own day, bear witness to the patent fact that God sees the truth but waits. The mystery now emerges not so much in the form of the question *how* God could effect this freedom, as, rather, in the form of the question *why* God would entrust to such a being such power! The answer to that is the same as the answer to all created mysteries in the world-view we have outlined: because He is Loving.

The atheist protestor in the name of human happiness cannot have his cake and eat it too. He cannot protest violently that man has too many handicaps against him and then proclaim that free man is worth the death of God. A modicum of prudent inspection of man's present state would surely rather elicit a terrified sense of impending catastrophe were the thinker to be compelled to accept this man as only lord of the cosmos. Nor does this statement strike equally at our own contention. For the Loving Creator need not infringe man's freedom in order to save the cosmos from destruction; he can precisely operate upon that very freedom itself, *by Love,* in the most interior and hidden node of that freedom's independence, to effect the analogue of that supreme love-relation whereby the humanity of Christ was conjoined to the Second Person of the Triune God. The cost is, of course, crucifixion, but the prize is resurrection of untrammeled freedom.

5. The Mystery of the Everlasting Crucifixion

Another great document of theism luminously expresses the mystery we have here sought to articulate:

> In the end when He completed on the cross the work of redemption, whereby He achieved salvation and true freedom for men, He also brought His revelation to completion. He bore witness to the truth, but He refused to impose the truth by force on those who spoke against it. Not by force of blows does His rule assert its claims. Rather, it is established by witnessing to the truth and by hearing the truth, and it extends its dominion by the love whereby Christ, lifted up on the cross, draws all men to Himself.[4]

Pre-eminently real himself, the Loving God calls to reality and respects reality, the reality He has mysteriously created. He respects it to the supreme degree, that of ratifying eternally that reality's choice even against himself. Thus, created reality viewed under the sign of strong Loving Creation, possesses a sobering and terrifying relative independence of its own. The document already cited explicitates this:

> If by the autonomy of earthly affairs we mean that created things and societies themselves enjoy their own laws and values which must be gradually deciphered, put to use, and regulated by men, then it is entirely right to demand that autonomy.[5]

Loving Creation then, initially, globally pleromizes the infinite, eternal, simple Act of Being; then, out of that pleromization, in mysterious free guidance of an ever increasingly free complexifying and interiorizing pleroma, the Creator eventually effects the birth of free conscious agents. From this moment forward, as Teilhard never tires of stressing, the further destiny of the evolving cosmos of which those free agents form part depends on the consent of those agents. This is the quintessence of created freedom: *the undetermined ability to consent to being in evolutionary context, in a fashion asymptotically approaching God's own utterly free consent to himself unobstructedly known.* The indeterminacy guaranteeing perfect freedom derives not from any ontological withdrawal of the divine action but, rather, from the very limitations of man himself and the obstructions intervening between his naked self, individual and generic, and the full knowledge of that self. Indeterminate created freedom is not a bonus mysteriously conferred on creatures set over against their Creator; it is, rather, a dreadful inherent parameter of their state.

If we attend in the proper spirit, the apparently whimsical interpretation of one of Christ's sayings becomes luminous with sobering meaning: "for without me ye can do nothing" (John 15:5 b). This implies not simply the negative incapacity to effect positive creative action; it suggests a pseudo-ability, very real indeed in its own dimension, to effect a relative reversal of the whole rhythmic pulse of being, to make a kind of nothingness. It is this again that Sartre has seen with perceptive penetration from his own strange angle of vision: rightly indeed he has noted that nothingness can inhere only in being; rightly, too, though in a mistaken context, he has articulated the need for man, the emergent for-itself, to tunnel a nothingness between himself and reality around him, in order to hide behind it in total independence. The mystery of the Incarnation shows, by witnessing in the flesh to the exact reverse, just how necessary such tunneling is for man's *total* independence, and just how stultifying and horror-producing. The freedom sought by Sartrean man is the freedom of God in the context of creaturehood. But if the creature seeks the totality of the freedom that is God's, in the context of man's own radical creatureliness, then man will shut himself off hopelessly from the very power that can impart to his imperfect striving the thrust of divinity. The one posture man must never assume, on pain of functioning as a destructive free agent, is the posture of *closedness-within-himself.* For creation of which man is the conscious free articulation is ultimately oriented not to self-sufficiency but to divinization: creation is radically open to union with the Creator in a thrust that renders it immortal without abolishing its real distinctness. Creation points beyond itself. This is at once the reason for the mysterious nature of its freedom and the promise of its ultimate glorification.

The human creature must surrender his will to his Creator and receive it back, powered by the divine Omnipotence, unto an everlasting crucifixion that is a progressive bursting of restrictive boundaries of centrifugal selfhood so that the true self of individual *and of cosmos* may at last be found in the Creator. Yet *in the executive dimension of his own real contribution,* man is ineluctably, egocentripetally alone, individually, generically, and even cosmogenetically. *Creation must do its part.* That part cannot and will not be done by the Creator because that would amount to a depression and violation of the very genuine reality imparted to the cosmos in creation and realized terminally in free, conscious man.

The ultimate level of our explicitation (*not explanation*) of the mystery of created freedom lies in the assertion that *this mind-staggering and appalling yet challenging freedom derives from the power of the Loving Creator to impart less than the fullness of His own act of Being.* In the Triune God the self-giving, the rhythmic pulse is total and the result is an utterly free, utterly perfect, *utterly self-contained and self-referring* reality. In the act of creation, the act is mysteriously dimensionalized, partialized, and the result is a created reality, radically open, *free precisely because unstable,* granted enough reality to chart its own course but not enough reality to rest within itself.

Augustine has been wretchedly mistranslated so often and the whole subtlety of his insight lost thereby. *Creasti nos ad te* does *not* mean "Thou hast created us *for* thyself" but "Thou hast created us *unto* thyself." Creation and man, in our cosmos its presently crowning product, *is* an open tendential thrust. It is the tension, till time be done, between the egocentripetal thrust of creation's genuine relative independence and the egocentrifugal thrust of creation's tendential yen that constitutes, in still another sense, the mystery of created freedom.

6. The Mystery of the Eschaton

We referred at the outset of our investigation to the evidence of God in creation. We contend that this evidence is present primarily in the cosmological dimension. To this dimension, some of the atheists we have examined (notably Sartre) show a bemusing indifference; others attend to it but miss a certain coloring (notably the Marxists and Nietzsche).

How can we fail to see [cries Teilhard] that, in the case of a *converg-*

ing universe such as I have delineated, far from being born from the fusion and confusion of the elemental centres it assembles, the universal centre of unification (precisely to fulfil its motive, collective and stabilizing function) must be conceived as preexisting and transcendent. A very real "pantheism" if you like (in the etymological meaning of the word) but an absolutely legitimate pantheism—for if, in the last resort, the reflective centres of the world are effectively "one with God," this state is obtained not by identification (God becoming all) but by the differentiating and communicating action of love (God all *in everyone*). And that is essentially orthodox and Christian.[6]

If time be truly taken seriously, if man be seen as an emergent of a drastically centering cosmos, intinct with a thrust to interiorizing complexification, then the coloring cast upon the universe by "the diaphany of the Divine in the heart of a universe aflame, of the Divine radiating from the depths of a Matter on fire"[7] will burst upon the observer like a radiant dawn, opening up to the human person a really unlimited horizon of creaturely development, the lost horizon betrayed out of existence by the persistent Narcissistic preoccupation with the technique of man's interior functioning, *illicitly split off from the whole thrust of evolution.*

We can here indeed make Teilhard's concluding words our own:

Among those who have attempted to read this book to the end, many will close it, dissatisfied and thoughtful, wondering whether I have been leading them through facts, through metaphysics or through dreams. But have those who still hesitate in this way really understood the rigorous and salutary conditions imposed on our reason by the coherence of the universe, now admitted by all? A mark appearing on a film; an electroscope discharging abnormally; that is enough to force physics to accept fantastic powers in the atom. Similarly, if we try to bring man, body and soul, within the framework of what is experimental, man obliges us to readjust completely to his measure the laws of time and space.

To make room for thought in the world, I have needed to "interiorize" matter; to imagine an energetics of the mind; to conceive a noogenesis rising upstream against the flow of entropy; to provide evolution with a direction, a line of advance and critical points; and finally to make all things double back upon *someone*.[8]

And to the atheist humanists who are sincerely interested above all else in the fate of the human person, we submit Teilhard's warning: "The only universe capable of containing the human person is an irreversibly 'personalising' universe."[9]

At the inception of the pleroma, then, and at the crux of man's tormented pilgrimage on Calvary, we are met by the mystery of love effecting the mystery of freedom. And it is the same at the end. The first document of modern theism we cited continues in eloquent phrases to foreshadow that end as we have reported it from the Holy Writings:

We do not know the time for the consummation of the earth and of humanity. Nor do we know how all things will be transformed. As deformed by sin, the shape of this world will pass away. But we are taught that God is preparing a new dwelling place and a new earth where justice will abide, and whose blessedness will answer and surpass all the longings for peace which spring up in the human heart.

Then, with death overcome, the sons of God will be raised up in Christ. What was sown in weakness and corruption will be clothed with incorruptibility. While charity and its fruits endure, all that creation which God made on man's account will be unchained from the bondage of vanity.

Therefore, while we are warned that it profits a man nothing if he gain the whole world and lose himself, the expectation of a new earth must not weaken but rather stimulate our concern for cultivating this one. For here grows the body of a new human family, a body which even now is able to give some kind of foreshadowing of the new age. Earthly progress must be carefully distinguished from the growth of Christ's kingdom. Nevertheless, to the extent that the former can contribute to the better ordering of human society, it is of vital concern to the kingdom of God.

For after we have obeyed the Lord, and in His Spirit nurtured on earth the values of human dignity, brotherhood and freedom, and indeed all the good fruits of our nature and enterprise, we will find them again, but freed of stain, burnished and transfigured.[10]

This stirring conclusion of an exhilarating document suggests already the direction of our own modest effort at that minimum of explication owed atheist listeners concerning the vexed problem of human freedom. For it puts before us most dramatically the call and the challenge to action in place of tormented meditation of mysteries too high for us. It sounds the trumpet for the building of the earth, the new earth, in the doughty love of man answering to the transfiguring power of Christ.

7. The Mystery of Revelation

This then is our vision. But how, the atheist listener may inquire, is this to be reconciled with the strange musty odors emanating from religious practice and sacrosanct traditions? Is this not rather an excursus into a revolutionary theologizing without any of the solidity of traditional theism? Where is there here to be espied the consistent trenchant preservation of the faith delivered to the saints? Indeed not a few theists may pose the same question. We must be prepared to give a reason for the faith that is in us. And we would here refer to still another document of Vatican II and a commentary on that document by a leading Scripture scholar of our day. *The Dogmatic Constitution on Divine Revelation,* promulgated by Pope Paul VI on November 18, 1965, states:

. . . the words of God, expressed in human language, have been made like human discourse, just as of old the Word of the eternal Father, when He took to Himself the weak flesh of humanity, became like other men.[11]

The commentator writes:

. . . a written record is a dead letter, needing constant interpretation and commentary in succeeding ages. It cannot of itself answer new questions, or explain what was once clear and has now become obscure. But the writings transmitted in a living community, from one generation to another, are accompanied by a continuous tradition of understanding and explanation, which preserves and re-expresses their meaning, and which applies them, from time to time, to the solving of new problems.[12]

In the dimension of revelation, as we have noticed throughout our investigation in so many other dimensions and areas, the damnable tendency to staticize has always been operative, the tendency among theists to endow the eternal dynamic God with the degrading staticity of human logical cogitation. The phenomenon of revelation is not a poetic odyssey of discovery whereby man by progressively refined efforts wrests from a faceless mindless will-less reality a dream of beauty and harmony which he articulates in ever changing and constantly refined poems. It is a speaking by the Loving God, out of the eternal dynamism that is His rhythmic pulse of being, to the evolving cosmos; and this Word of the Lord is *given with power*. It is not simply a flat, static, layered unveiling of static strengths and qualities; it is a continuous creative act, geared far more to revealing to man those mysteries of his own being which derive from his openness to God on which he cannot look and live until he has been caught up himself into eternity. Thus the dynamic of revelation will keep pace exactly with the dynamic of the evolution of the cosmos whose present crown is man in his still larval stage but whose ultimate state, that of perfect creature, bridging galactic gulfs of space and uniting all intelligent awarenesses everywhere in this cosmos at least (this cosmos that may well be but one of many), is not yet even imaginable to present-day man.

There is sound evidence that we live in a thrilling age of *Zeitwandel,* though every age indeed is to some extent a *Zeitwandel,* for temporal reality is constantly changing. Because of our strange position in the Time-dimension, a position at once exhilarating and terrifying, a point-instant of great and drastic transition, there are many who fear that old certainties are disappearing, fading like an autumn sunset, dissolving like salt grains into a dreadful amorphous uncertainty. It is not so. But the caterpillar contemplating the butterfly could scarcely recognize himself therein; and seeing a pupa, he must conclude that this is his final demise.

This malaise of our age is by no means confined to theists. *The Pastoral Constitution on the Church in the Modern World,* promulgated by Pope Paul VI on December 7, 1965, signally summarizes this malaise, precariously balanced on the razor's edge between fey optimism and blackest paralyzing pessimism:

> . . . the modern world shows itself at once powerful and weak, capable of the noblest deeds or the foulest. Before it lies the path to freedom or to slavery, to progress or retreat, to brotherhood or hatred. Moreover, man is becoming aware that it is his responsibility to guide aright the forces which he has unleashed and which can enslave him or minister to him. . . . Thus, on the one hand, as a creature, he experiences his limitations in a multitude of ways. On the other, he feels himself to be boundless in his desires and summoned to a higher life.[13]

8. The Triune Age of the Earth

In such a climactic age, there is a special need for faith. This faith must be temporally oriented rather than a mere atemporal acceptance of allegedly eternal truths (the trouble with these "eternal truths" being that they are indeed true in eternity but must be constantly asymptotically more accurately restated to keep them even analogically relevant to advancing time). This faith, then, must contain an element of trusting forward-thrusting conviction that the battle is worth the effort, that the outcome *could* at least be victory and the satisfaction of the longings of man's heart. It is precisely in this dimension of the faith-phenomenon that Protestant Christianity has made its signal contribution, a contribution supremely relevant to our present purpose. For that Protestant tradition has continually proclaimed faith to be a personal trust in a personal Savior. And we here proclaim faith in God to involve a crucial trust in a supremely real Tri-Personal Loving Creator-Redeemer-Sanctifier. This Loving God is not simply making *truths about himself* ever clearer to His creation, now centered and focused in man; He is making *himself* clearer and ever more powerfully operative, within the limits imposed by man's skittish freedom, to that creation with whom He has, temporally considered, been conducting such a long, passionate, and poignant love-affair. As Creator, His relation to creation was (and of course continues to be!) the most intimate conceivable and yet precisely inconceivable because it is in the order of existence which is unconceptualizable. As Redeemer, His relation to creation was the more tensional though more conceivable one of Crucifixion-Resurrection. As Sanctifier, His relation to creation again swings inward to a new intimacy, as intense as the Creator-relationship but both conceivable and overwhelmingly personal, since *mediated* in a very real sense by the free acceptance of the redeemed creature. In the temporal dimension, the first truth to be impressed upon the free creature's heart, and on all creation via that free creature, was the truth that there was a Creator. Hence in the earliest temporal dispensation the stress in revelation was most often on man's comparative nothingness, so that essentially primitive but exuberant man would not go astray into paths of sterile God-games, playing at being the God he could never be. In the next dispensation, that of redemption, the stress in the over-all phenomenon of revelation was most often on man's indisputable sinfulness, his capacity to "do nothing" in alienation from God. In the third dispensation, that of sanctification, the stress is most often on man's potential for participated Godhood.

It would be utterly erroneous to imagine these three ages as successive and mutually exclusive. Creation contains already potential
redemption and sanctification; sanctification involves continuing creation and redemption. Yet I believe that, in a very real sense, if the
figure be properly understood, one can say that the age of sanctification is just beginning in our own day. I am well aware of the theological (and indeed atheistic!) objections that could be entered against
this contention. I protest that it is not a strictly theological or anthro-
pological articulation but, rather, a cosmological observation on the
borderline between theology and anthropology.

Creation is a point-instant act and yet likewise a continuing operation. Redemption is a point-instant act (effected on Calvary and in
the garden of Joseph at dawn) but it perdures. Sanctification is of
course, on one reading, a supratemporal act commencing with the
descent of the Holy Spirit in the immediate wake of the redemption.
Yet the most orthodox Christian theistic tradition holds that redemption is not and can never be automatic, precisely because of the
combined operation of the parameters of created freedom *and time.*
Christ's redemptive act, we are told, must be *appropriated* to each
successive human individual; and once again, in a dual sense: initially
absolutely for that individual, in baptism (i.e., no human being can
be actually redeemed before he actually exists!) and again, more
subtly, along the time-line of that fallible human evolution to the
great moment of death when that individual crosses into eternity.
There is thus in redemption, perhaps even more clearly than in creation (though that could be traced, too) a peculiarly multidimensional
dynamic: the *will* to redemption is present from the instant of man's
fall; but only when the *fullness of time* is come does the redemptive
point-instant act occur; and this point-instant act is again temporalized along the time-line of each individual life and along the vaster
time-line of the evolving life of the genus. May it not then be so
likewise with sanctification, in a fashion proper precisely to and specified by the nature of the sanctifying act? Even as creation (in an
utterly impenetrable mystery) presupposes the nadir of utter nothingness of what is to be created; even as redemption presupposes another kind of nadir, when man has given full proof of his sinfulness
and reached a state of morbid despair because of that frailty; so

sanctification might be held to presuppose, for the inception of its full actualization, for, as it were, the moment of turning on of its full power in the executive operative dimension of the genus, a nadir of Godlessness and destructive nullifying power. I mean Godlessness here in the psychologico-personal sense, not primarily in the moral; a state of widespread loss of contact with God, the Loving Source of Life, a state precipitated certainly to a great extent by human sinfulness of the past and present which thrusts between the individual and his God the awful curtain of the pain and outrage inseparable from wickedness, but due also in no small measure to the peculiar phenomenon of maturation which leads man to imagine his own power as so extensive and potentially all-embracing as to abolish any need for a Creator. Man's destructive nullifying power here signifies not his constant capacity as free creature to corrupt the cosmos by sin but, rather, his more specific physical power, derived from the fission of the atom, to destroy physically his own spaceship-home. If I were therefore asked the moment at which the age of sanctification in the intensive operative executive sense began, I should unhesitatingly select the moment of the true beginning of the atomic age, the moment at which the first atomic bomb plunged to earth in Hiroshima, signaling man's proved executive capacity to destroy the world.

At this moment the Loving Creator cannot, without violation of His own creature, forcibly intervene with any drastic apocalypse. He can only commence in time to pour out a more abundant rain of His Spirit, offering most insistently to man the apotheosis he craves at the very moment man stands as moral agent at the antipodes of the Loving Creator God.

In this last extremity of his checkered career, man needs more than continuing creation, more than redemption; he needs sanctification, he needs to be rendered divine, he needs to be brought into the dimension of the Loving Creator, he needs to be aided to love. Over Hiroshima and Nagasaki has been written in mushroom clouds of fire: *Love one another or perish!* This is the true and deepest sign of our age: not mere search for new and deeper wisdom, not mere struggle for greater control of the forces of nature, but the supreme wisdom of the heart, the grace to use this wisdom and that control *in a service of Love.*

9. The Call to Our Future

Because of this passionate conviction and a concomitant persuasion that time is short indeed if we would avert disaster, I can never consent to the notion that a fruitful dialogue between theists and atheists can occur in abstraction from the God-question. Nor do I for an instant believe that the dialogue cannot be sincere unless the theist abandons his firm persuasion of the supreme relevance of God. Nor, finally, do I believe that the atheist is being degraded, by a dialogue instituted in the fashion I propose, to the dubious status of a potential convert or a marginal commentator on secondary aspects of the situation.

The atheist of our day has a far more important and deeper-cutting contribution to make to theist-atheist dialogue than simply a gadfly prodding of theists to live up to their faith. He can and must make the supreme contribution of *compelling theists to take creation seriously.* For it is more than high time theists did this. As long as they do not, they are fumbling the crucial question of man's very survival and of the forward movement of evolution on our planet, *the cardinal contribution of free created agents to the economy of God's guidance of creation to the perfection it can attain in and as our cosmos.*

The theist, on the other hand, himself degenerates to a truly dubious status if he does not realize and articulate his own obligation to endeavor *to cause the atheist to take God seriously.* It is not our purpose here to discuss the whole dimension of the creature's *duty* to his Creator; I am persuaded that God thinks far more in terms of love freely given as duty nobly done. But I am concerned to specify quite precisely just why I believe the atheist should take God seriously. It is because man cannot otherwise be preserved in this moment of doom. If man persists in scratching in the radically open circle that is his own created being for the sense of his own destiny, if man persists in scrabbling to close the open ring of becoming that is the totality of creation, if man persists in seeking in the spring-fed cistern of his own selfhood for living water while he resolutely seals that cistern off from the spring that feeds it, then not only disappointment but disaster will descend upon us all. This is not an effort at intimidation, except as one tries to "intimidate" the adventurous child playing on the edge of an active volcano. It is a passionate manifesto of personal conviction of fact. On the other hand, the instant that man refrains from that closing action, the grace of God, the power that is His Spirit will pour into our human race, so long God's tragic darlings, and we shall experience a springtime of love, more powerful than Satan.

Not theism of the supertranscendental sort, nor atheism of the restrictive and bumptious sort will save the earth; only the new vision, fed in the temporal order precisely by the confrontation between those who take creation desperately seriously and those who take God trustfully seriously, can effect humanity's required contribution to the sanctification now being offered us. As Teilhard puts it:

> The sense of earth opening and flowering upwards in the sense of God, and the sense of God rooted and nourished from below in the sense of earth. The transcendent personal God and the universe in evolution no longer forming two antagonistic poles of attraction, but entering into a hierarchic conjunction to uplift the human mass in a single tide.[14]

The same Teilhard urgently defines the need of our day in the dimension of human relations and of human goal-setting:

> It is not our heads or our bodies which we must bring together but our hearts. The generating principle of our unification is not finally to be found in the single contemplation of the same truth or in the single desire awakened by something, but in the single attraction exercised by the same Someone.[15]

Let Being be known as Loving and the heart of the world is healed. There remains the long battle to win through simultaneously to the shyly hidden heart of the creature and the massive pulsing Heart of God. Suspended between the two, mortal man can pursue his struggle to unite them. Then will the theist nevermore connive with oppression or sacrifice fear-stricken children to the Moloch of a God doubly horrible because first anthropomorphized and then totally transcendentalized; then will the atheist nevermore deliberately extinguish in that child's eyes the hope of a permanence of that worth that makes him inviolable. Then will the sanctifying God's voice be heard, as He spoke through His prophet:

> Yea, I have loved thee with an everlasting love;
> therefore with loving kindness have I drawn thee.
> JEREMIAH 31:3b

NOTES

1 FAITH AND THE ATHEIST: MYSTERIES AND IMPONDERABLES

1. Pierre Teilhard de Chardin, *Building the Earth* (Wilkes-Barre, Pa.: Dimension Books, 1965), pp. 119 f.
2. Leslie Dewart, *The Future of Belief* (New York: Herder and Herder, 1966), p. 63.
3. *Ibid.*
4. *Ibid.*, p. 64.
5. *Ibid.*, p. 63.
6. Cornelio Fabro, *God in Exile: Modern Atheism* (New York: Paulist-Newman, 1968), pp. 7 ff.
7. Gustav Wetter, *Dialectical Materialism* (London: Routledge and Kegan Paul, 1958), pp. 558 f.
8. J. A. Gunn, *The Problem of Time* (New York: R. Smith, 1930), p. 16.
9. Albert Camus, *The Rebel* (New York: Vintage Books, Random House, and Alfred A. Knopf, 1956), p. 73.
10. Samuel Alexander, *Space, Time and Deity,* The Gifford Lectures at Glasgow 1916-1918. 2 vols. (New York: Dover Publications, 1966).
11. Harvey Cox, cited on the dust cover of Leslie Dewart's *The Future of Belief.*

2 FAITH IN FREEDOM

1. Jean-Paul Sartre, *Being and Nothingness,* translated and with an Introduction by Hazel E. Barnes (New York: Washington Square Press, 1966), p. 26.
2. *Ibid.*, p. 30.
3. John Macquarrie, *Twentieth Century Religious Thought* (New York: Harper & Row, 1963), p. 358.
4. James Collins, *God in Modern Philosophy* (Chicago: Henry Regnery Company, 1959), p. 370.
5. *Ibid.*, p. 371.
6. Sartre, *op. cit.*, p. lxxviii.
7. *Ibid.*, p. 90.
8. *Ibid.*, p. 94.
9. *Ibid.*, p. lxxix.
10. *Ibid.*, p. 90.
11. *Ibid.*, p. 91.
12. *Ibid.*, p. lxxix.
13. *Ibid.*, p. 136.
14. *Ibid.*, p. 165.
15. *Ibid.*, p. lxxix.
16. *Ibid.*, pp. 93 f.
17. *Ibid.*, chap. 2, pp. 371-440, especially pp. 430-433.
18. *Ibid.*, p. 94.
19. *Ibid.*, p. 95.
20. *Ibid.*, p. 27.
21. *Ibid.*, p. lxxx.
22. The phrase is Sartre's, *op. cit.*, p. 541.
23. *Ibid.*, p. 27.
24. *Ibid.*, p. 28.
25. *Ibid.*, p. 30.
26. *Ibid.*
27. *Ibid.*
28. *Ibid.*
29. *Ibid.*, p. 535.
30. *Ibid.*, p. 537.
31. *Ibid.*, p. 583.
32. *Ibid.*, pp. 586 f.
33. *Ibid.*, pp. 606 f.
34. *Ibid.*, pp. 677 f.
35. Hans Hellmut Kirst, *The Seventh Day* (New York: Ace Books, 1959), p. 6.
36. *Ibid.*, pp. 318 f.
37. Hazel Barnes, "Translator's Introduction" to Sartre, *op. cit.*, p. xxxix.
38. *Ibid.*, p. xxxv.
39. Sartre, *op. cit.*, p. 100.
40. *Ibid.*, p. 536.
41. Collins, *op. cit.*, p. 370.

42. A theme from *Huis Clos*, cited in *The Philosophy of Jean-Paul Sartre*, ed. Robert Denoon Cumming (New York: Random House, 1965), p. 185.
43. Régis Jolivet, *Sartre, The Theology of the Absurd* (Glen Rock, N.J.: Newman Press, 1967), p. 78.
44. *Ibid.*, p. 81.
45. *The Philosophy of Jean-Paul Sartre*, p. 26.
46. Sartre, *Being and Nothingness*, pp. 476 f.
47. *Ibid.*, p. 483.
48. *Ibid.*, pp. 488-489.
49. *Ibid.*, pp. 495, 496 f.
50. *Ibid.*, p. 649.
51. *Ibid.*, p. 499.
52. *Ibid.*, p. 501.
53. Jolivet, *op. cit.*, p. 108.
54. Jean-Paul Sartre, *The Words*, translated by Bernard Frechtman (New York: Braziller, 1964), p. 253.
55. Jolivet, *op. cit.*, p. 106.
56. *Ibid.*
57. *Webster's New World Dictionary, College Edition*, (Toronto: Nelson, Forster and Scott, 1964), p. 1464.
58. Sartre, *Being and Nothingness*, p. 754.
59. *Ibid.*, p. 705.
60. *Ibid.*, pp. 693 f.
61. *Ibid.*, pp. 98 f.
62. *Ibid.*, p. 754.
63. *Ibid.*, p. xxxvii.
64. *Ibid.*, p. 748.
65. *Ibid.*, p. 744.
66. *Ibid.*, p. 746.
67. *Ibid.*, p. 747.
68. *Ibid.*, p. 748.
69. Genesis 2:7, Douay Version. The RSV and others have "dust" and the original Hebrew stresses indeed the dryness and hardness. Yet Douay is justified in using "slime" with its overtones of liquidity, for the material in the myth must be sufficiently damp to be molded!

3 FAITH IN SEX

1. Henry Miller, *The World of Sex* (*WS*), (New York: Grove Press, 1965), p. 12.
2. *Ibid.*, p. 18.
3. *Ibid.*, p. 27.
4. Henry Miller, *The Rosy Crucifixion, Sexus* (*S*), (New York: Grove Press, 1965), p. 283.
5. *Ibid.*, pp. 205 f.
6. *Ibid.*, p. 208.
7. *Ibid.*, pp. 13, 15.
8. *Ibid.*, p. 35.
9. *Ibid.*, pp. 161 f.
10. *WS*, p. 39.
11. *S*, pp. 425 f.
12. Henry Miller, *The Rosy Crucifixion, Plexus* (*P*), (New York: Grove Press, 1965), p. 57.
13. *Ibid.*, pp. 321 f.
14. *Ibid.*, pp. 348, 349 f.
15. Cf. *P*, p. 572.
16. *P*, p. 630.
17. Henry Miller, *The Rosy Crucifixion, Nexus* (*N*), (New York: Grove Press, 1965), p. 39.
18. Henry Miller, *Remember to Remember* (*R to R*), (New York: New Directions, 1947), p. xxxvii.
19. Henry Miller, *Big Sur and the Oranges of Hieronymus Bosch* (*Big Sur*), (New York: New Directions, 1957), p. 57.
20. Henry Miller, *The Wisdom of the Heart* (*WH*), (New York: New Directions, 1960), p. 43.
21. Henry Miller, *The Cosmological Eye* (*CE*), (New York: New Directions, 1939), p. 180.
22. *R to R*, pp. 179 f.
23. *CE*, p. 151.
24. *S*, p. 273.
25. *Ibid.*, p. 280.
26. *Ibid.*, p. 420.
27. *Ibid.*, p. 422.
28. *Ibid.*, p. 423.
29. *WH*, p. 89.
30. *S*, p. 269.
31. *Ibid.*, pp. 289 f.
32. *N*, p. 176.
33. *S*, p. 418.
34. *CE*, pp. 290 f.
35. *P*, p. 417.
36. *R to R*, p. 305; cf. *CE*, pp. 133 f. for the uneasy impression of an ultimate domination of the female, the Molly Bloom syndrome.
37. *P*, p. 44.
38. *Ibid.*, p. 612 f.
39. *Ibid.*, p. 89.
40. Henry Miller, *The Colossus of Maroussi* (New York: New Directions, 1958), p. 241.
41. *N*, p. 177.
42. *S*, p. 430.
43. *Big Sur*, p. 57.

44. *P*, p. 87.
45. *Big Sur*, pp. 236 f.
46. *WS*, pp. 12 f.
47. *Ibid.*, p. 17.
48. *Ibid.*, p. 20.
49. *Ibid.*, pp. 22-24.
50. *Ibid.*, pp. 79 f.
51. *Ibid.*, p. 107.
52. *Ibid.*, p. 110.
53. *Ibid.*, p. 119.

4 FAITH IN DEATH

1. Albert Camus, *The Outsider* (Harmondsworth, England: Penguin Books, 1966), p. 118.
2. *Ibid.*, pp. 118 f.
3. Albert Camus, *The Rebel* (New York: Vintage Books, 1956).
4. *Ibid.*, p. 22.
5. *Ibid.*, p. 296.
6. Albert Camus, *Caligula and Three Other Plays* (New York: Vintage Books, 1958), p. 41.
7. *Ibid.*, p. 71.
8. Albert Camus, *The Myth of Sisyphus* (New York: Vintage Books, 1955), pp. 111 f.
9. *Ibid.*, p. 91.
10. *Ibid.*, p. 87.
11. *The Rebel*, p. 303.
12. *Ibid.*, p. 79.
13. *Ibid.*, p. 306.
14. *Ibid.*, pp. 77 f.
15. *Ibid.*, p. 306.
16. *The Myth of Sisyphus*, p. 113.
17. *The Rebel*, p. 305.
18. Rachel Bespaloff, "The World of Men Condemned to Death," *Camus, a Collection of Critical Essays*, edited by Germaine Brée, (Englewood Cliffs, N.J.: Prentice-Hall, 1962), p. 99.
19. *Ibid.*, p. 100.
20. Albert Camus, *The Plague* (Harmondsworth, England: Penguin Books, 1966), p. 252. Italics mine—A.G.
21. *Ibid.*, p. 246.
22. *Ibid.*, p. 178.
23. *Ibid.*, p. 179.
24. *The Myth of Sisyphus*, p. 116.
25. *Ibid.*, p. 119.
26. *Ibid.*, p. 136.
27. *Ibid.*, p. 137.
28. *Ibid.*, p. 142.
29. *Ibid.*, p. 144.
30. Albert Camus, *Resistance, Re-*

bellion and Death (New York: Random House—Modern Library, 1960), pp. 28 f.
31. *The Myth of Sisyphus*, p. 44.
32. Rachel Bespaloff, in *Camus, a Collection of Critical Essays*, p. 93.
33. *Ibid.*, pp. 93 ff.
34. Adele King, *Camus* (Edinburgh and London: Oliver and Boyd, 1964), p. 23.
35. *Camus, a Collection of Critical Essays*, p. 55.
36. Cited in Adele King, *Camus*, p. 105.
37. *Camus, a Collection of Critical Essays*, p. 58.
38. *Resistance, Rebellion and Death*, p. 22.
39. *Ibid.*, p. 53.
40. *The Plague*, p. 178.
41. *Ibid.*, p. 83.
42. *Ibid.*, pp. 186 f.
43. *Resistance, Rebellion and Death*, pp. 52 f.
44. *The Plague*, p. 187.
45. Albert Camus, *Essais* (Paris: Gallimard, 1965), p. 15. I have made my own translation of this and all other selections cited from this volume—A.G.
46. Adele King, *Camus*, p. 23.
47. *Essais*, p. 65.
48. *Ibid.*, p. 87.
49. *Ibid.*, p. 835.
50. *Ibid.*, pp. 843-844.
51. *Ibid.*, p. 850.
52. *The Plague*, pp. 107 f.
53. *Resistance, Rebellion and Death*, p. x.
54. *Ibid.*, pp. 11 f.

5 FAITH IN MATTER

1. Gustav Wetter, *Dialectical Materialism* (London: Routledge and Kegan Paul, 1958), p. 558.
2. Leslie Dewart, *The Future of Belief* (New York: Herder and Herder, 1966), p. 54.
3. *Ibid.*, p. 55.
4. George Berkeley, *A Treatise concerning the Principles of Human Knowledge*, Part I, paragraph 92, in *Berkeley's Works*, Vol. I, ed. A. C. Fraser (Oxford, 1901), p. 309.
5. Frederick Copleston, S.J., *A History of Philosophy*, Vol. 7, Part I, (Garden City, New York: Image

Books, Doubleday and Company, 1965), p. 208.
6. *Ibid.*, p. 209.
7. *Ibid.*, pp. 216 f.
8. *Ibid.*, p. 231.
9. *Ibid.*, pp. 241 f.
10. *Ibid.*, p. 242.
11. *Ibid.*, p. 217.
12. G. Wetter, *op. cit.*, p. 4.
13. Copleston, *op. cit.*, p. 238.
14. G. Wetter, *op. cit.*, p. 284.
15. *Ibid.*, p. 556.
16. *Ibid.*, pp. 558 f.
17. K. Marx and F. Engels, *On Religion* (Moscow: Foreign Languages Publishing House, 1955), pp. 173 f.
18. V. I. Lenin, *Materialism and Empirio-Criticism* (Moscow: Foreign Languages Publishing House, n.d.).
19. Cf. G. Wetter, *op. cit.*, pp. 294 f.
20. V. I. Lenin, *op. cit.*, pp. 260 f.
21. *Ibid.*, p. 261.
22. *Ibid.*, p. 265. Italics mine—A.G.
23. *Ibid.*, p. 266. Italics mine—A.G.
24. *Ibid.*, p. 267.
25. *Ibid.*, Lenin citing Valentinov.
26. G. Wetter, *op. cit.*, p. 289.
27. *Ibid.*, p. 295.
28. V. I. Lenin, *op. cit.*, p. 270.
29. *Ibid.*, pp. 270 f.
30. *Ibid.*, p. 271.
31. *Ibid.*, p. 269.
32. E. Gilson, *Elements of Christian Philosophy* (Garden City, N.Y.: Doubleday and Company, 1960), p. 134.
33. G. Wetter, *op. cit.*, p. 289.
34. *Ibid.*, p. 294.
35. V. I. Lenin, *op. cit.*, p. 270.
36. *Ibid.*, p. 269. Italics in original.
37. *Ibid.*, p. 271. Italics in original.
38. *Ibid.*, p. 276.
39. G. Wetter, *op. cit.*, p. 286.
40. *Ibid.*, p. 288.
41. V. I. Lenin, *op. cit.*, p. 292. Italics mine—A.G.
42. J. Stalin, *Problems of Leninism* (Moscow-London, 1947), p. 721.
43. *Ibid.*, p. 713.
44. Roger Garaudy, *From Anathema to Dialogue* (New York: Herder and Herder, 1965), p. 72.
45. *Ibid.*, p. 73.
46. *Ibid.*, p. 80.

47. G. Wetter, *op. cit.*, p. 295.
48. *Ibid.*, p. 284.
49. *The Concept of Matter*, ed. Ernan McMullin (Notre Dame, Indiana: University of Notre Dame Press, 1963).

6 FAITH IN FINITUDE

1. R. J. Hollingdale, in his Introduction to his translation of Nietzsche, *Thus Spoke Zarathustra* (Harmondsworth, England: Penguin Books, 1961), pp. 22 and 12.
2. James Collins, *God in Modern Philosophy* (Chicago: Henry Regnery Company, 1959), pp. 266, 268.
3. Hollingdale, *op. cit.*, p. 18.
4. Crane Brinton, *Nietzsche* (Cambridge, Mass.: Harvard University Press, 1948), pp. 76, 140.
5. *Nietzsche: An Anthology of His Works*, edited, newly translated, and with critical Introductions by Otto Manthey-Zorn (New York: Washington Square Press, 1964), p. 77.
6. Hollingdale, *op. cit.*, p. 24.
7. Collins, *op. cit.*, p. 267.
8. Friedrich Nietzsche, *The Joyful Wisdom*, translated by Thomas Common, with an Introduction by Kurt F. Reinhardt (New York: Frederick Ungar, 1964), p. 168 (para. 125).
9. *Ibid.*, p. 173 (para. 132).
10. Hollingdale, *op. cit.*, pp. 24 f.
11. Brinton, *op. cit.*, p. 141.
12. Nietzsche, *The Joyful Wisdom*, para. 343, p. 276 of the English translation cited above.
13. Collins, *op. cit.*, p. 267.
14. "Notes on the Eternal Recurrence," para. 42 in Nietzsche, *Die Unschuld des Werdens* (edited by A. Baeumler), II, para. 1351.
15. *Nietzsche: An Anthology of His Works*, p. 90.
16. *Ibid.*
17. *Ibid.*
18. The reference is to Goethe's *Faust*, Part I:

Wenn ich zum Augenblicke sage:
Verweile doch, Du bist so schön

(If to the fleeting moment, I say:
O linger on, thou art so fair!)

Faust is speaking to Mephistopheles, and the rest of the quatrain is significant:

Da magst Du mich in Fesseln schlagen
Da werd' ich gern zu Grunde gehn

(Then may you chain me on that day Then will I gladly perish there).

What seems to us a fatality would be greeted by Nietzsche as the "great hope of hopelessness," the price to be paid for the self-sufficiency of the finite, prerequisite of its inviolable autonomy!

19. Ernst Bertram, *Nietzsche, Versuch einer Mythologie* (Berlin: Georg Bondi, 1919), p. 236.
20. Nietzsche, *The Joyful Wisdom,* pp. 152 f. (para. 109).
21. *Ibid.,* p. 213 (para. 276).
22. *Ibid.,* pp. 270 f. (para. 341).
23. *Ibid.,* pp. 271 f. (para. 342).
24. Nietzsche, *Thus Spoke Zarathustra,* p. 167.
25. *Ibid.,* pp. 178 f.
26. *Ibid.,* p. 180.
27. Hollingdale, *op. cit.,* p. 33.
28. Nietzsche, *Thus Spoke Zarathustra,* p. 234.
29. *Ibid.,* p. 236.
30. *Ibid.,* p. 333.
31. *Ibid.,* pp. 331 f.
32. Nietzsche, *The Joyful Wisdom,* p. 309.
33. *Ibid.,* p. 341.
34. *Ibid.,* p. 353.
35. Kurt Reinhardt, in his Introduction to *The Joyful Wisdom,* pp. 7 f.
36. The reference is to *The Joyful Wisdom,* p. 266 (para. 338).
37. Reinhardt, *op. cit.,* p. 12.
38. Nietzsche, *The Joyful Wisdom,* p. 287.
39. Brinton, *op. cit.,* p. 243.
40. Martin Heidegger, *The Question of Being,* translated with an Introduction by Jean T. Wilde and William Kluback (New Haven: College and University Press, 1958), p. 107.
41. Martin Heidegger, "Der Spruch Anaximanders," *Holzwege* (Frankfurt a. M.: Klostermann, 1950).
42. Cornelio Fabro, *God in Exile* (New York: Paulist-Newman, 1968), pp. 886, 893.
43. Albert Camus, *The Rebel* (New York: Vintage Books, 1956), p. 74.
44. K. Löwith, *Dio, uomo e mondo da Cartesio a Nietzsche* (Naples, 1966), p. 103.
45. Collins, *op. cit.,* p. 268, especially the "youthful poem" of Nietzsche to the unknown God, there cited.
46. Karl Jaspers, *Nietzsche und das Christentum* (Hameln, 1948), pp. 5 f.
47. Fabro, *op. cit.,* p. 880.
48. Ignace Lepp, *Psychanalyse de l'atheisme moderne* (Paris: Grasset, 1961).
49. Nietzsche, *The Antichrist,* para. 18, in *The Portable Nietzsche,* (New York: Viking Books, 1959), pp. 585 f.
50. Nietzsche, *The Joyful Wisdom,* p. 172 (para. 130).

7 FAITH IN TIME

1. Samuel Alexander, *Space, Time and Deity,* Vol. II (New York: Dover Publications, 1966), p. 341.
2. *Ibid.,* p. 342.
3. *Ibid.,* p. 345.
4. *Ibid.,* Vol. I, p. xxxix.
5. Cornelio Fabro, *God in Exile* (New York: Paulist-Newman, 1968), pp. 803.
6. Charles Hartshorne, *Philosophers Speak of God* (Chicago: University of Chicago Press, 1953), p. 366.
7. John Macquarrie, *Twentieth Century Religious Thought* (New York: Harper & Row, 1963), p. 261.
8. Rudolf Metz, *A Hundred Years of British Philosophy* (London: Allen and Unwin, 1950), p. 624.
9. Samuel Alexander, *Philosophical and Literary Pieces* (London: Macmillan, 1939), p. 73.
10. S. Alexander, *Space, Time and Deity,* p. x. (Dorothy Emmet's Foreword to the 1966 edition.)
11. Alfred North Whitehead, *Science in the Modern World* (New York: Macmillan, 1929), p. xi. The Whiteheadian dependence on and development of Alexander's thought is treated at length in Donald B. Kuspit's "Whitehead on Divinity," *Archiv für Philosophie,* XI, pp. 74 f.

12. S. Alexander, *Space, Time and Deity*, Vol. II, p. 40.
13. *Ibid.*, p. 41.
14. *Ibid.*, pp. 38 f.
15. *Ibid.*, p. 44.
16. *Ibid.*, pp. 49-50.
17. *Ibid.*, p. 49.
18. *Ibid.*, pp. 54 f.
19. *Ibid.*, pp. 337 f.
20. J. A. Gunn, *The Problem of Time* (New York: R. Smith, 1930), p. 257.
21. A. N. Whitehead, *Process and Reality* (New York: Harper Torchbook, 1960), p. 517.
22. *Ibid.*, pp. 516 f.
23. *Ibid.*, p. 519.
24. *Ibid.*
25. *Ibid.*, pp. 520 f.
26. *Ibid.*, p. 521.
27. *Ibid.*, p. 524.
28. *Ibid.*, p. 529.
29. Macquarrie, *op. cit.*, p. 277.
30. *Ibid.*
31. James Collins, *God in Modern Philosophy* (Chicago: Henry Regnery Company, 1959), p. 322.
32. Whitehead, *op. cit.*, p. 532.
33. For an appreciation of the complexity of the problem, cf. Adolf Grünbaum, *Philosophical Problems of Space and Time* (New York: Alfred A. Knopf, 1963).
34. Howard Moss, *The Magic Lantern of Marcel Proust* (New York: The Universal Library published by Grosset & Dunlap, 1966), p. 109.
35. Marcel Proust, *Swann's Way* (New York: Random House, 1956), p. 65.
36. Moss, *op. cit.*, p. 83.
37. Proust, *Swann's Way*, p. 93.
38. Moss, *op. cit.*, p. 111.
39. Milton Hindus, *The Proustian Vision* (Carbondale and Edwardsville: University of Illinois Press, Arcturus Books, 1967), p. 101.
40. Marcel Proust, *The Sweet Cheat Gone* (New York: Random House, 1957), p. 47.
41. Marcel Proust, *The Past Recaptured* (New York: Random House, 1932), pp. 400 f.
42. *Ibid.*, p. 402.
43. Hindus, *op. cit.*, pp. 277 f.
44. Jean Guitton, *Man in Time* (Notre Dame: University of Notre Dame Press, 1966), pp. 136 f.

45. Herbert Dingle, "Time in Relativity Theory: Measurement or Coordinate?" in *The Voices of Time*, ed. J. T. Fraser (New York: George Braziller, 1966), p. 472.
46. G. A. Whitrow, "Time and the Universe," *The Voices of Time*, p. 581.
47. Satosi Watanabe, "Time and the Probabilistic View of the World," *The Voices of Time*, pp. 560, 563.
48. J. L. Russell, S.J., "Time in Christian Thought," *The Voices of Time*, p. 76.
49. Friedrich Kümmel, "Time as Succession and the Problem of Duration," *The Voices of Time*, pp. 45, 54.
50. Edmund Parsons, *Time Devoured* (London: Allen and Unwin, 1964), p. 94.

8 FAITH IN GOD

1. Herbert Richardson, *Toward an American Theology* (New York: Harper & Row, 1967).
2. Robert Browning, "An Epistle of Kharshish."
3. *Pastoral Constitution on the Church in the Modern World*, para. 14. In *The Documents of Vatican II*, Walter M. Abbott, S.J., General Editor (New York: Herder and Herder, 1966), p. 212.
4. *Declaration on Religious Freedom*, para. 11. *Ibid.*, p. 691.
5. *Ibid.*, para. 36, p. 233.
6. Pierre Teilhard de Chardin, *The Phenomenon of Man* (New York: Harper & Row, 1959), p. 338.
7. Pierre Teilhard de Chardin, *Le coeur de la matière*.
8. *The Phenomenon of Man*, p. 318.
9. *Ibid.*
10. *Pastoral Constitution on the Church in the Modern World*, para. 39, *The Documents of Vatican II*, p. 237.
11. Para. 13, *The Documents of Vatican II*, p. 121.
12. *Documents of Vatican II*, p. 109.
13. Para. 9, 10. *Ibid.*, p. 207.
14. Pierre Teilhard de Chardin, *Building the Earth*, p. 117.
15. *Ibid.*, p. 111.